FREAK LIKE ME

confessions of a 90s pop groupie

MALCOLM McLEAN

RedDoor

Published by RedDoor
www.reddoorpublishing.com

© 2019 Malcolm McLean

ISBN 978-1-910453-69-8

A CIP catalogue record for this book is available
from the British Library

Cover design: Clare Connie Shepherd
www.clareconnieshepherd.com

Typesetting: Tutis Innovative E-Solutions Pvt. Ltd

Printed and bound in BZGraf S.A.

Prologue

February 1999

'I can't believe it... we've got in! That was so easy. We're actually here!' I thought to myself. I'm trying my best to look blasé and important, but my excited eyes, darting around the room, are telling a different story. At least it's dark in here.

'Oh my God, that's Boy George! And there's Mark Owen!' Gemma squeals as we casually start to wander round the room.

'CALM DOWN, GUYS,' Steph urges. 'Just be cool.' She was older and wiser than the rest of us. She was leading this whole escapade... and I was one of her accomplices.

'I can see some of Five!' Charlotte exclaims. 'And that's Sharleen from Texas!'

We shuffle in a big loop around the arena, all six of us. Up we walk, through each tier of candlelit tables, the hubbub of small talk and cutlery clinking on porcelain, interspersed with corks popping and staff in black waistcoats asking 'Red or white, madam?' My mind's going crazy. This is *utter* madness. It's Tuesday evening of half term and I'm fifteen years old! And what if we get caught? What would they do to us? At least if we get thrown out now this will still have been the most ridiculous thirty minutes of my entire life. There we were, roaming around undetected, with fake passes around our necks at the biggest showbiz event in the music calendar – where few fans had ever gone before – the *BRIT Awards*. Unfortunately, other than 'get in', there was no plan.

We keep walking, milling past table after table of industry execs. 'Shit, that food looks good right now!' Charlotte says, clutching her stomach. I'm not even hungry. We're all acting unnaturally; trying to look relaxed and important, that was the main thing we discussed outside. 'Don't look nervous!' – I can hear Steph's pep talk from the car park going round and round in my head. It's a lot to think about when you're swaggering past waiters and Security, trying hard not to trip over each other.

We weren't the sons and daughters of pop stars or industry bigwigs, we'd *made* this happen ourselves – the impossible. I can't believe we've fooled everyone with these forged passes. Access All Areas! Who do they think we are? We'd all wanted to go so badly, for as long as we could remember, years before Ginger Spice had stepped out on that stage in her Union Jack dress, two years ago.

'Right, let's try to go backstage,' Steph said, boldly.

'Okay, why not? Let's just do it!' replied Charlotte.

We'd got this far, so we thought we might as well try our luck.

'I think I know the way. Follow *me*...' said Paul.

'No, he's wrong! I saw it on the way in. Follow me,' Gemma assured. She was always confident, but it usually worked.

So, there we were, six music-loving teenagers who'd hit the jackpot. We were possessed by pop. But we didn't just want to listen to it, we wanted to live it. Whatever it took to get close to our favourite bands. Devious tricks, careful planning, steely determination or just sheer luck. By skipping school or sleeping in train stations, airports or Hyde Park we'd managed to meet anyone who was anyone in the pop industry. It was all a far cry from my dull suburban life at home.

1

I'll Be There for You

Secondary school is a human zoo of hormones. A teenage day prison, with marginally less violence. The first few weeks are make or break, establishing the pecking order for all the years that follow: show them you won't take any shit and you'll be fine. But I wasn't that kind of person in 1994. As a shy eleven-year-old, who had moved to a new town and started secondary school as The New Kid, I adopted the desperate 'keep-your-head-down' approach as my survival tactic. However, when the first festive season arrived – and I'd acquired a couple of friends I could hover on the edges of the playground with – I made the brave but ill-advised decision to *volunteer* to open the school's Christmas carol concert. Clearly, I wasn't blessed with common sense, but I was quite a musical child. I mean, I played no instruments, but growing up, I'd liked dancing to Mum's Donna Summer LPs, could recite most songs from her Rodgers and Hammerstein VHS collection, and had literally *competed* with other boys at primary school to win the part of singing 'Walking in the Air'

1

from *The Snowman* in the final-year carol service. My Year Six classmates had thought I was fantastic for it. *I really think this'll clinch my popularity*, I thought, as I volunteered at my new school, despite literally no one else putting themselves forward. Funny that.

On the big night, I sang a window-shattering falsetto solo of 'Once in Royal David's City', looking angelic holding a candle and pretending to read music from a stand covered in holly. Even our RE teacher Mrs Casha (think Miss Trunchbull from *Matilda*, but with a buzz cut) was crying in the front row. I guessed they were tears of joy. In hindsight she was probably envisaging me getting my head kicked in a couple of years later.

I'd be lying if I said I hadn't loved the attention. I liked standing out from the other kids who couldn't sing for shit. Though hardly Aled Jones, I could warble in tune, even if my soprano tones were never going to nab me a Charlotte Church five-album opera deal. Some kids made the odd cruel comment afterwards, but in general, as eleven-year-olds, most kids are too young to have found their voice and strength yet, and I was able to brush them off and bask in the minor praise I got from the more musical of my peers. I was too busy loving my five minutes of fame in a world where the football team ruled the school and all other boys were ignored. Afterwards, I was longing to do it all again; to lap up the applause and see their smiling faces. To let my inner performer shine. Unfortunately, puberty had other ideas.

◆ ◆ ◆

All I ever knew, growing up, was suburban Surrey. Mile after mile of mock Tudor, privet hedges and block-paved driveways. We lived on Rosefield Gardens. It was a road to nowhere (literally, it was a cul-de-sac). The quaint name belies a sinister world of curtain-twitching septuagenarians existing on a diet of *Daily Telegraph*, lawn bowls and boredom. As a child I was oblivious to this. All I cared about was the fact I was now old enough to have a room of my own, free from the shackles of an older sister obsessed with Alan Shearer. Football wasn't on my radar. I was more into Disney songs and hanging out with my nan.

We grew up in a village called Ottershaw, sandwiched between Chertsey and Woking. It was not what most people would call a village, more a suburb of a suburb, separated by golf courses and the odd paddock, thereby earning itself the right to a separate identity. It's under a mile from Ottershaw to the M25, but the divide it created might as well have been a hundred wide. It separated civilisation from barbarism; world city from provincial backwater – and we were plonked on the wrong side of it. You could never escape the constant whirring hum; it was the aural backdrop to my childhood. The motorway even lopped off a corner of the school playing fields, selling short one vision of the future in the name of another. All that separated us from it was a flimsy wire fence – I'm sure that was great for my asthma.

Apart from bike racing and roller skating around the close, we passed the time browsing the labyrinth of floor-to-ceiling VHSs to rent at Ottershaw Wines. This was not just an off-licence, it was almost a department store with bottles of mediocre wines at the back, and the whole front of the shop dedicated to videocassettes. *Sleepless in Seattle* sandwiched between the toffee popcorn and their extensive porn section.

Pre-Internet, our lives revolved around telly. Saturday nights in the nineties were spent flicking between *Noel's House Party*, *Stars in Their Eyes*, and if we were really desperate, *Big Break*. This was the age in which blokes potting balls in comedy waistcoats constituted entertainment.

My dad, Ron, was a manager at a local copper tube company. Riveting! Despite this being well into the nineties he still hadn't got rid of his Tom Selleck moustache. Looks-wise, he was a cross between Father Ted and Ned Flanders. Personality-wise too, come to think of it. Dad is one of the loveliest men you could ever meet. He would do anything for us.

But, The Flanders we weren't. We were undeniably Simpsons. My sister Anja, a year above me at school, was a studious book-lover, although definitely wilder than Lisa Simpson. I was like Bart in that I spent most of the nineties playing out in the cul-de-sac with our little sister Sophie: our favourite pastime involved tying the skateboard to my BMX and pulling her down the road at a rapid rate of knots until she flew off when I took a sharp corner. That, or the mattress-down-the-stairs game when Mum asked me to babysit. Sophie and I were close. She was my toy, my pet and my best friend all rolled into one little tomboyish bundle of fun.

Liz, my mum, was every inch a gay icon. She had the hair of Liza Minnelli, the voice of Julie Andrews and the cheekbones of Cher. Mum played all the lead roles in the musicals of a local theatre company: Maria in *The Sound of Music*, Anna in *The King & I*, Nancy in *Oliver!*, Grace Farrell in *Annie*. The Beyoncé of the Surrey am-dram world, Mum always got the lead.

Our bungalow was one of the shabbiest on the street, full of bodged jobs and with a greenhouse with broken windows, a lasting memory from the time Anja roller skated down the path into it, hands-first. It was all just a bit crap. But I was also very lucky; there are a lot worse places to grow up than the slightly downtrodden part of Surrey.

♦ ♦ ♦

Our school, Salesians (pronounced *Suh-leeee-zhuns*), had a 'great reputation', priding itself on its 'strong, traditional values' and a strict adherence to Christianity and school uniforms. I know, it sounds like a 1950s Conservative manifesto but it ticked boxes for a lot of parents.

Despite its rather grand-sounding name, Salesians had all the visual charm of an industrial estate on a wet Sunday in February. Concrete and brick blocks surrounded by a sea of pale grey mobile classrooms. It was an unmistakably *Grange Hill*-esque mix of fluorescent strip-lit classrooms decked out with pubic carpet and Formica tables (the underside of which had a thick crust of dried-up chewing gum). The walls were covered with kitsch displays about The Tudors and DNA, while in the canteen, grey-faced women in floral tabards lovingly served up a selection of beige chips, beige burgers, beige hash browns and lurid fizzy drinks. It was your classic nineties suburban comprehensive, except it had a twist. This, being a Catholic school, meant there were still a few decrepit monks and nuns kicking around.

Sister Act 2 though, it wasn't. There was no Deloris Van Cartier to bring glamour, shade and street cred to our grey secondary school. Since moving to this new area and getting a bigger house, the downside was there were none of our old primary school friends we had loved so much. Anja and I were unknown weirdos from a school no one had heard of, possibly just made up, despite being just five miles away. I managed to survive by latching onto a couple of other quiet, geeky boys and generally keeping my head down (other than my festive singing exploits). I wasn't popular, but I survived my first year without making too many enemies.

Come Year Eight, EVERYTHING changed. No longer would I be stuck in the corner, making small talk with the official rejects: Conor, my best friend from primary school, was transferring to Salesians. I was delighted we'd be reunited. Conor was also pansyish and into music and theatre. At last I would have a genuine friend there; someone I had something in common with. My wallflower days were over! We were placed in all the same classes and whiled away the days secretly laughing at the popular kids who were afraid to be who they really were, unlike our fabulous selves. We flocked together like birds of a feather (more Sharon and Tracey, definitely not Dorien) and had a riot from the second he arrived. Suddenly it felt like big school was going to be okay after all.

Quicker than a ray of light, things started to change though. Puberty was now in hideous full flow, except for the unlucky few, and almost overnight everyone was cottoning on to how different Conor and I were to the other boys. We didn't like football, which meant we were seen as freakish oddballs in a sea of *normal* boys with the usual *macho* interests. We were just us. But lads can sense that feminine sensitivity some boys have. With hindsight, we were pretty camp, and we definitely loved reciting Céline Dion and M People hits more than the other kids.

Conor was a tiny, bespectacled geek (sorry, Conor!), well spoken and a bit of a swot. But he had a sharper tongue than Lily Savage, and brutally put down all who dared pick on him. It always worked. I, on the other hand, was taller and more lanky, and secretly felt like the other kids ought to think *I* was the cooler one – they didn't. Unlike Conor, I was too scared to bite back. Quite rapidly, I became the easiest target out of the hundreds of students in our year in the first few months of Year Eight.

How the fuck had this happened? I'd slipped down the hierarchy faster than Shampoo's short-lived pop career. The bullying quickly got out of control: boys tripped me up wherever I went, slung abuse at me, in and out of class, and I could no longer cross the playground without balls flying at my head.

Behind my back, Conor had divulged the torrent of abuse to my parents. One morning, we both got hauled out of RE class to go to the head of the lower school's office. I had absolutely no idea what was going on – I thought we were in trouble, which seemed unlikely, considering our A-grade loser status. As I nervously entered Brother John's office, my palms dripping with cold sweat, I saw Mum and Dad sitting next to this monk in a robe.

I sat there red-faced, stuttering through every homophobic slur I'd had hurled at me.

'Umm... shirt-lifter... Er... gay boy, faggot, poofter, dirty queer... Erm... Julian Clary...'

'Well, thank you for sharing those with us all, Malcolm,' said Brother John, thinly veiling his shock and awkwardness with a tone of compassion.

You could see the language was a bit much for a monk on a Tuesday morning. I pleaded with my parents to just leave it and let it go away, telling them I could handle it myself, but Conor intervened and gave the names of the ringleaders anyway. I didn't blame him – he wanted his best mate to stop being called a 'fucking queer' in every lesson. But inside, I didn't believe that it would change a thing.

The worst offenders were called out of class that same day, punished and given strong warnings. For a few days the abuse was replaced with glares and passive aggressive comments. I *knew* it wasn't over. Before long they'd started up again, some of them charged with a new anger from being singled out.

As the months went by, the hounding continued. I would endure gay bashing from girls with greased-back ponytails and boys with less intelligence than the petri dishes in the science labs. The teachers did nothing, of course, despite our school having a 'zero tolerance policy to bullying' (you have to laugh). Things were very different back then. Because of Section 28, the teachers never spoke out against homophobia in class, so why would the kids stop? 'Section 28' was part of the Local Government Act 1988, brought in by the Thatcher government. It prevented local authorities and schools from 'promoting' homosexuality, banning them from providing literature to support gay people, or funding gay rights groups. It made schools turn a blind eye to any playground homophobia for fear of breaking the law and reinforced the notion that gay people were second-class citizens.

Internally, I was struggling with my sexuality. As puberty hit I realised I didn't want to be with girls, but I wasn't sure what my feelings were telling me. All I could see were negative portrayals of gay people in the media and hateful attitudes at school. The very few gay characters on TV only ever had AIDS-related storylines or complex problems as a result of their sexuality, and when anyone was 'outed' in the tabloids it was as though they had committed some sort of heinous crime. Back then the only really prominent gay pop star was Elton John and kids at school used to spread stories about his 'sordid' antics. One Sir Elton rumour circulating the playground claimed he had a secret swimming pool, lined with ceramic picture tiles of naked men, so that he could swim underwater to look at the perverted photos and play with his tiny dancer.

◆ ◆ ◆

Although my sister Anja is only eighteen months older than me, she got into pop music much earlier than I did. Aged seven, she let me dance to Kylie's debut album, *Kylie*, with her. Years later, she loved Britpop and early nineties dance. Anja taped songs off the radio and had acquired copies of the *Now!* compilations on cassette – all the stuff that saturated the airwaves back then. Like every girl, she'd put in a brief stint as a massive Take That fan and, in 1993, she once redecorated her bedroom overnight with floor-to-ceiling Mark Owen posters. I couldn't understand why she'd wanted to damage her wallpaper with such cheap, tacky posters of Mark, plus Shane from *Home & Away* and some actor called Leo. My bedroom was immaculate – I couldn't imagine having it like hers! I didn't see the attraction, other than the envy I had of all those boys with their tanned abs and luscious gelled curtains. My barnet was so thick and wiry; I couldn't get it to grow down – it only grew outwards, like a toilet brush. I'd tried to tame it with handfuls of gloopy blue hair gel that Mum bought me from the supermarket, but one knock to the head and it would crumble away into powder.

Anja was always blaring 95.8 Capital FM out of the tinny, crackly ghetto blaster in her room and we'd have the radio on in the car when we weren't listening to Mum's *Flashdance* soundtrack and other eighties cassettes. I could belt out a couple of Whitney and Mariah songs she'd played to death, and knew bits of Ace of Base and M People hits, but I was utterly clueless about the bands, the videos or their chart positions. I knew Take That and East 17 were big rivals – for example – but the rest was all a blur.

Anja and I were your classic warring siblings. We bonded only in thirty-minute intervals, confined to the screen time of Australian soap operas, *The Fresh Prince of Bel-Air* and *Blossom*, laughing in unison at niche American jokes we weren't sure we'd understood, and scandalous plot twists on Ramsay Street (*Neighbours*). When the credits rolled, it was business as usual, back to pretending we hated each other and asking Mum when dinner was ready.

Like most teenage boys, when everyone was out, I'd creep into my sister's bedroom and read her *Just Seventeen* and *More!*

magazines to educate myself about sex, pop music and the embarrassing teen issues on the problem pages. I didn't *need* to know the pros and cons of tampons vs. towels, and what boys *really* meant when they asked you over for an evening revision session, but it was all helpful, to be honest. Pre-Internet, if you didn't have a big sister with a thumbed-through stack of these mags in her bedroom, you were screwed. It wasn't just the problem pages, I never knew any of the bands in them either. Kids at school or the church youth club (which was as fun as it sounds) would discuss the charts and I was left feeling clueless.

In the winter of 1995, a few months into the start of my Year Eight hell at school, Anja and I were sitting in the front room watching TV. She was in the prime position: the threadbare spot on the sofa, directly in front of the telly. The nineties R&B girl group Eternal was appearing on the BBC1 show, Gary Wilmot's *Showstoppers*, a naff Sunday afternoon nan favourite, where he performed songs from musicals with West End stars and special guests. The three Eternal girls were dressed in pantomime costumes for their song: garish corsets, ill-fitting dresses and feather boas. But beyond the polyester outfits, to me they stood out from all the other drivel on the show. They were stunningly beautiful and glamorous, despite the raw deal from the BBC wardrobe department, and were great vocalists to boot. Who *were* these girls? When sweet, doe-eyed Kelle hit a high note that only dogs could hear, during their version of 'Mama, I Want to Sing', I was captivated.

I muttered something about it being amazing and Anja shot me a typical teenage sister's reaction of, 'Yeah, so what? They're not *that* pretty and talented!'

But I went away feeling like I'd discovered some hidden gem, not realising the band had been wildly successful for a couple of years and had already shed a member! A few weeks later, they popped up on something else I was watching, looking far more glam this time, like *proper* pop stars. Anja told me nonchalantly that they had a Christmas single out: a 'soppy ballad' called 'I Am Blessed'.

'They were so much better before Louise left. They dressed *way* cooler back then, in their baggy trousers and boots,' Anja casually threw out there, knowing I wouldn't have the faintest idea what she was talking about.

'Who's Louise?! Was there another girl? I don't understand,' I whined, desperate to know the score on the sultry trio.

'Yes!' she said with a sly grin and an eye roll. 'Louise Nurding left Eternal the same week Robbie left Take That. Now she's a singer on her own. Duh!'

I had no idea what she was talking about, but I needed to find out more.

◆ ◆ ◆

One night in early December, half the household went out to a family friend's Christmas do nearby. I opted to babysit Sophie rather than endure the tedious chit-chat. While they were out, I did what every respectable teenager does and opened up my present from Anja, which was already sitting under the tree. We all know what a James Bond job it is to remove the Sellotape *so* carefully so as to not rip the wrapping paper. Anja would definitely have reported me for ruining Christmas if she discovered I'd opened my present early, so the pressure was immense. From the thickness of it, I could already tell it was a CD single and I was *dying* to know what she'd chosen. I managed to break into it and, after a few gentle taps, the Eternal single from a couple of months ago, 'Power of a Woman', fell into my sweaty palm. They looked so raunchy in the artwork. I can still see it now:

they're wearing jeans and little silk shirts, posing provocatively, their crotches pushed together. These glamorous girls amazed me with their sass and perfection – a world away from anyone I'd ever seen on the streets of Woking. I'd never paid any attention to pop music artwork in the shops until then, and here this CD was, *screaming* out to me.

I popped it on the stereo player in the lounge (the best speakers in the house) and cranked up the volume. The opening piano bars hit me like a bitch slap in the face. Then the note-bending harmonised vocals kicked in, with the girls singing 'DO-YOU DO-YOU DO-YOU DO-YOU-FEEL THE POWWWWER?' I was hypnotised.

It's basically four minutes of fabulousness and as a twelve-year-old boy fairly in touch with his feminine side, it *really* excited me. I couldn't get over how empowered these three women, singing this captivating pop song, were. I secretly recorded it to a cassette on my hi-fi and re-wrapped the CD, placing it back under the tree in the same position for it to remain until 9 a.m. Christmas morning. For the next couple of weeks, I listened to the song and its B-side obsessively in secret.

When Christmas Day arrived, I was strangely excited about being reunited with my present, longing to look at the cover art again and hold the precious object in my hands. I played along, excitedly telling Anja how happy I was with it. Chuffed with her choice of gift, she grinned and said, 'I think you're really gonna like it,' to which I nodded and smiled, thinking, *I know I will, bitch. I listen to it twenty times a day!* I spent Christmas 1995 consuming its three tracks in my bedroom until, in the dull, dead days between Boxing Day and New Year, I begged Dad to drive me to Woolworths in West Byfleet, where I bought the full Eternal album of the same name with my Christmas money, so that I could see what else they had to offer.

In the following months I went from mild admiration to full-on fixation. It wasn't just them I'd been opened up to, though. I began listening to the radio throughout the week to hear the latest songs and devour the Top 40 countdown every Sunday. All along I had just needed a way in, one group I knew quite well, and now that I did, I was hooked! Chart pop became my world and Eternal were the biggest territory on the map.

♦ ♦ ♦

The year 1996 didn't start too well for quite a few people. Charles and Diana were finally getting divorced, the Tories were getting their knickers in a twist over Europe (some things never change) and the rest of the nation was panicking about mad cows. I, meanwhile, found myself turning to the world of pop to shut out the incessant bullying at school. The deeper I gazed into that world, the more captivated I became with Eternal.

But how could I find out more about my trio of pop heroines? I needed more, I was an addict searching for the next hit. But there was nothing on them in that week's *Smash Hits* and they weren't on TV promoting new music. I had to make do with the CDs that brought me so much joy, introducing colour to my grey life each time I pushed the play button on my bedroom hi-fi.

That January, under a cloak of darkness, Dad took me to his office late one evening to use the World Wide Web for some Miss Marple-ing. I logged onto Eternal's official website, which, once we'd left it for twenty minutes and had a cup of tea, had finally unveiled the three pictures it contained. Dad generously printed them off for me in colour so I could stick them to my bedroom wall. As the printer noisily whirred away, the faces of Kelle and the Bennett sisters, Easther and Vernie, slowly emerged, pixelated line by pixelated line. I looked up at Dad in anticipation and he responded with a beaming grin. The ink needed replenishing, so, as the prints progressed, the technicolor icons faded to a muted mix of green and white. The quality was atrocious, and the photos tackier than the pictures of the good-looking soap stars adorning Anja's bedroom walls, but these were my *first* posters!

A little into the New Year I found out exactly who this Louise character was. She burst into my life while I wolfed down my Coco Pops one Saturday, on some terrible kids' TV show. I scrambled around the TV cabinet to find a VHS to record her segment on. I settled on 'MUM'S KILROY TAPE', praying she'd watched the episodes on it and wasn't compiling some sort of 'best of' collection for her TV and ironing sessions. As I caught the second half of Louise's performance of 'In Walked Love', her syrupy-sweet new single, I was captivated by her overenthusiastic dance routine, the magnificently layered keyboard solo and the breathy backing vocals. Love really had walked into my life, although probably not in the way most lads reacted when they watched her bounce round the stage in a skimpy vest top. The song only managed Number 17 in the charts, so maybe the rest of the country was slightly more discerning than thirteen-year-old Malcolm. Re-watching old footage of the performance, the song itself, and accompanying dance routine, is so naff it wouldn't have looked out of place as one of the closing numbers at the end of *Eurotrash*.

One evening after school, as I immersed myself in one of my Eternal CDs, I discovered via the sleeve notes that there was an official VHS available. I almost spilt my glass of squash: I *needed* it. Needless to say, it was more difficult to acquire merchandise in the mid-nineties before the stress-free luxury of Amazon One-Day delivery. The Information Superhighway was yet to master online sales, so I had to really hunt it down. After wasting only half a day phoning every branch of Woolworths in Surrey,

Hampshire and Berkshire I could find in the Yellow Pages, I managed to locate the VHS in a shop a few towns away, and Mum agreed to drive me over there to buy the only copy in store. For the coming months, my precious treasure lived in the video player, or on top of it, and was screened almost daily that spring and summer. It had all the music videos, interview excerpts and live performances by Eternal, from back when Louise was still in the band. I thought every minute of baggy-trousered, flat-cap-wearing grainy footage was gold, and repeatedly paused and rewound my favourite bits till those sections of the tape grew wobbly and grey, as it slowly wore out.

My Eternal and Louise obsessions only grew as the spring of 1996 gave way to summer. Conor was now into them too (although not nearly as much as me). He saw in the back of one of his mum's magazines that Eternal were going on tour soon. After a week's worth of discussion and persuasion, our parents allowed us to attend Eternal's Wembley Arena concert in a few weeks. WEM-BER-LEYYY! The pinnacle of any band's career, which only the very biggest acts got to headline. And, aged twelve, we were being allowed to go alone to see this with our own eyes! I perched on our wooden kitchen bench next to Dad as he rang Ticketmaster's call centre and bought us the best seats of the limited ones still available – a bargain at £15 a ticket. I probably would have been happy with the worst ones! Even sitting in the back row behind a 6'7" bloke, and seeing nothing but the ceiling of the arena, would have been good enough for me – anything to just *be there*.

Our excitement reached fever pitch as the Wembley week drew near. The girls were popping up on all the usual kids' TV and crap daytime shows to promote their latest single, 'Good Thing', in between tour dates, so as to hopefully rack up another Top 10 single. Five days to go! By Tuesday morning, Vernie and Kelle from the band appeared on TV without lead singer Easther as she wasn't feeling well. 'She's just resting her voice before Wembley on Sunday,' Kelle said reassuringly to a nodding, faux-concerned Anne Diamond. They even cancelled a couple of dates during the week so as not to jeopardise the big one.

As Sunday approached, I became more and more electrified. My stomach filled with butterflies. I could scarcely believe that these goddesses who had occupied so much of my time the past few months would be stood there, in front of me, belting out those anthemic songs. Would we get a good view? Might we get to meet them somehow? What if Dad's car broke down and we couldn't make it? My head was about to explode!

Finally, the day arrived. After a night of broken sleep, the wait was over. I donned my favourite Joe Bloggs T-shirt and, unusually for me, was ready early. I bounded into Dad's car and we made our way over to Conor's, listening to one cassette on the journey, knowing that, as each track ended, the next time I would hear it would be live and in the flesh. We pulled onto the tarmac drive and Conor ran out to meet us in his Sunday best, a freshly ironed shirt and waistcoat. Immediately, I knew from the despondent look in his eyes that something was amiss.

'IT'S CANCELLED!' he wailed. 'It's cancelled; Easther's got laryngitis. I heard it on the radio, they're telling everyone to turn back and go home.'

A wave of shock passed through my body before the news could set in. It gave way to disbelief before the upset hit me like a thunderous blow. I felt the blood drain from my limbs as I responded in a broken voice with 'How?' 'Why?' My eyes filled with a watery glaze. Dad tried to comfort me by suggesting they would probably reschedule it, but I already knew they were flying to Japan a few days later for the Asian leg of the tour.

That evening I consoled myself with my blessed VHS and stared up at my grainy homemade posters. Somehow they'd lost their lustre. I had this feeling it wasn't meant to be... that I'd never get to see them, let alone meet them.

2

2 Become 1

It was a Sunday, on one of those long June afternoons, when Conor rang me with the devastating news that he wasn't going to youth club that evening. No sooner had I put the phone down, annoyed that I'd be spending the evening trapped at home, when he rang back, this time with even bigger news: he and his family were moving to Belfast that August. As the news sunk in that I'd be losing my best friend, I felt sick in the pit of my stomach. I sat at the kitchen table, gazing at the peeling sunflower wallpaper and tapping my fingers anxiously, wondering what I was going to do without him around. We'd been best friends since we were three, and the past year at school had only been bearable because he was there with me. This was a jagged little pill to swallow.

♦ ♦ ♦

A few weeks later, we went on a family holiday to Boston, USA. It was the first time Anja, Sophie and I were getting on an aeroplane, so, naturally, we were thrilled. But my excitement was dampened when I worked out that the trip would coincide with my favourite pop band appearing everywhere to promote their new single. Eternal had been chosen to sing the theme for Disney's summer blockbuster, *The Hunchback of Notre Dame*: a sickly-sweet mega-ballad called 'Someday'. Back in the days before YouTube or catch-up TV, I had to provide Conor with a strict itinerary of all their performances, which he needed to record onto VHS in my absence (as if, with his family moving to another country, he had nothing more pressing to think about). I spent the entire holiday imagining Britain going wild with Eternal fever.

Little did I know that Eternal's big moment was being wildly overshadowed by the appearance of five decidedly more spicy young ladies. It seemed that in-yer-face catchy pop, rather than mellow ballads, was what the world really, really wanted that summer.

When we got back from America, I switched on the TV to find out via Ceefax where Eternal had charted, but the world was only interested in these new wannabes. My girls had been truly eclipsed by the Spice Girls and I was fuming. The world's media was full of the feisty five sticking their tongues out and shouting about female empowerment. I was livid! Eternal had (only a few months earlier) released 'Power of a Woman'. And Shampoo had released a single *called* 'Girl Power'. Somehow, nobody on *The O-Zone* or in *Smash Hits* had noticed, though.

There was a new source of pop news that was telling it like it really was: Dial-up Internet! After a number of lengthy phone calls to various call centres and a mile of phone wires and bulky equipment being mailed to us, Dad linked us up to the World Wide Web and I started to discover quaint homemade Eternal fan sites, full of pixelated photos, Hit Counters and painful moving WordArt in neon green and blue. Just loading each page would take about fifteen minutes, but it was worth it to get exclusive access to the latest gossip.

When the Spice Girls arrived, however, fan websites reached a whole new level. Media-savvy kids were logging onto GeoCities (a prehistoric Tumblr) by their thousands to create their own bit of the Internet, dedicated to their obsession with the recently christened Scary, Sporty, Posh, Baby and Ginger.

Through these early sites I discovered I wasn't the only one thinking it was a travesty that this manufactured gang of girls were stealing Kelle, Easther and Vernie's thunder. One site in particular, with Eternal and Louise forums, caught my attention. But this wasn't like Reddit: it was simply a massive group email list. You'd just hit 'Reply to All' and send a message about how much you loved the B-side to Eternal's third single and it would appear in the inbox of hundreds of similarly obsessive fans across the Continent. I found a whole new world where everyone shared my love: a place where I wasn't the odd boy, the target for a football or a crass insult.

Back at school that September I entered Year Nine unaided, left to fend for myself without Conor. We'd had an emotional farewell that August, and sworn we'd phone each other every week with all the latest gossip. It was like someone had sliced off an arm – even worse, it was the one carrying my trusty, bespectacled shield. As my school days became lonely and even harder, more and more I felt like these people online weren't just names on a list, they were my cyber friends, and I spent hours chatting to them about the minutiae of Vernie trivia and Louise gossip when I wasn't batting off insults in the playground.

◆ ◆ ◆

Christmas arrived a few weeks later, and the world was witnessing peak *Evita* – the long-awaited big-screen version of Andrew Lloyd Webber's musical, starring a late-thirties and slightly pregnant Madonna. I wasn't interested in the film or the soundtrack but I remember very clearly the first time I heard the 'Miami Mix' of Madge's version of 'Don't Cry for Me Argentina'. Madonna claimed she'd always wanted to put her own spin on the widely covered song, and so put out a Latin-dance version that is so gay, it's one of the campest things she has ever done. I twirled around with my cordless headphones on to its thumping beats, Spanish guitar and cascading piano in secret, with my imaginary castanets, imagining what it would be like to hear in the clubs it was made for.

Unfortunately, Eternal's festive offering was about as inspiring as an overcooked Brussels sprout. It came in the shape of 'Secrets', the fourth single wrung out from their current album, *Power of a Woman*. Faced with the Spice Girls and their rather more exciting addition to the Christmas Buffet, '2 Become 1', it was like they'd given up and gone home. Instead, the world lapped up the candlelit anthem to safe sex, propelling the spices to the much-coveted Christmas Number 1 on their first attempt.

The Spice Girls were caricatures, in the best possible way. Each one had a totally distinct image and personality, and all possessing a cheeky rebelliousness that guaranteed them column inches and ensuing record sales. They may not have had the greatest voices, but they certainly had the greatest range of merchandise. Within months of their arrival, shopping centres and supermarkets were piled high with Spice Girl branded crisps, deodorant, and even tins of custard creams. They were a total phenomenon.

But I wasn't about to switch my allegiance that easily. To me, the Spice Girls felt less slick and talented than my Eternal girls, although for reasons unknown I was fixated on the outspoken, buxom 'ginger one'. Geraldine Estelle Halliwell was simply unlike any other pop star on the planet: her hair, ridiculous dress sense, the amount of crap she talked, her over-the-top make-up. She was the first drag act I ever loved. And that's not an insult – Geri's been quite honest about what a drag queen cartoon she was in her Spice days. In a society that brushed a lot of issues under the rug, she was a breath of fresh air. The Spices were all larger than life in their own way but, something about Ginger just spoke to me, in a way that no one else did.

◆ ◆ ◆

In early 1997 I was gagging to listen to Eternal's long-awaited new album, *Before the Rain*. It was to be their first release since the Spice Girls had taken the pop world by storm. The five-piece were, by this point, reaching the end of their debut album's campaign and had buggered off to the US to make it over there. This left the door open for Eternal to reclaim their pop crown, and I was sure they would, with a fantastic album that would show everyone they were just as talented and original as their recent challengers.

When the album arrived, it was decidedly more 'grown-up'. Upbeat, soulful pop mostly made way for melancholy R&B. Were they trying to set themselves apart as something more credible than their rivals, or simply attempting to break the US market? Either way, it gained them a whole new set of fans – noticeably older than me and my peers online. But, at the same time, they were shedding younger fans who were gripped by power pop's resurgence. At the time I was blind to this, and decided to demonstrate my love through creativity. I bought a selection of gloss paints from B&Q and painted a magnificent mural, a leopard-print vision copied from Eternal's album's cover, across my bedroom radiator. For a week my perfectionist eye spent hours after school, carefully examining the cover and replicating its every detail, ensuring the ripples on the radiator's surface wouldn't distort the perspective. It also had the unintended consequence of making my thirteen-year-old's bedroom look like Bet Lynch's boudoir! Mum and Dad were surprisingly relaxed about me defacing their home. I guess they thought they'd repaint it before they ever sold the house. That didn't happen. I'm sure it was a real selling point.

A few weeks later, a largely indifferent world hadn't taken much notice of Eternal's comeback when their young upstart rivals decided to launch their latest single in a *slightly* more memorable fashion. At the 1997 BRIT Awards a titian-haired goddess, clad in a bold Union Jack number, strutted down the catwalk in a pair of bright-red platform boots. This unforgettably Cool Britannia meant business. I sat gobsmacked on the sofa as the five of them broke into 'Who Do You Think You Are'. Suddenly, I saw what all the fuss was about. The song ended and the crowd went wild. Only then did I realise that Eternal had missed the boat.

♦ ♦ ♦

The highlight of the summer holidays in 1997 was when I flew over to Belfast to see Conor for two weeks. We went on adventures every day. Particularly memorable was a trip to Derry, where we saw a stretched Mercedes with blacked-out windows. Conor said, 'You'll love this, Mal. That's Gloria Estefan's limo, she keeps it here for when she comes to Northern Ireland.' My mind was blown. I spent the rest of the day in a state of confusion. Did Gloria have a limo in every country around the world, on the off-chance she's popping in? Do ALL celebs have a limo in every country? If so, where's Cher's Northern Irish limo? And where does Gloria keep her English one? I quickly realised this was stupid, and thought they must obviously share these international limos, a Rent-A-Car for the rich and famous.

The next morning, my mind was blown again. I woke up violently to Conor's little brother Stephen walking over me on the sofa bed, yelling, 'PRINCESS DIANA'S DEAD! PRINCESS DIANA'S DEAD!' Even as a fourteen-year-old, I knew this was big news, but was more captivated by the spectacle than weeping into a box of Kleenex.

That afternoon I flew back from Belfast and on the plane all I could think about was how the summer was over. That was it – the only thing on the horizon was going back to school in Year Ten with no real friends, no interest in my upcoming GCSEs, and the prospect of everyone at school treating me like a freak. Back to normality then. When I got home I switched the radio on, in preparation for the Sunday evening ritual of listening to the Top 40 Chart, only to discover it had been cancelled as a mark of respect for Diana. In fact, the nation had taken the news so badly that for a couple of weeks Capital FM only played 'Everybody Hurts', 'Nothing Compares 2 U', 'You Have Been Loved' and other tearjerkers on an hourly cycle. We heard from relatives that it was like this all over the country. It was unlike anything I'd ever witnessed.

Eventually, the weepy tunes became less frequent and things returned to normal, although I don't think poor little Sophie realised. My little sister still cried daily at the car radio whenever The Verve's 'The Drugs Don't Work' came on, hysterically questioning us as to why there was 'a cat in a bag waiting to drown' while we all tried to mask our hysterics.

And, like a drowning cat, the first week back at school was as slow and painful as I expected. The only thing that seemed to get me through it was plonking myself in front of the computer as soon as I got home and escaping into the realm of the Internet, chatting to the only people who got me: my fellow pop-loving Eternal and Louise fans. One evening, after a particularly soul-destroying day in the classroom, I made a decision that would change the course of my pop-loving future forever.

3

Angel of Mine

Friday, 3 October 1997. Another horrible day at school. The only thing I was looking forward to was that Eternal's new single, 'Angel of Mine', would be charting that Sunday. I'd had two action-packed weeks of Smash Hits Q&As and interviews on *Live & Kicking* and *Blue Peter*. And Louise had released the first single – 'Arms Around the World' – off her second album, *Woman in Me*, the week before. I'd been spoilt.

Maths was the last lesson of the week. One final boring hour of Pythagoras' theorem before the bell would ring and I'd be free. Mum picked me up in her clapped-out Polo from a side road a few minutes' walk away: her carefully chosen location, away from the chaos of hundreds of parents picking up their juvenile offspring at 3.40 p.m. I was happy for her to park as far away as possible to spare her overhearing the shower of names I was heckled with on my walk out. If there's one thing worse than being called a 'faggot' by acne-ridden adolescents outside the school gates, it's your mum hearing it and confronting the tormenters.

At home I made myself my usual platter of Golden Syrup sandwiches before plonking myself in front of our beige-grey Hewlett Packard computer. I dialled up the Internet, with its loud whirring beeping sounds. 'Don't be long, please! You know it's expensive before six!' Mum bellowed from the lounge. 'Okay!' I shouted back, as if that was going to stop me catching up on the day's gossip on the Eternal and Louise mailing list emails. Everyone was excited about Louise's *Top of the Pops* appearance later that night, and how well we all thought Eternal would do in Sunday's charts.

Mum threw together an early dinner of pork pies and cold baked beans (which was, bizarrely, one of our favourites) before she took Sophie swimming. I settled down to watch *Top of the Pops*, vigilantly making sure I had the video player and my 'MALCOLM'S LOUISE TAPE – DO *NOT* TAPE OVER' VHS ready to record the performance I'd been waiting all week for. I was surprisingly organised and always ready with my finger on the button by 7.25 p.m., patiently sitting through a pre-facelift Anne Robinson and co-presenter Alice Beer keenly reading out the final updates on a defective Hoover recall or mis-sold Teletext holiday insurance on BBC1's *Watchdog*.

Louise's Asian-themed performance of 'Arms Around the World' was the highlight of my week thus far. To capture the song's eastern influences, in one corner there were women doing Bollywood dancing on the spot, and in another, a man pretending to play a sitar. Louise was dressed like Lewisham's answer to Princess Jasmine, with a high ponytail and gold jewellery up her arms and around her neck. It was a cultural mishmash that at the time I thought was *so* cosmopolitan.

Anja sat on the sofa behind me, giving her two-pence worth during the whole thing. Her main gibe was that the song was a 'blatant rip-off' of Janet Jackson's hit the previous year, 'Runaway'. I told her at the time to piss off; they were totally different. Since emerging from the blind adulation and unwavering love for Louise, I can now admit that the two songs are a *tad* similar!

We ended up having an argument about it. Anja loved making fun of the things I held dearest in my life. But then I slagged off her beloved Newcastle United whenever I got the chance, so we both knew how to torment each other. I stormed upstairs to listen to Louise and console myself. What did she know? For Christ's sake, don't get me into all this worshipping-of-pop-queens malarkey, then tell me how shit they all are!

♦ ♦ ♦

After fifteen minutes shut away in my room I heard the phone ring. Probably one of Mum's friends – it was never for me. Then I heard a knock at the door.

'Malcolm!' Anja called.

'What do you want?!' I snapped, still not over our Louise spat.

'Is there a girl in your class called Kelly?'

'Go away, I don't care!'

'IS THERE OR ISN'T THERE? There's someone on the phone for you.' Anja upped her sense of urgency this time.

'Well, yes... But she wouldn't be ringing me.'

'Then I don't know how to tell you this, but I think Kelle from Eternal is on the phone for you,' Anja announced, in the most serious face I've ever seen her make.

My brows started trembling and I looked straight into Anja's eyes. 'My *letter*. She must have got my letter!!!' I screamed, as I ran past her, swooping down the stairs towards the grey handset resting on the kitchen table, its curly cord stretching over to the grubby phone on the wall.

I clutched it close to my chest, whispering, 'I wrote her a fan letter last week. I never thought she reads them!'

'QUICK – speak to her!' Anja yelled.

'Hellllllo?' I said suspiciously.

'Hi.'

'Who's this?'

'It's Kelle.'

'Kelle who?' I asked, biting my lower lip, looking up to the ceiling in disbelief.

'Kelle!'

'Kelle from Eternal?'

She paused. 'Yeah. It's me! How are you doing? I got your letter, I've got it here in front of me.' She sounded so friendly and calm compared with the manic euphoria I was going through. 'We just arrived back from Holland this evening, where the girls and I were doing promo for "Angel of Mine" and I stopped by the label to pick up my mail. Your letter was so lovely and I just wanted to pick up the phone and say hi.'

As if this was actually happening to me! I couldn't contain my delirium. I'd never had any interaction with a pop star in my life. In the days before Twitter and Instagram, the popstar-fan relationship was totally different – completely one-sided. This was blowing my mind! There I was, sitting in our shabby kitchen in Ottershaw, talking to one of the people I admired most in the world. A glitzy pop star was taking time out from her showbiz life to ring ME!

We chatted for twenty-five minutes about all sorts. She told me about how she liked to hang out with her mum, then I told her about how I liked to hang out with mine. She told me about Eternal's recent trip to Holland and I told her about learning Pythagoras. We even had an in-depth discussion about Northern Ireland Secretary Mo Mowlam and the peace process. I loved every surreal second. And I really wanted to hang out with her and her mum.

As I hung up the phone I fell on the floor in a heap and cried uncontrollably for a very long time. I was a lonely kid going through dark times at school, and it meant *so* much to me that this international pop star, *my idol*, had chosen to ring me to chat about Sinn Fein and Woking. Anja put her arm around me, grinning, 'This is amazing! Your dreams have come true!'

Mum and Sophie arrived home from swimming class and I was still crying hysterically, almost hyperventilating. I walked out into the street, where they were getting out of the car, and Mum worriedly asked what the hell was going on. I just kept crying. 'What's happened? What's wrong?' she shouted. Anja intervened, explaining the events of the last thirty minutes and that I was, in fact, very happy.

Mum rolled her eyes and said, 'Thank God – I thought something serious had happened to you both!' Sophie was less restrained, screaming with bloody murder, 'AAAAAAH! OH MY GOD!!! What?!!' We all laughed about it in the street and once I'd calmed down later on, I told the whole family in minute detail every last thing that had been said.

I also explained that with the most recent letter I'd enclosed a butchered photo of me and Mum on holiday in Cornwall that I'd cut out of the family album. I don't think she has quite forgiven me for that, but I'd have sacrificed many a photo of us looking our seaside-best for the chance to relive that phone call.

That Sunday, 'Angel of Mine' charted at Number 4. Never mind... Kelle, you're still my angel!

♦ ♦ ♦

While speaking to Kelle, I told her I'd been chatting to other Eternal fans on the unofficial email list. The Internet back then was the preserve of tech geeks and obsessive teenagers on fan sites. Some others online said they were planning to watch Eternal record their appearance on *Top of the Pops* the following week. I told Kelle I was thinking of coming. 'Yeah! Come down and say hi if you can. Definitely!... As long as your parents are okay with it' (Spoiler alert! This is not a book about me being groomed by a sixty-eight-year-old man masquerading as a devotee of the Bennett sisters. We were all much more naïve and innocent back then.)

The few lucky classmates of mine fortunate enough to have 56 kbps streaming into their PCs were all addicted to Yahoo! chat rooms. It was a gateway to every corner of the globe, chatting about the Spice Girls and homework with kids from North Dakota, or Barrow-in-Furness, or a suburb of Dortmund. Mum and Dad were happy for us to chat on there, but they certainly didn't want us to arrange to meet these total strangers. They definitely wouldn't want their fourteen-year-old son travelling to the other side of London to spend a day with a whole group of people he'd met online discussing what Louise's favourite breed of dog is. Particularly on a school day. Hmm, how could I possibly convince them? I went for the classic teenage tactics of guilt trips, badgering and tantrums.

Over the next five days, after endless tears and pleading I finally wore them down. Mum begrudgingly agreed to let me have a half-day at school, provided I didn't tell my teachers where I was going and caught up on the lessons I would miss. Dad even had to book the afternoon off work. I was extremely appreciative and respecting of the conditions: Yeah, yeah... blah blah... OH MY GOD I'M GOING TO THE ACTUAL *TOP OF THE POPS* STUDIOS! Someone slap me, this can't be real!

I checked with the fans on the email list where it was: 'Elstree Studios in Borehamwood' someone had written. Where the hell's that? That's not the place with the bouncing ball on the opening credits of *Live & Kicking*! I finally tracked it down in the very top corner of a page of the out-of-date *A–Z* Dad kept in his glove box. Turns out Borehamwood is not round the corner from Mayfair, it's not even on the Tube. In fact, it's so far out of London, it's in bloody Hertfordshire! It made me even more curious to visit this mythical land that must be jam-packed with A-listers, like the Home Counties Hollywood.

♦ ♦ ♦

The morning of the recording I nervously prepared myself for the expedition ahead of me. I shoved some supplies into my school rucksack: Club biscuit: tick; camera and a spare roll of film: tick; CDs to get signed: tick. Then, in a moment of genius, I realised that I needed to get noticed – I had to stand out from the crowd. I scoured my wardrobe for something that would make me visible to ensure Eternal, and the TV cameras, couldn't miss me. Blue Adidas T-shirt? Too dull. Grey Joe Bloggs shirt? No. Massive lime green Day-Glo T-shirt? Perfect! I then rummaged through my other drawers and pulled out a lime green woolly hat. And some lime green trainers (same ones that Mel C was currently wearing for the 'Spice Up Your Life' CD artwork). I was to be a vision in lime. Subtle it wasn't, and perhaps a bit premature for Nu Rave, but at least everyone would see me.

Dad and I then set off around the M25. I followed the journey all the way on his *A–Z*. For those of you who have never had the pleasure of visiting Borehamwood, it's a prime example of nominative determinism. Yes, it's home to some of the best-known television shows in Britain, but the studios are not surrounded by the mansions of the rich and famous, as in Hollywood. Instead, it's a rather ordinary suburban town wedged between the M25 and the last straggling fringes of London. This came as something of a shock to me as Dad pulled off the motorway and we drove along the high street, where, stood outside the local branch of Superdrug, was a man in a black fleece selling laminated posters of Melinda Messenger and the Spice Girls in bikinis for £2 each. We turned down a residential street and my heart filled with a combination of excitement and bewilderment as I realised that the studios were just at the end of the road. Was this really the home of *Top of the Pops*? Was it *really* the location of the MDF Albert Square?

Barely at a halt, I jumped out of Dad's Vauxhall estate. 'Okay, bye! Yeah, I'll call your office from a payphone later!' I shouted as I leapt out of the passenger seat. Standing on the roadside opposite were three nervous misfits staring at me. I immediately recognised them from the one lo-res photo each of them had put online: late-twenties, practically dressed, socially awkward. We weren't exactly similar, but they took me under their wing and the fact they loved Eternal made me think I'd found some kindred spirits. And they really loved Eternal. They could recount endless inane facts about them, from their shoe sizes to Taiwanese chart positions. In 1997, fourteen-year-old me thought that I was the first person ever to meet someone from the World Wide Web. I was crazy! I felt more futuristic than a feature on *Tomorrow's World*. They were very different times; unlike today, there wasn't the fear about meeting people from the Internet because no one really did it back then.

We huddled together against the drizzle by the gate like a group of penguins, but with fewer social skills. The TV studios were surrounded by a high metal fence with all the staff and stars within it, and, unfortunately, we were stood on the wrong side of it. I gawped with amazement as Pat Butcher (Pam St Clement) rolled past in a Volvo on her way to film some gripping storylines at the Queen Vic. And just a few moments later Pauline Fowler (Wendy Richard) gave us a royal wave from a Ford Mondeo. What kind of parallel universe was this?

Some rival Eternal groupies also rocked up, who clearly thought they were bigger fans than us, as they strutted through the car park in their puffer jackets with greased-back ponytails. I recognised these four girls – Tracy, Lisa, Anthea and some other hard-looking late teen – from watching *Top of the Pops*. They would always be on the front row whenever Eternal were performing. And the band knew them. I wished the whole band knew me too. These four adolescent Eternal groupies seemed so much cooler and more streetwise than me – shy and nervous, dressed head-to-toe like a bloody citrus fruit! Inside, I just kept thinking, *Let me in your gang and I'll ditch the Millets-clad misfits. I'm one of you!*

My fellow Internet dweebs knew the story of Kelle ringing me, as I'd plastered it all over the email list that same evening in glee, but I recounted it once more for the other groupie girls. They were notably less-impressed but still happy for me. 'Yeah, that's a very Kelle thing to do,' Lisa said. It didn't take a genius to see that Kelle was not as popular among these girls as Easther and Vernie, the Bennett sisters. I couldn't really get my head around this, as to me, Kelle was the one with the beaming personality and permanent grin, whereas the two sisters had a reputation in interviews for being the ice maidens of UK pop.

The Groupie Girls gloated to me, 'Kel's not all she seems. I can see why people think that from TV and stuff, but she's not really like that in person.' I bit back, 'She might have bad days! Maybe you caught her at the wrong time?' Lisa kept going, 'Yeah, well, she doesn't have many groupies who really like her now, so I think she's trying harder with people.' How dare she suggest my beloved Kelle was ringing me out of desperation!

After lunch, some of the bands started arriving. A car with three long-haired blonde girls turned up – it was the Hanson Brothers. Members of post-Britpop band The Seahorses strolled in and out to down Carling and pork scratchings at the pub around the corner in between rehearsals. Finally, the Eternal girls were driven past in their blacked-out silver Mercedes. I nearly soiled myself with excitement. After an hour or so the Bennett sisters came out and said 'hi' to us all as they were being ushered to another rehearsal. Kelle wasn't with them, which was gutting. Perhaps the Groupie Girls were right – maybe she wasn't interested in the fans. Maybe she thought she was better than us. Easther said she didn't even know where Kelle was. I was starting to realise how divided the band was. I was desperate to see Kelle and tell her it was me – the boy she rang last Friday night. Would she remember me? Or was she too busy being a pop star to actually care?

♦ ♦ ♦

As the day drew on and the studios got busier I became increasingly nervous that I wouldn't actually get in to watch the show. We needed to find people with spare tickets, but were clueless about where to wait. The rival Groupie Girls got theirs pretty quickly – they just casually strolled up to the nearest guy and nonchalantly asked him for tickets. Soon, there were hundreds of audience members, but there were also now loads of other chancers playing the same game as us. As time passed more and more glammed-up late teenage girls from Stevenage and Hemel Hempstead got dropped off by their dads, scavenging for tickets. *Shit! I don't think this is going to happen!* I thought. Every time we asked people arriving they gave us a pitiful smile and shook their heads with expressions that said 'No chance, mate'. Hope was ebbing away. Was seeing Wendy Richard drive past really going to be the highlight of my day?

Night fell and there were swarms of men in horrible shirts and women in horrible skirts in a queue going right around the street. I felt increasingly out of my depth, a schoolboy in an adult's world. I was standing tall, my chest pushed out and less smiley, to try desperately to look older, like a real bloke who'd be going to *Top of the Pops* with his girlfriend, but inside I felt like a vulnerable fourteen-year-old with his school bag. Even if we scored some spare tickets, would my doctored birth certificate even pass as ID? As the queue finally started to disappear through the gates into the studios, I prepared myself for disappointment and a sad call home to Mum and Dad.

Apparently, they cut the queue off when the studio gets too full anyway. However, that evening, they were still slightly under capacity as the last cold girls in boob tubes, denim jackets and strappy heels filed through. Security were minutes away from shutting the gates and I was gutted I'd come this far and wouldn't get to see Eternal perform, to tell Kelle I made it all the way to see her.

With two minutes to go, two girls and a guy ran around the corner. We begged them for any spare tickets, pleading like our lives depended on it. One of the girls rummaged around in her handbag, eventually pulling out a brown envelope. She flicked through the contents and unceremoniously handed us three spare tickets. 'There you go! Have a good night!' I looked down at my hand to check I really had that ticket and hadn't either (a) imagined it, or (b) been handed a blank bit of paper by someone taking us for a ride. They seemed to be the genuine article. Overjoyed, we stood nervously behind them in the queue as they were flagged through by Security. And then it was our turn: we did our best to look hopeful (but not too desperate) at the gate. Our ticket numbers were cross-checked and the emotionless security guard waved us through. 'You're the last ones. Very lucky!' he said as the green steel gate clanged shut. 'Follow them and put your stuff in the cloakroom. Quickly, please.'

We grabbed each other's arms in glee and let out a silent scream as we finally ventured beyond the big iron gates we'd been staring through longingly all day. We were about to be a part of the most iconic music TV show of all time. I thought of the decades of bands through the ages, the classic image of Jimmy Savile smoking a cigar (little did we know...), the icons of pop doing dodgy mimes to the biggest songs of the last fifty years. I'd watched religiously every week for the last two years, obsessing over every performance and piece of trivia fed to me through the television. I was just an imposter kid out on a school night. Was this really happening?

♦ ♦ ♦

Inside was a large room with bright fluorescent lighting. This was basically a holding pen for girls touching up their lip gloss and twisty-hair 'up-dos'. It was wall-to-wall Kookai tops, a plethora of feather boas, with the odd bored-looking bloke in an ill-fitting Ben Sherman shirt interspersed among them. The atmosphere was a cross between a provincial nightclub and the boarding gate for a Thomas Cook flight to Faliraki.

People were already queuing around the outside of the room to get into the studios. We quickly checked in our bags and coats, then joined the back of the queue. Two women at the far end of the room opened a set of doors and everyone was marched through a maze of cold concrete corridors to the studio. Fragments of TV backdrops were dotted around us. I was star-struck as I passed The Arches – home of the Mitchell brothers' mechanics, and bits of the *Kilroy* set, casually dumped out in the damp passageway. My mum had little interest in my pop obsession, but I'd found the one thing that would excite her when I got home.

At the end of the concrete wind tunnel were the studio doors, the comforting sound of breakbeat reverberating out from within. Again, we were led through more corridors, this time made of high, black curtains: a never-ending labyrinth into the inner sanctum of pop. We turned a corner and there it was. Like I'd gone through the television set and ended up on the other side, right there in my favourite programme. The crowd were herded around the main stage as dark and grimy speed garage anthem 'Gunman' was blasted out to the buzzing crowd. Immediately I was struck by the unbelievable cold – I just wished I'd worn a couple more lime layers to insulate me.

Two warm-up guys, cockney geezer double-act Mark and Danny, got the audience dancing immediately to the heavy bassline as they talked us through what was in store that evening. They insisted, despite the intolerable coldness at the start of the night, we would all get significantly warmer as the evening went on. There was a lot of screaming as the acts were read out, then more when we were told that the best dancer would win... wait for it...TEN CDs. TEN! Holy shit, we'd better crack out our best moves for this challenge!

At this point I'd never set foot in a nightclub before, but imagined this was sort of what it was like. I thought if no one at school was ever going to invite me out clubbing, maybe I could just come here instead for nights out. Despite my lack of clubbing experience, I'd still studied the way the audience moved on *Top of the Pops* every week, so I broke into a nineties sidestep bop-and-occasional-clap (I thought it more suitable than my full *Pan's People*-esque routine.)

Mark and Danny complimented the girls in the audience as they also bopped clumsily from side to side. Some of the compliments were a little gauche. They were half-Beavis and Butthead, half-Chas and Dave, cracking shit jokes we all laughed at as we carried on throwing shapes, this time to chart-friendly drum'n'bass, courtesy of Adam F's 'Circles'.

The studio had four stages – the main stage where the biggest bands would usually perform, the 'White Stage' (reserved usually for the alternative artists), another one opposite which seemed to be mostly for urban acts and one at the back tucked in the corner for pure pop. Occasionally they'd get a big name artist to perform on the floor, invariably perched on a bar stool, surrounded by the audience.

As the last ones into the studio, we were stuck right at the back. Yes, we'd made it, but even in the most garish clothing in the whole room, I was never going to be visible on TV behind two hundred people. Imagine my delight then when the crew asked everyone to turn around to face the second stage, where the first band would be performing. I rotated to discover I was now on the front row: my small-screen debut was about to commence.

The first band on were Catch, a totally forgotten British boy band consisting of three posh sixth-formers who played their own instruments (still quite a revelation in the pop industry in

1997, after trailblazers Hanson had conquered the world that summer). As the opening bars of their song 'Bingo' were played, it didn't matter that I'd never heard it before, this was it! My lime green pixelated image would be beamed to ten million households across the nation.

As they burst into the chorus I listened to the lyrics and felt like they were singing about me, there and then...

Yes, I went there... BINGO! ... *and* I found out.
Yes, I discovered... BINGO!... what the fuss is about!

It all felt so deep and profound to fourteen-year-old me. Shortly afterwards, I discovered that this deep and meaningful song about self-discovery was in fact a tale of losing your virginity in a red-light district. I felt cheap and used. It will forever be the moment I lost my *Top of the Pops* virginity. Simultaneously life-changing and memorable while also slightly awkward and disappointing. And it only lasted three minutes and twenty seconds.

They were basically an early Busted prototype, spanning the gap between a genuine band, in the 'school mates jamming in their parents' garage' mould, and a manufactured attempt by a big label to replicate that in a more saleable format.

This was Catch's first – and last – Top 40 hit. Clearly, the world wasn't quite ready for a Britpop boy band. Except, it seems, Indonesia – where they were massive. They do have one reason to for ever be a footnote in musical history – their video for 'Bingo' was being played in the graveyard slot on ITV in the early hours of 31 August 1997, only to be rudely interrupted by a newsflash announcing the death of Princess Diana. I don't actually remember their follow-up single, 'Dive In', which didn't make the Top 40 – they pretty much disappeared without a trace. Alas, their legend burned out long before their candle ever did.

As 'Bingo' faded out, rather than a seamless ten-second link fronted by the evening's presenter, Mark Lamarr, the studio audience were subjected to grumpy floor managers herding us around like cattle as we did our best to avoid tripping up on the miles of camera cables strewn across the floor. Meanwhile, Mark and Danny were back, desperate to keep everyone upbeat and looking cheery while the technicians prepared the next act on a stage at the other side of the room.

Eventually, Hanson were ready to perform. Teenage me was excited to see them as they were the boy band of the moment. Now, when one gets the opportunity to see Hanson play, there's only one song you want to listen to. Unfortunately, this being *Top of the Pops*, you just got their latest single and sadly for us, 'MMMBop' was months ago. Desperate not to be a One Hit Wonder, the boys were playing their third single that night: a rousing, wintry ballad, 'I Will Come to You'. Harmonies, key changes and even a string section.

Luckily for us, they weren't coming back to these shores for a while and after filming their performance, the group announced they were also recording their Christmas *Top of the Pops* performance of 'MMMBop'! Hurrah! Sorry to spoil the magic, kids, but sometimes for the purposes of television, celebs are forced to don jumpers and scarves in mid-June and sweat their way through a set filled with fake snow and mince pies, all to save the BBC a bit of cash. Hanson's performance of 'MMMBop' was exactly as you'd imagine: energetic, fun and lyrically indecipherable. The Millets crew and I loved it.

As we crowded around the front of the stage, an angry cameraman in a polo shirt, wearing an earpiece, starting yelling from behind us to move out of the way. An unwieldy two-ton camera on a crane, mounted on a makeshift railway track, was hurtling towards us. It was a mad rush to save ourselves, pushing over nineteen-year-olds in stilettos to avoid losing a leg.

Britpop dregs The Seahorses followed them, with their atmospheric indie tune, 'Love Me and Leave Me' on the White Stage. I hated Britpop at the time – that was more Anja's bag – but to me, just being there and seeing anyone was mind-blowing.

In between takes, a blonde woman would run on stage to touch up the performers' foundation and lipstick. Imperceptible on screen, most bands, however masculine, were caked in the stuff: like half a dozen skinny pantomime dames dressed in Fred Perry and parkas. Just as we'd been promised, the studio heated up. Seriously. Even in the depths of winter, the lights and crowds of people would turn this black box into the biggest sauna in Borehamwood.

Ordinarily, *Top of the Pops* would end with a performance from whoever was that week's Number 1. However, this was halfway through Elton John's seven-week stint at the top with his inescapable tribute to Diana, 'Candle in the Wind 1997'. Instead of a live performance, the programme would cut to a sombre video of news footage. The Princess's death had thrown the entire nation into a period of mourning and wreaked havoc on the House of Windsor. It even led the Spice Girls to postpone the release of their new single, 'Spice Up Your Life', as the world wasn't ready for an up-tempo party number just yet.

♦ ♦ ♦

The penultimate act on was rock 'n' soul act Roachford, on one of the side stages, but by this point most of us Eternal fans were getting distracted by the crew setting up three microphone stands on the Main Stage. The Groupie Girls had no interest in watching his performance of 'The Way I Feel', choosing instead to pitch themselves at the front row of Eternal's stage in preparation. They were *Top of the Pops* regulars, so weren't awestruck by every act like I was. I diligently stood there through Roachford, enjoying his performance with a growing sense of anticipation for the main act.

As his performance ended and everyone broke into applause I knew I had to quickly get my lime-green arse across the studio floor if I was to get close enough to the front to get on telly. I managed to squeeze myself to the front, opposite the left-hand mic – the one that Kelle had used in other performances of the song on TV. Please God let it be the one she's using tonight! After a few final minutes of bullshit jokes for the crowd and the girl with the biggest tits in the audience being awarded the 'Best Dancer' prize, the moment of truth had arrived.

'Right, can you put your hands together, please... a massive round of applause for our very special, last act of the night. The one... and only... ETERNAL!' Danny, the warm-up guy, announced. The crowd went crazy one last time and my heart raced as the girls strutted out onto the stage; visions in white under the heavenly blinding blue lights. My three angels!

Their new-look wardrobe was questionable. They'd gone from baggy armywear for their first album to sassy for the second, then mumsy chic for the recent one: lots of long coats. Fans were underwhelmed, especially as the Spice Girls were decidedly more jazzed up. Dorothy Perkins would no longer suffice. Even new girls All Saints had been branded with a trademark look: evoking early Eternal with their vest tops and combat trousers. That night though, the Eternal girls had obviously made an effort: they'd clearly upped their game, each with a stylish variation on the theme of white, as though they were taking part in the Daz Doorstep Challenge.

The Groupie Girls gossiped with Easther and Vernie, as Kelle smiled and looked on, without joining in. There was definitely something going on here. She looked isolated in the corner while the sisters lapped up the attention of their small army of self-proclaimed 'biggest fans'. There wasn't time for me to try to get Kelle's attention though; the next minute we were cheering again and the opening guitar strums of their breathy, current smash 'Angel of Mine' were played out. For those three minutes I was in ecstasy, swaying in the crowd as the girls sang their heavenly pop. Well, the backing vocals looked to be mimed, but this was the nineties – a live vocal in any form was a rare treat.

After they had performed it once, Mark and Danny came on to let the band know if they'd got what they wanted. The girls smiled at the quiet crowd again, as they waited to get the all-clear. Right, this was my chance. Now or never...

'Kelle!' I screamed.

She looked around to see where the shouts were coming from, partially blinded by the glare of the stage lights. 'KELLE!' I bellowed again. I caught her attention finally.

'You phoned me!' I said with a beaming smile. Easther and Vernie were now staring at me, as well as the surrounding crowd, who had turned to see the brazen fan trying to talk to them. She looked back blankly and gave a vague, awkward smile. 'It's me! Malcolm! You rang me last Friday!' I yelled, using my little finger and thumb to mimic a telephone, worried that my one chance to connect in the flesh and prove it had all happened was falling apart around me very fast. The audience started giving me weird looks and murmuring. FUCK! If she didn't remember, everyone would think I'd made it up. That's worse than never getting to talk to her! She looked me in the eye for a few more seconds (which felt like an eternity), the cogs turning in her head. Then suddenly the penny dropped.

'OH! Oh, it's you! Sorry, I was miles away. You made it here!' Now her smile was beaming back at me. 'It's so nice to see you, thanks for coming down. Give my love to your mum!' The audience and the Bennett sisters looked on in bizarre bewilderment as I let out a huge inner sigh of relief. We swapped knowing grins and I told her how happy I was to get to see them perform.

'Wow, she phoned you?' the girl next to me said. 'That's so lovely!' For a moment, I felt like I was the famous one. There was more murmuring from the audience, who'd now turned back to talk to their friends. Mark and Danny apologised and said they wanted to record another take to get some more shots. They launched into the song again and this time Kelle looked at me throughout, smiling and singing me my own private concert. It was overwhelming. We cheered and they bade us goodbye, Kelle giving me one last wave as she left the stage.

It was over, I had done it! As soon as Eternal had cleared the stage, a rotund man with a clipboard ushered us out of the studio as unceremoniously as we'd been let in. We'd barely left the room before the crew were clearing the floor of cameras and cables, the fluorescent strip lights destroying any illusion that I was anywhere other than a warehouse by the M25 on the very edge of London.

Once outside in the dark night again, I stood with my Internet buddies, recounting every last moment of the night, all of us on such a high. There was talk of people going to the ITV studios the next day to try and see the girls record their appearance on *Light Lunch* (featuring two lovely young presenters called Mel and Sue).

Sure enough though, like the mom in *Almost Famous* honking her car horn, picking her young son up after his first brush with fame at a rock gig, there was Dad, politely beeping. Time to return home to my black-and-white life in Kansas.

♦ ♦ ♦

Back at school I had a spring in my step for a change as word spread that I 'reckoned' I'd attended *Top of the Pops* the night before. No one's insults or doubts could hurt me. I'd already seen the light at the end of this tunnel; experienced a world way bigger than they knew about. They would see me on TV and wonder how the most bullied kid had pulled something like this off, with almost no friends.

That Friday night, as I settled into my TV dinner during *Top of the Pops*, I couldn't help but reflect on how much had happened since Kelle's call. Watching my lime-green self in the audience, with the whole family crowding around the TV set, was the icing on the cake. There I was, forever recorded in time: my lanky body bopping side to side in my massive T-shirt. Even Anja and I called a truce during those hallowed thirty minutes. No arguments; just laughter. Mum and Dad said I had a knack for blagging. Maybe this was my true calling?

4

Life Ain't Easy

On the Monday morning after my *Top of the Pops* telly debut I swaggered up the school driveway, grinning like Brian Harvey on a heavy night out. Would people finally realise how cool I was? No. Barely anyone was interested in the appearance of me, or my lime-green T-shirt, during a British TV institution. Those who were just thought I was even weirder. *Oh, Malcolm, you're too good for these small-town nobodies!*

It made me even more desperate to escape from Ottershaw, to spend my time hanging out with international musicians, or other fans at the very least. I assumed that, as Mum and Dad had allowed me a day off school to meet my idols once, they'd be letting me go to everything. But they had other ideas. Dad said they'd been more than fair; that I'd 'had my fun' and, after one measly day off as a special treat, I now needed to knuckle down and concentrate on doing well in my GCSEs (which were eighteen months away). I couldn't wait that long!

♦ ♦ ♦

Mum, meanwhile, wasn't having an easy time. Granny, her mum, was in the final stages of throat cancer. Mum was going back and forth to Grantham to visit her in a nursing home. Granny was always a fuller-figured woman, the embodiment of Hyacinth Bucket: a twin-set-and-pearl clad busybody with a lacquered perm and a lust for social climbing. When we went up in November 1997, six months after us grandkids had seen her last, she looked like a completely different person: weak and withered, with ghostly white hair, and barely able to stand. I was stunned into silence.

Mum had been protecting us from the grim transformation she'd been through in the past few months. This was supposed to be a 'nice catch-up' but we all knew it was one last goodbye. Granny died a couple of weeks later, in December, and her funeral was likely to be held close to Christmas.

Since summer, though, the main thing on my mind wasn't the ailing health of my grandmother but Louise's upcoming Wembley Arena gig (sorry, Granny). It was set to be the biggest show of her career and I'd managed to secure amazing seats for me and one of my classmates, Kathi. We'd bonded over our mutual love of pop during lessons, discussing each week's interviews in *Smash Hits*. She too was a bit of a misfit. Her scraped-back brunette hair wouldn't pass muster with the cooler girls, so she sought solace in Boyzone.

As the day crept closer, it looked worryingly like I might have to miss it for Granny's funeral. WHY?! Another cruel hand of fate at Wembley! Thankfully though they didn't clash (I'm pretty sure I know what fourteen-year-old me would have opted for). On the big night, Dad dropped us off outside the arena among a hectic crowd of fans. Our mood dropped when we piled out of the car to see the grim concrete arena, looking more like a warehouse than a glittering showbiz venue, with a shoddy plastic 'LOUISE' banner casually draped across the front. I surrendered six months' pocket money at the merch stand on inferior T-shirts, mugs and posters, while overdressed girls queued up in droves for the Formica toilet cubicles. On our way to the front we bumped into the Eternal Groupie Girls from *Top of the Pops*, which, after a brief chat with them, made Kathi think I was now some sort of big cheese on the pop scene. The audience of 10,000 screaming teenage girls, a few gay guys and some drooling straight men loved it; whether for the music or the kitsch factor.

As I had phoned up early to get tickets, I'd had my pick of locations. Instead of choosing some fantastic seats in Row B, slap bang in the middle of the stage, I ignored all the friendly lady's advice over the phone and went for the two remaining tickets in ROW A!!! I'd bagged front-row seats for my pop idol! I thought I was so much better than the fans at the back as we were ushered past everyone to our places. I don't remember much of the concert, possibly thanks to the giant stack of speakers obstructing our view. We'd traded having some of the best seats in the house for front-row status. We didn't care though, as Louise made momentary eye contact and waved right at us.

As we made our way out of the gig, we wondered what new heights 1998 would bring for Louise. Little did we know it would be her swansong though, just as my groupie career was kicking off. The following year, her crown would be challenged by a whole bunch of other hungry competitors.

That winter, while Mum was at Granny's house in Grantham clearing out eighty years of doilies and pearl necklaces from her tallboy, I was learning what a fickle business pop is. A new band called All Saints were suddenly taking Britain by storm with their moody R&B, and blowing Eternal out of the water. Overnight, the music-buying public abandoned them in favour of these four girls. Eternal's success was less than eternal – I'm sure I was mourning them more than Granny.

♦ ♦ ♦

In 1998, it felt like forever until spring half term when Kathi and I could go to *Top of the Pops* from morning to midnight! Kathi, also an avid viewer, didn't require much persuading to get her down there. We were in the same form group at school but didn't hang out all the time. Our friendship seemed to exist mainly during morning registration and online on the Eternal and Louise email lists with the other geeks.

For the first time we went by train, feeling a bit more grown-up and streetwise on this trip, rather than Dad pulling up to the studios in front of all the other teens scouting for tickets. It was a really convoluted journey. This was well before smartphones and travel apps, so I'd had to rely on the London Travel Information phoneline. You'd ring up and someone in an office would flick through a book and recite the best train times.

When we finally arrived at the little street leading to the studios, still bright-eyed and chirpy, there were some other pop fans loitering by the security barrier, in the same spot I'd waited all day on my first visit. We didn't talk to them initially, preferring to stand far away enough so that we could wilfully ignore their existence. However, after a few silent minutes of slyly looking each other up and down, Kathi and I decided it was going to be a *very* long, awkward day on the concrete pavement slabs if we didn't utter a word to them, so we bit the bullet and to thaw the ice, stiffly asked who they were waiting for. They weren't there for anyone in particular, just to try to meet pop stars on their half term and get into the show that evening. Oh, same! Perhaps we could just hang out together rather than be bitter rivals? They were a group of four girls: a pair of tiny brunette twins and two bubbly blonde girls. All from the hinterlands of Luton; all of them *Top of the Pops* regulars who, it also turned out, knew some Eternal fans Kathi and I had chatted to online.

We were both fourteen. These Luton girls were all sixteen or seventeen – practically adults to us. (You *technically* had to be seventeen to get into *Top of the Pops,* but my butchered birth certificate helped me overcome this hurdle. Kathi had one too – we all did!) There were also a few mouthy local kids hanging around, presumably just fed up and looking for something to do during half term; maybe see an *EastEnders* star walk out to grab some lunch.

Once we'd gotten over our initial awkwardness of teenage small talk and minor one-upmanship, we got on like a house on fire. All gawky, teenage oddballs in our own ways, we just wanted a little brush with the stars at the studios whenever we could. It was better than being stuck in dismal shopping centres and bowling alleys, causing trouble with all the other bored kids in our hometowns.

After several chilly hours on a suburban street corner, dissecting our favourite celeb haircuts and crushes, we all scored spare tickets off incoming audience members. We ambled up the high street to Burger King so the girls could get dolled up for the show in the toilets, the glamorous smell of fried beef infusing with their White Musk Body Shop sprays.

I waited patiently at a greasy table, snacking on insipid chips, while they went into the loos to slap on more lip gloss and change out of their jeans and jumpers into strappy tops and miniskirts. Were they talking about me? I really hoped they all liked me.

After twenty minutes of intensive glamorising, they emerged and joined me, then each added a generous serving of glitter glue (like the stuff you made cards for your nan with), which was lacquered on everywhere: their hair, around their eyes, up their arms, you name it. In the late nineties the glittery, lubed-up look was rampant among teenage girls.

This was *all* new to me, having never been on a real night out before, with a group of girls (or anyone, to be honest), and been part of all the make-up, clothes and boy-chat that takes place before a night on the tiles (or studio floor). I felt so at ease with our new friends, despite having only spent a few freezing hours together. There wasn't a moment where I felt like they were taking me for a ride, like so many of the girls at school who would feign interest one minute, then snigger at me with the boy bullies the next: I felt accepted.

Back in the queue, I fretted about whether we'd still get in, what with standing out on the street all day with all the local kids. The Luton Girls were less wary. When we reached the front of the queue the security team at the gate glanced at our fake IDs and waved us through. The Luton lot, all regulars, said that the BBC staff weren't bothered about people waiting outside all day; they reckoned there was this weird, unspoken rule, that, so long as you cleared off for a while and dolled yourself up to look like a 'real' audience member before trying your luck in the queue, you'd have no issues getting waved in, however young you looked or dodgy your fake ID.

I *lived for* all the tacky hairstyles and shimmery outfits on the girls in the audience when we got into the waiting room inside the studios. They interested me much more than what the guys were wearing. Mens' clothes in the nineties were *so* drab! Ill-fitting short-sleeved shirts in khaki or white. Grey T-shirts with sportswear logos. Baggy blue jeans. Nothingness with added pockets and logos. Cute blokes that had their hair in curtains, like Nick Carter from Backstreet Boys, or twisted, sloppy-gelled spikes, like a member of Five or 911, were the only ones that caught my eye. I didn't think I fancied them at the time – I'd suppressed all those feelings so deep inside me, I usually just wanted their awful hair!

By now I'd realised that the warm-up guys, Mark and Danny, cracked the *exact* same jokes *every* week. The audience cackled as we stood at the side, eye-rolling at every dad gag, like we were such old-hands already. After enduring their well-rehearsed routine they introduced the bands we'd be seeing that night. We kicked off the evening with Natalie Imbruglia's attempts to defy One Hit Wonder status with her new single. Kathi and I both loved 'Torn' a bit too much, so we immediately made a beeline to see the former star of *Neighbours* perform her second single, 'Big Mistake'. Although it sounded amazing with a full live band, it lacked the pop genius of 'Torn'.

After the floor manager told Natalie they needed to do another take in a few minutes, the Luton Girls rushed over to talk to her at the side of the stage, only to be met with a slightly frosty reception. She probably had her mind on the job and didn't want to be pestered by teenagers asking inane questions, but her reaction riled Kathi enough for her to declare, 'She's a right cow! I'm not buying her records again.' Fourteen-year-old me was of course on the girls' side, and in solidarity I swore I'd never purchase another of Natalie's musical offerings. She didn't end up sustaining that level of greatness, so it wasn't *too* difficult for us to keep our promise.

Some performances that night took us completely out of our comfort zone. Instead of the jolly pop we loved, four acts were certainly on the alternative end of the spectrum, namely: mellow French electro duo Air; Natalie's rumoured squeeze,

Finley Quaye; Welsh rockers Stereophonics and mediocre indie boys The Bluetones. While it might not have been the music we were really into, these acts broadened our horizons, playing us songs we would never ordinarily watch live or even listen to on the radio.

Cornershop were up next, with 'Brimful of Asha'. The song had received masses of radio play in the last month, thanks to Fatboy Slim's up-tempo remix, and, sadly for Cornershop, it was that rendition that the entire audience was expecting. Instead, we endured the mellow original version that no one recognised or could figure out how to dance to – we were *not* happy shoppers. As they put down their instruments, Danny the warm-up guy announced, embarrassingly while the band were still on stage, 'Don't worry, everyone, they're coming back later on to play the version you *actually* like!' One of the Luton twins and I shot each other an awkward wince. But Danny was right, the audience much preferred the remix, the lads and ladettes all chanting 'everybody needs a bosom for a pillow' for the rest of the night.

US soul-pop newbie Lutricia McNeal was on next, followed by the last act on the bill – M People. Conor and I used to love listening to them on the way home from school, and *finally*, I was getting to see them in the flesh! That night they were performing their mediocre new single 'Angel St'. Unfortunately, by this point Heather had lost her legendary pineapple barnet, and with it, the band seemed less than totally tropical. A bit like Samson once he'd lost his massive mane, the heavenly hits had gone with the hairdo. As soon as they finished and received a half-decent round of applause we all filed out to get our coats and fast food for the journey home.

Kathi and I followed the crowds and went to the proper chippy up the road, our Lutonian buddies still in tow. By that point I felt like we'd known each other for years, and as though I'd actually found some friends who didn't just see me as the hideous freak at school. We exchanged landlines and postal addresses, promising to stay in touch and meet up at *Top of the Pops* again soon. Inside though, part of me was worried that they would somehow find out about what everyone at school thought of me, and then they too would ditch me for being a lanky, tragic, shirt-lifter.

♦ ♦ ♦

By the time the spring of 1998 had finally sprung I'd blown my reserves of pocket money on singles and shoddy merchandise. I'd begged, stolen or borrowed from Mum, Dad, Anja and even seven-year-old Sophie to fund my trips around London. I was desperate for more cash, especially as I needed some new outfits to show off on *Top of the Pops*. More money would also mean more independence, so I answered an advert for a paper round vacancy in the village newsagent's, *Coopers News*. My first job! That £9 a week was going to be so sweet. Dad – a paper-round veteran from back in the fifties – and Mum – both mocked me, claiming to 'know what I'm like' and that I'd never stick it out. *Puh-lease! This is the new, responsible, hard-grafting Malcolm.*

The day before my first shift, Mr Cooper, of the eponymous establishment, took me on a driving tour of the route. It seemed *really* long. And *really* complicated. First off were the pensioners' bungalows, then down the main road to another cul-de-sac that I didn't even know existed; back to the main road; a couple of left and right turns; out past some fields and down a dirt track to an obscure farmhouse that looked fresh off the set of *The Darling Buds of May*; then along a posh avenue of semis, and on, and on, and on. By the time we got back to the newsagent's

I had completely forgotten the route, having spent most of the journey daydreaming about what I would spend my hard-earned cash on.

I was a spoilt wimp aged fourteen and already freaking out about the effort this would be: the early starts, the bad weather, and getting totally confused between Mrs Johnson at No. 8 who took *The Times*, and Mr Johnson at No. 18 who only read *The Telegraph*.

The first morning I fell out of bed while it was still dark outside, the milk float pootling past my window. I nervously cycled the deserted streets, desperately trying to find all those obscure little *Closes* and *Avenues* and *Drives* to deposit my back-breaking load. I couldn't find 40 per cent of the houses though and returned to the shop, stressed out, dumping a pile of undelivered *Daily Mails* and *Expresses*, before legging it to school unwashed.

That afternoon, a slightly frustrated Mr Cooper gave me the previous day's tour again, to make sure I remembered it this time. Yep, definitely got it! I made some vague excuse about accidentally taking the *first* right past the telephone box, rather than the *second*, and that was where it had all gone wrong.

The second day, less cold but slightly rainier, I returned from my round with 10 per cent of the papers undelivered, again flustered and knackered. I had a dawning realisation that this might not be my calling. I rode home to get ready for school, and as I walked through the back door, I yelled at Mum and Dad that I was quitting. What a weight off my mind, although it *killed* me inside to admit defeat! I'd tell the shop later that day and then that would be that.

'I KNEW IT!' Mum bellowed. 'I don't care *what* you do, you're going to finish the whole week you signed up for, out of respect for Mr and Mrs Cooper. They're such lovely people.'

'NOO!' I wailed, as I devoured my jam on toast. 'That is SO unfair!'

Even Mr Cooper laughed at my pathetic perseverance when I awkwardly handed in my notice that afternoon. I begrudgingly made it to the end of the week though, earning my £9 for what equated to be less than 80p an hour. *Screw this!* I opted instead to resort to the Bank of Mum and Dad with their weekly £6 pocket money hand-outs – I'd just have to make do with those tired old T-shirts for a bit longer.

◆ ◆ ◆

An event rocked the world of pop to its core that March. No, it wasn't Chumbawumba throwing a bucket of ice over Deputy PM John Prescott at the BRIT Awards, or easy-listening pin-ups Texas duetting with the Wu-Tang Clan (although that *was* fucking weird!). The Spice Girls released their seventh single, aptly titled 'Stop', and it DIDN'T MAKE NUMBER 1. It entered at Number 2, then slowly dropped down the ranks. *Spicepocalypse*! They hadn't done their usual media assault of semi-fictitious tabloid-fodder stories and boisterous interviews on daytime TV shows for the Motown-influenced number, mostly because they were busy rehearsing for their epic world tour. While the nation was still lapping up the Spice Girls' brand, they were a bit jaded from similar-sounding songs, especially one going head-to-head with Jason Nevins' remix of Run DMC's 'It's Like That'. It was as though millions of people suddenly realised that what their life was actually missing was break dancing.

I, however, didn't want to spin on my head or have dance-offs in a car park. 'Stop' was my favourite single the Spice Girls had released so far, so I was slightly bemused at that song in particular failing to clinch the top spot.

Back then, its Number 2 spot hung over it like a black cloud, as if it marked the beginning of the end. It seemed 'Spice' had saturated the market, and people were already getting sick of it.

◆ ◆ ◆

In late March Louise released her single 'All That Matters'. It sounded like the backing track to a Weight Watchers' advert, but I blindly adored it, of course, and was determined to finally get to meet her when she performed at *Top of the Pops*. Mum and Dad were equally determined that I was not to miss any more lessons. A row ensued. Doors were slammed. I'd only be missing our Sponsored Walk Day, after all. Eventually they agreed, after I promised this would be the last time I would miss any school.

I wanted to show Louise how much she meant to me, and also make sure she'd never forget me, so I decided to make her a really personal gift – her portrait painted in acrylics. She'd never be able to forget me once I'd presented her with the *Mona Louisa*. I was really chuffed with the portrait, staying up late the night before the recording to perfect Ms Nurding's big beautiful eyes.

I ventured up on the first off-peak train to Elstree & Borehamwood, with my school bag packed with supplies and the portrait. Neither Kathi nor any of the Luton Girls could go that week, so I was going to be on my own.

I walked to the station and waited impatiently on the platform, repeatedly checking the time, making sure I was getting on the right train, running through in my head where I needed to change. I felt like an imposter, like everyone in my carriage was looking at me, thinking, 'Where does that kid think he's going?' So much of my early teens felt like that: convincing myself and others I was almost an adult, only to have my inner child tell me I wasn't part of the grown-up world yet.

When I got to the studio there was another fan waiting alone. He was a cocky lad named Paul, reeling off many tall tales about his encounters with the lovely Louise. Almost two years older, Paul didn't have to be at school (living the dream). He had a mop of blond hair and a restless energy that manifested in him talking incessantly. We got on well, had lots in common and he even knew the Luton Girls.

We didn't have long to wait before Louise's navy blue Beemer whizzed round the corner to where we were waiting, in front of the security barrier. 'Here she is,' Paul declared. The car slowed as we waved frantically at it. The passenger window was lowered and a slightly bleary-looking Louise came into view.

'Morning, boys,' she said cheerily.

'Hi, Louise!' we answered in united enchantment.

After a couple of minutes of initial chit-chat, Paul and I pulled some CDs out of our bags to get signed.

'I've also painted you a picture,' I nervously muttered.

'Oh, lovely,' she replied in her chirpy Sarff Landan accent, as I handed *actual* Louise my work of art.

It wasn't an exact likeness, it definitely had a touch of *Changing Rooms*' Carol Smillie about it, but she seemed delighted with it. She showed it off to her manager, Wendy, on the seat next to her, as I lapped up every second of Louise enjoying the fruits of my labour. Before long, she zoomed off again, into the depths of Elstree Studios to have her morning coffee and make-up (and to show off her painting to anyone she came into contact with, I assumed). We wasted the rest of the day hanging out on the table next to Aussie pop duo Savage Garden at Burger King, and later scabbed spare tickets for the recording off people as they turned up.

Inside the studio that night we were treated to a selection of genre-spanning Top 20 hits. The Matalan of boy bands, 911, were performing 'All I Want Is You', the front row made up entirely of besotted girls. German DJ Sash! ticked the dance box for the evening, while Ian Brown provided the late Britpop.

Last on was our showstopper of the night: Louise, looking predictably dazzling in pinstripe office trousers – worn under a long-sleeved maroon dress with one arm cut-off and a shirt collar on top, just for something extra. There was a lot going on. It looked like she had caught her sleeve in a door en route from the dressing room and half the outfit tore off. It didn't quite come together, even for 1998, but Louise is the kind of girl who could have worn an Iceland carrier bag and looked chic! It was just brilliant to see her sing live up-close, I was in heaven. She spent the whole song looking at each one of us in the front row; even thanking me, in between takes, for my 'amazing painting', which made feel giddy inside. Paul, already happy to speak his mind with me, was 'sick of hearing about that bloody painting' by the time she exited the stage. But I was so pleased – everything had gone to plan.

At home I filed a full report of the day's antics back to my fellow geeks on the Louise email list before heading to bed very late, an irremovable grin still slapped across my face. I could feel my confidence growing with every toe I dipped into the pop world.

5

So Young

The following morning, I was giddy as I headed into school. I had met my beloved Louise the day before, and there were only a few hours of classroom boredom left until the Easter holidays. *Two whole weeks* away from the chain-link fences and the idiots who made my life hell; spending every day immersed in music. And after that, I'd have only a few months of Year Ten left.

As usual, the teachers had reserved the last day of term for a special treat. Instead of lacklustre attempts to make us memorise the periodic table, an oversized TV would be wheeled in from a storeroom and a VHS of *Mrs. Doubtfire* played to the class. At last, the bell rang, and it was time to get out of the place. As I strolled through the playground, a guy from my class ran up behind me, looking pleased with himself. He was also regularly the target of mindless name calling, his crime being his ginger hair and large build. I assumed he was going to wish me a happy Easter. Instead, I was pushed to the ground and a kick landed square in my stomach – 'Fucking queer!' I barely had time to realise what had happened, or to catch my breath, before he struck me again. I glanced up and saw some Year Nines looking on at me, laughing. Where had this come from? He'd barely called me names before; we were allies. But I was clearly below him even in the pecking order. He scarpered before anyone caught him, safe in the knowledge that by the time the holidays were over it would be long forgotten.

I got up, brushed the gravel from my uniform and picked up my rucksack. I hated this place, I hated these people. Just a few hours before I had been so happy with my new mates: people who weren't ashamed to speak to me, people who were interested in my life. As I approached Mum's Polo I wiped my eyes with my blazer, brushed myself down and took a deep breath.

◆ ◆ ◆

On 21 May, a few days after mine and Kathi's fifteenth birthdays, we both made the pilgrimage up to *Top of the Pops* after school. Clare, one of the Luton Girls, had finally trusted me with the phone number for the security guard's hut by the front gate. Now, this was the Holy Grail. The morning before each recording, Security would be given a piece of paper listing the artists performing that day. As long as you sweet-talked the guards, they'd pass on the information to us fans when we phoned up.

I nervously rang the number, and a deep-voiced man with an Estuary accent read out the stellar line-up: a World Cup 1998 song, Natalie Imbruglia, emerging pop titans Steps, Lutricia McNeal, Imaani (UK's Eurovision entry from the week before, and runner-up to Dana International) and a performance by the Spice Girls. A wave of excitement shot through me. I would *finally* be seeing the iconic quintet in the flesh! My love for Eternal had so far prevented me from falling head-over-platforms for the biggest band on the planet, but I was fascinated by their prowess, especially Ginger Spice. They weren't just a pop group – those five were international A-listers. Even Nelson Mandela was honoured to meet them.

First up, we saw Steps drive by in their people carrier, with their vaguely manic perma-grins, but they were playing second fiddle today. *Everyone* was awaiting the late arrival of the pop goddesses. How would we know it was their cars? Maybe they were arriving by helicopter? Perhaps they *did* own a big bus driven by Meat Loaf? When the convoy of five gleaming, silver Mercedes turned the corner, there was no mistaking them.

Posh, Baby, Scary, Sporty and Ginger all had their windows down for the fresh air, and to lap up our rapturous welcome. I was totally star-struck – these ubiquitous faces had been everywhere for the past two years. And I soon got swept up in the electric atmosphere and joined in with the screaming. For the first time in my life, I could honestly say I knew what it must feel like for a Brazilian nun to meet the Pope. They responded with enthusiastic waves and cheesy grins while their cars were individually stopped at Security – though surely the guards could recognise their famous mugs? Bringing up the rear was my favourite: Geri. A cheeky kiss blown at me from those overdrawn lips would have made my year. She was reading a book and indifferently glanced up at us, looking forlorn and dazed. She mustered a limp wave and a weak smile, a world away from the animated hellos that the others next to her had managed for us before they drove by.

'What's wrong with Geri?' I asked the others. Clare and Sarah had met the Spice Girls many times outside TV and radio shows in the past two years.

'I dunno. She's not normally like that. She's always just... Geri,' Sarah said insightfully. 'You know, crazy and over-the-top.'

'Probably just tired and on her period,' Clare said, reassuringly.

I was disheartened by the lacklustre initiation Ginger gave me into the Spice World, but still looking forward to their performance and all the other acts on the night's bill. First up were Bus Stop, with their nineties update of the seventies disco hit 'Kung Fu Fighting'. Frontman 'Daz' looked more like a dodgy wedding DJ than an international pop superstar. We wouldn't get to hear the full horrors of his oeuvre until 2006, when he represented us in Eurovision, surrounded by a posse of schoolgirls.

Lutricia, Space and Shed Seven were next up, followed by the climax of the evening. We gathered around the Main Stage and, after a brief introduction, the Spice Girls appeared from the wings. They were clearly trying to escape from their caricatures by this point. Pouting Posh had been replaced by a robotic-looking, grinning Victoria. There was no Union Jack dress, no tracksuit, no leopard print and no pigtails. I was taken aback; instead of the teen idols I was anticipating, I was confronted by a rather pedestrian-looking band in trouser suits and dull dresses.

Geri, in particular, had been transformed from an exuberant vision into a washed-out strawberry blonde shadow of her former self. Dressed like a mourner at a funeral in a black cardigan and lengthy, black skirt, while the other girls smiled and chatted with fans, Ginger was noticeably despondent. The Luton Girls and I stood in front of her, trying to say hello and ask her questions, but she responded only with a glazed look and vague, one-word answers. She didn't even come to life as they mimed their way through the pre-record of upcoming single 'Viva Forever'. As they left the stage we were promised that they'd be back later to sing again. Hopefully then we'd get to see something with a bit of zing.

If they hadn't brought any effervescent energy to the stage, pop newbies Steps certainly made up for it with a beaming performance of their new cheesy anthem, 'Last Thing on My Mind'. With their unwavering Butlins Redcoat smiles, they were happy to chat to us in the front row and teach us their dance moves (which we all knew already!).

One of that summer's many World Cup 1998 songs was on after that. The performance was being recorded weeks before its release, so the name Fat Les didn't mean anything to us. A ramshackle bunch of misfits, who filled the Main Stage in their dozens, belting out the ridiculously catchy 'Vindaloo'. At last, somebody was bringing some spice to the night. There were fat comedians dressed as babies in Y-fronts, a kids' choir, a drunk woman whose breasts fell out of her top during the performance, a young Matt Lucas and David Walliams – all led by Keith Allen (Lily's dad). It was total carnage, but this lot singing 'We're gonna score one more than you' was probably the best thing we saw all night.

After a couple of other acts the Spice Girls returned to the stage to perform their other new single: the official World Cup 1998 song for England. For '(How Does it Feel to Be) on Top of the World?' the girls had teamed up with a host of middle-of-the-road indie bands: Space; Ocean Colour Scene and Echo & the Bunnymen to form 'England United'. They looked the antithesis of a supergroup, and both the song title and the band name had an irony that surely wasn't lost on a malcontent Geri as she cracked out mumsy dance moves.

After the filming, the girls jetted out to Scandinavia for a couple of tour dates. Each day after school I would log onto our Dial-up Internet and visit the few unofficial Spice Girls fan sites and forums, waiting ten minutes for each 'Word Art'-filled page to load to catch the latest gossip about their antics in Denmark and Finland.

♦ ♦ ♦

In those pre-Netflix days, primetime telly was a load of balls. The National Lottery's bi-weekly shows were a big fixture in people's lives, the show's games, global A-list music guests and dragged-out draws watched by millions at home. The Spice Girls, desperate to ensure their latest release was a success, flew back between Scandinavian dates, a few days after their as yet unscreened *Top of the Pops* recording, to appear on it.

Clare and Sarah, my groupie mates, were heading there to see their idols again, hoping for bubbly and brash business as usual this time. I had to make do with watching it from home, nearly exploding with curiosity when only four of the girls appeared on stage. 'Get well soon, Geri!' urged Sporty Spice in her mellow Scouse accent, staring deep into the camera lens, as TV's Carol Smillie, a nineties vision in a metallic satin jacket, quizzed the girls on the absence of the legendary redhead. The official line was a dicky tummy.

I rang Sarah late that evening for the goss. Apparently, Security had banned the fans outside from taking photos of the group, and an altercation erupted when a paparazzo breached the rule. I was lapping up the drama, and as soon as I got off the phone I scoured the Internet for any information. These days it would be all over Twitter in an instant, but back then, the Information Superhighway was slower to respond.

The next evening when I logged on a Norwegian fan had posted up a grainy photo of the doors of the Oslo venue, where the girls were performing that night. A handwritten note pinned to the door explained that, once again, the world would have to make do with a quartet. The thread was filled with rumours. Was Geri really ill? Had there been a huge bust-up? On the one hand, I was loving watching this car crash. On the other, I was increasingly concerned about the fate of one of the world's most iconic pop stars. The press were jubilant, almost euphoric, at their fall from grace.

On Sunday morning I woke up to the Radio 1 news: the Spice Girls would be making a formal announcement that afternoon. What would it be? All over the world fans, journalists and random people were giving their two-pence worth.

I sat inches from the TV to watch the announcement: 'Geri Halliwell has left the Spice Girls'. The last few days had all been building up to those seven words. The official announcement naffly ended with the line, 'Friendship Never Ends'.

Motionless, I sat there stunned at the realisation Ginger was never coming back. I was also transfixed by the drama of the real-life pop soap opera that had played out over the last few days on our TV screens and newspapers – red top and broadsheets – across the world. Back at school that Monday, kids actually wanted to know my opinion on it. As well as exhausting debates about the band's future, newsreaders kept talking about their 'final UK performance as a quintet' at *Top of the Pops.* Then it dawned on me: 'Viva Forever' hadn't even been their final performance here. It was their doomed and dismal World Cup song, as forgettable as a nil–nil draw. How tragic!

Geri's departure rocked the world. Kids from Indiana to Indonesia were inconsolable. Even the band's label EMI reportedly saw 3 per cent knocked off their share price as their biggest act looked on the verge of total collapse. With an eye-watering price tag increasing by the day for a single paparazzi snap of her since jumping off the spice rack, Geri fled. She'd killed off Ginger Spice and escaped the country, successfully making herself more elusive than Lord Lucan.

♦ ♦ ♦

For the rest of us, life carried on as normal. I continued my Thursday night escapades in Borehamwood until school was out for summer.

One June Thursday had perhaps the oddest line-up I'd seen there. It started with an assault on the senses: yet another sodding World Cup song! This time it was 'Carnaval de Paris', Dario G's cultural mash-up of every conceivable nation into a three-minute Eurodance bastardisation of 'Oh My Darling, Clementine'. Onto the stage poured bagpipe players, Jamaican steel drums, accordions played by onion-clad beret wearers and some miscellaneous instruments I thought looked vaguely Turkish. It was like Eurovision on speed – I loved it.

Ian Brown popped up on the bill again, as did Garbage, Karen Ramirez, who spent most of the summer dispassionately 'Looking for Love', Neneh's sharp-sighted little bro, Eagle-Eye Cherry, as well as Eurovision's victorious diva Dana International.

With the entire Western world's insatiable appetite for girl bands still not over, the Spices in turmoil and All Saints approaching the end of their in-vogue honeymoon, four delightful ladies from the Emerald Isle were poised to step in and inject some *loife* into the charts. Step up, B*Witched, whose debut song, 'C'est la Vie', got stuck in our heads for the rest of the year. When I saw them they were sitting pretty (in denim) at the top of the charts for an outrageous third week. They had more energy than Aqua, early Spice Girls, and every World Cup performance put together, jumping around the flower-clad stage while making vague threats about 'fighting like their dads'. The

Luton Girls were full-on into B*Witched and chatted to them in between takes, which I tried to join in with. I usually liked my pop slick and soulful, but with Eternal AWOL, I could feel myself transitioning into a shameless, bubblegum pop bitch.

The last act on that night was an American girl group performing their second single. I couldn't see that these girls would ever make it in the UK with their serious R&B, so, as Laura, one of the Luton Girls, and I watched them sing their decidedly un-poppy song 'With Me' (which limped into the charts at Number 19), I thought it might be the last we'd hear of these 'Destiny's Child' girls. Fresh-faced with an average age of sixteen, the girls were quiet and more polite than an eighty-year-old *Telegraph* reader at a vicar's tea party. Before the producers gave them the okay to begin, the band's lead singer, Beyoncé, smiled at me in the front row, just a few feet in front of her.

'Don't you love the colour of his shirt?' she gestured to bandmate Kelly Rowland.

'What?' Kelly asked, taking out her earpiece to hear better.

I raised an eyebrow at Laura next to me, who, like the rest of the audience, looked at me with bemusement.

'*I said*, I love his shirt. The colour of it. Don't you like it?' Beyoncé repeated.

'Oh, yes,' Kelly said, nodding in firm agreement. 'That colour is *gorgeous*.'

The object of their desire was a baggy mint green shirt that I had paid a whole £3 for at the Woking branch of Mad House. I can only imagine the beautiful tone was enhanced by the beetroot red my face had turned.

As they performed the song their lead singer (Ms Knowles) kept gyrating in my direction and staring into my eyes as she sang the suggestive lyrics. 'He's with me,' she declared, pointing directly at gawky me and my verdant shirt.

Destiny's Child's next venture didn't fare any better in the UK charts. Stuck on the bottom rungs of the pop world domination ladder, Beyoncé and co. were (mis)informed that their next move should be singing backing vocals and reading out love life advice on upcoming pop luminary and ex-*Coronation Street* B-lister Matthew Marsden's second (and final) single, 'She's Gone'. Despite the future biggest-girl-band-in-the-world lending their honey-sweet vocals to the R&B-lite stinker, it tanked at Number 24 and poor Matthew was never seen lurking around the bottom half of the Top 40 again. I'm guessing Beyoncé has long since removed it from her LinkedIn – although you can bet it's still on Matthew's.

◆ ◆ ◆

With even Kathi embarrassed to be seen hanging out with me much at school, I found a fellow weirdo to befriend: a Goth called Roseanna ('Zanna' to her friends). We were chalk and cheese, pop and metal, but within days after crossing paths, we were getting on like a house on fire, mocking the 'cool' kids who rejected us, like I'd done years ago with Conor. But by this point, I'd stopped caring about school, now I had all my pop friends.

With a month to go until summer, my beloved school forced us to partake in one week's work experience at a place of our choosing. Despite my best efforts, I'd received refusal letters from *Smash Hits*, Capital FM *and* Radio 1 – hell, I even applied to every mum's favourite, Heart FM, in desperation. I did get a 'Yes' from a local FM radio station in Surrey, who listed all the fun and varied stuff I'd be getting up to in my action-packed week. Mum and Dad said it was an amazing opportunity, but I thought it too provincial and accepted my other offer – a week of unpaid shop-floor work in Woking's Virgin Megastore, which I thought would bring me closer to the action of the pop industry. I learned my lesson the hard way, returning home dead-eyed and vacant after the fifth day of my silent shelf-stacking purgatory. The only vaguely rock'n'roll moment was on the first morning, when the manager gave me a strange warning about not keeping marijuana in my staff locker.

I did manage to squeeze two pop extravaganzas into the following week. Conor flew over from Belfast for *Party in the Park*, held in Hyde Park. My old primary school buddy and I were reunited for a day of watching twenty of the world's biggest pop acts at the colossal concert, including All Saints, Tom Jones, Boyzone, Eternal and lyrical genius Des'ree among many others. Like Mel Blatt's baby bump, the gig was so big that, the next day, pictures and gossip from it were all over the papers.

A few days after that, Dad and I did some father-and-son bonding at a midweek Whitney concert. Dad (also a Ms Houston fan) had agreed to take me after school, which was really kind of him, especially as it was a four-hour trip each way to Manchester. The concert was really epic, even if we were sitting in the gods. We then drove home straight after. It seemed like a great plan until Dad fell asleep on the M6 and almost careered into the central reservation. Dad was woken from his slumber by the siren of a passing police car that had watched us drift across the motorway. The constable gave him some friendly advice to have a nap and then get a strong coffee at the next Welcome Break. Fortunately, we made it home alive and I was able to brag about my exploits on a geography field trip the next day.

◆ ◆ ◆

Once school was out, nobody could stop me spending all day every day cavorting around the South East of England. I decided

I would make summer 1998 my Summer of Love. I could already picture it: scorching sunshine, a child's travelcard in my wallet, a 35mm camera and black permanent marker as constant companions. I started researching online where I could go and keeping notes in my diary of all the events I couldn't miss. On the free days in between, Zanna and I agreed to keep each other company, either loitering in the local park or watching MTV at her mum's house.

I voyaged to *Top of the Pops* eight times over the next eleven weeks. I witnessed intimate performances of some of the biggest songs that summer, including: Another Level ('Freak Me'), Placebo ('Pure Morning'), Boyzone ('No Matter What'), Foo Fighters, Robbie Williams (performing 'Millennium' in a glittery, gold dress), Faithless ('God is a DJ'), All Saints ('Bootie Call'), Honeyz ('Finally Found'), Five, Hole (featuring an inebriated-looking Courtney Love performing 'Celebrity Skin'), the Manics ('If You Tolerate This Your Children Will Be Next'), Steps ('One for Sorrow'), Alisha's Attic, the Bee Gees (performing a greatest hits set), Jennifer Paige ('Crush'), Pulp, The Mavericks, blonde-dreadlocked Icelandic oddity Alda ('Real Good Time'), Cypress Hill, PJ Harvey, ladette-pop personified, Republica, The Beautiful South ('Perfect 10'), Culture Club, country-pop goddess Shania Twain and some diva called Celine, to name just a few...

Because of all the pre-recordings they did, I was guaranteed to be in the audience on every programme well into autumn. My young cousins up in Grantham thought there was something wrong if they didn't spot me on TV as they ate their dinner every Friday night.

The weekly ritual involved getting there early, chatting by the gate while we waited for the stars, getting ready in the Burger King toilets, pushing to the front for the performances and finishing off the night at the chippy. Unlike plenty of the boys from school, I didn't want to be fooling around with girls in the car parks of Walton-on-Thames or bravely kicking other boys' heads in on the mean streets of Chertsey.

Between these exploits though, there were still days on end sitting on the sofa with Sophie, watching kids' TV, or playing out in the street with her till it got dark and Mum told me off as it was past her bedtime. Every day I'd while away hours waiting for emails about pop to load, conscious that every minute I spent online would rack up an even larger phone bill.

♦ ♦ ♦

In between jaunts to Borehamwood and days hanging out at the shopping centre in Woking, I managed to fit in a family holiday to Kefalonia. I'd been dreading it ever since Mum and Dad told us all we were going away a couple of months previously. Anja moaned every time the upcoming holiday was mentioned. I made it clear to Mum and Dad how unhappy I was about missing a fortnight of potential pop excursions in London. They wanted a break from the daily grind, to create precious memories with their kids, and we were just pissing on their moussaka.

Mum and Dad probably thought our whining was going to be the worst thing about the holiday, but they hadn't seen the accommodation yet. A bald, brutish Greek woman, the boss of the chalets, 'greeted' us with some shouting and grunts as she handed over the keys. Two (cold) outdoor showers for all the families to use and an absence of air-con and mosquito nets didn't lift our despondent dispositions as the coach sped off, leaving us for dust in the midday sun.

The island itself was actually majestically beautiful (not that I was much aware of this at the time) and once we'd unpacked (or I'd strewn my belongings across the floor of our concrete box), we headed down to the glistening turquoise sea to stake a place on the baking beach for the fortnight ahead. Like a lot of boys, gangly and pasty was how I viewed my fifteen-year-old body. I was excruciatingly self-conscious about exposing it when running around with Sophie on the sand and among the waves, or when Mum would yell at me from across the beach at the top of her lungs, for her hourly application of Factor 50 to my bony shoulders.

Sophie was oblivious to my insecurities. It wasn't just my freckly skin and lack of muscles I was trying to hide though; while Anja was getting attention from hot Greek boys, I had no interest in the girls on the beach that Mum and Dad encouraged me to speak to and repressed my perplexing feelings for the bronzed Adonises in charge of the sunbeds.

I should have just relaxed and enjoyed myself, but it was a confusing time. Aside from sexuality struggles, I was at a difficult age: too young to drink, too old to play with the kids. Stuck between two worlds. There I was, on a pedalo in forty-two degrees heat, performing Spice Girls' songs, with eight-year-old Sophie to keep us entertained. This was the year when Sophie, like so many other children, spent the summer months running around singing 'I'M HORNY, ALL NIGHT LONG; I'M HORNY, ALL NIGHT LONG', much to the despair of most parents in England.

After a whole week away I was missing my new friends back home. Instead, I was spending the day swimming in the Med on the majestic Myrtos Beach. I'd just clambered up to our spot after a thrash around in the crystal blue waves, and was raiding the picnic bag for snacks, when Mum attempted to introduce me to the fantastically glamorous lady on the sunbed next to her. 'Okay, hi! Nice to meet you,' I said, wolfing down a bag of

Lay's crisps. Mum had been chatting to her while I was having a dip and it turned out that she was a music video producer *and* had just finished making the video for Scary Spice's debut single, featuring Missy Elliott! Okay, *now* she had my attention! And, just like that, there I was. Back in the bubble again, chatting to this interesting and incredibly beautiful lady from LA, who'd worked with Janet Jackson and was giving *me* the lowdown on the stars and her video shoots, as I sat there in my speedos, trying to cover up.

◆ ◆ ◆

After a delayed flight full of ruddy-faced Brits we returned to the slightly less sweltering Surrey. As soon as I'd got through the door I switched on the computer to catch up on two weeks of goings-on in the pop world. At the front of my mind was the status of the seemingly moribund Eternal. After loading for an eternity, I opened an email from their fan mailing list. While I'd been sunning myself in Greece, the Bennett sisters had been faxing the tabloids with a statement confirming my beloved Kelle was no longer a member of the band. Unfortunately, they'd forgotten to fax the statement to Kelle, and she only discovered her departure when she read about it on page seventeen of *The Mirror*!

Compared with Ginger Spice walking out in anger on the biggest band in the world, mid-tour, it was nothing – a minor story one day, chip wrapping the next. I wasn't surprised by the news, as the band seemed to be getting more shambolic, but I didn't realise things had got so toxic. I was saddened at how they'd fallen apart, and also how the world seemed to have ditched them. But I'd already realised the music industry was fickle. Online, the main discussion between fans was about how they'd managed to hide their personal grievances so well. The press had always painted the Bennetts as the Ugly Sisters to Kelle's Cinderella, and that was certainly how I felt towards them that August evening. As I trawled through the online email forum feeling dismal, I remembered there were only three weeks of summer left before I would have to return to school.

◆ ◆ ◆

With a week of summer left before Year Eleven, I made my final visit to the hallowed *Top of the Pops* studios in the knowledge that once September came, I'd have to knuckle down and wouldn't be allowed to spend my Thursday evenings in a TV studio. Once again, the main topic of conversation was the Spice Girls. This time it was about their upcoming Wembley Stadium dates, which every pop fan on the planet seemed to be going to.

I was going to sorely miss what had become a weekly ritual: the stages getting set up with props and unplugged instruments, wind machines put in position for glamorous divas. Then the artists would wait around after walking on stage, either looking tired and bored, or bright-eyed and chatty with audience members. Sometimes we'd sneak an autograph in between takes or get hugs and kisses as we chatted to them when they left the stage. It was never just about watching the performances – there was so much that went on in that studio each week, the un-filmed action all part of the magic.

Between takes we'd chat to the presenters, boring them with questions about which stages the acts would be on and who their favourite members of pop bands were. Hosting duties that summer predominantly fell upon Jayne Middlemiss, interspersed with Kate Thornton and Zoe Ball. Unfortunately, for them (and us) they had to record links not only for the main programme, but for the various long-forgotten spin-offs, such as *Top of the Pops Extra*, *Top of the Pops Italy* and *Top of the Pops Late*. Every edition required half a dozen links, in varying locations around the studio, each with a backdrop of excited-looking teenagers. What seemed on TV to be a fun and glamorous presenting job was, in reality, hours of repetitive intros to bands that had pre-recorded performances weeks earlier.

As the last act that August unpinned their microphones and shuffled off stage, we too shuffled out of the sweltering studio, into the warm evening air. I shared a portion of chips with one of the Luton Girls and lamented that it was all over. Next time I saw them it would probably be autumn, by which point I'd know whether the Spice Girls would survive as a quartet, if the Bennett sisters would miraculously resuscitate Eternal – and whether everyone at school would still be shouting Julian Clary at me across the classroom.

6

I Don't Want to Miss a Thing

After the reprieve of a training day on the Monday, I trudged my way into school on the first Tuesday of September 1998. Despite the blue sky, the wind was chilly. An ominous reminder that I was heading back to that prison – HMP Salesian – for another year. At last, it was my final year there. I'd had the best summer of my entire fifteen years with my Luton friends, clinching fleeting encounters with *Smash Hits* C-listers up and down the streets of Borehamwood, but we had to go back to our real lives. I didn't attempt to mask my sadness at returning to the playground: I was one for sorrow, and it was too, *too* bad.

I was resigned to the fact that Mum and Dad wouldn't let me return to *Top of the Pops* until half term. After a miserable first day back, with the same old bullies hurling the same old terms of endearment towards me, I went home and sulked about not being allowed to follow my dreams and see my *real* friends. *Perhaps it wouldn't be too much to go just once*, I thought, in that quiet, first week back. I raised the topic over the dinner table, expecting to storm out when Dad refused, but, unexpectedly, he softly replied, 'Okay, sure. You're old enough now. As long as you get your work done, we don't mind you going from time to time.' I nearly fell off the rickety kitchen bench. 'For real?!' I was over the moon. The old gang reunited. Just like the heady days of... last week.

The minute the bell rang on Thursday afternoon I dashed to the train station, still surrounded by hordes of mocking schoolkids. I wouldn't lose them till we pulled out of Staines – they'd get nosebleeds if they ventured beyond there. As I reached Borehamwood the light grey clouds seemed to part and the sun shone bright while I greeted Laura by the security gate. The summer's biggest hitmakers were all on offer that night: Jennifer Paige, All Saints and T-Spoon (of 'Sex on the Beach' fame), to name a few. It was like summer had never ended. We partied late into the evening and, while T-Spoon belted out that crass, if unforgettable, Europop chorus (one of the anthems of my celibate fortnight in Kefalonia), we bashed beach balls around the studio and palm tree-clad stage in defiance at autumn's imminent return. Laura and I had chips on the way home and agreed we'd definitely be back seven days later.

Maybe Year Eleven wouldn't be so bad after all.

◆ ◆ ◆

Later that week the press went into Spice Girl overload for the first time since Geri's dramatic exit. Not only were they playing two colossal nights at Wembley Stadium the following weekend, but there was a rumour doing the rounds that The Artist Formerly Known As Ginger would join them for a special farewell appearance. Mel B had also just become the first shacked-up spice. The media were less interested in whether she was wearing a leopard-print dress than whether she would ditch the 'B' for a 'G'.

After Scary's first solo *Top of the Pops* performance a few days later, at which the Luton Girls and I were stood at the front, along with a couple of other fans I managed to get my CD single signed. 'She's Mel *G*! She's not Mel B anymore,' Sarah said, tapping me manically on the shoulder. I struggled to hear her over the crowd but eventually the penny dropped as I looked down at my CD. A murmur of excitement passed around our group, which caught the attention of an undercover paparazzo in the audience. And just like Richard O'Brien's 'tabloid tormentor' in *Spice World: The Movie*, he slyly removed a small camera from his pocket and paid one of the other fans £300 for a snapshot of the CD with Mel's scrawly handwriting. If we were stunned by Scary Spice's new identity, we were green with envy that one of the other fans had just got paid hundreds for a photo of it. I was still bitter the next morning, when, as I passed Cooper's News en route to school, I clocked a story in *The Sun* with *that photo* of *that signature*.

◆ ◆ ◆

That weekend I travelled with Kathi to the Spice Girls' much-anticipated Wembley Stadium concerts, the grand finale of their Spiceworld Tour – which had spanned continents and seasons, and pocketed tens of millions of pounds, while losing their unbroken run of Number 1s and a band member in the process. Supporting them were Cleopatra (*Comin' Atcha!*) and Björn Again (no, I can't believe it either). That night we would find out whether all the press speculation about a special Ginger appearance was true.

There was an amazing atmosphere in the stadium, a sea of fans under the shadow of the famous towers. The whole event was punctuated by the crowd chanting, 'We want Ginger!' Sadly, the greatest pop moment that could have been never materialised: Geri did *not* say she'll be there. Instead, she stayed at home in Hertfordshire, plotting her revenge. The remaining four put on an impressive performance, and made themselves look like they'd been in the business decades, rather than just two manic years. The tour was over, and so, it seemed, was any hope of a reunification.

♦ ♦ ♦

When Mum and Dad had agreed I could occasionally go to *Top of the Pops*, I'd taken that as 'Malcolm, you are free to bunk school at will, to waste every weekend outside TV studios and radio stations to meet C-list pop stars'. Unlike most people in the fan world, at this point I didn't really have a group to follow that I could call 'my band': a favourite act to devotedly meet at every possible opportunity.

I decided to do something about that.

On 24 September 1998 I headed to Elstree after school as usual. The Luton Girls weren't going, despite their favourites B*Witched performing 'Rollercoaster' that night. So I arranged to go with Paul instead.

I met Paul's friends first in the queue outside. I recognised them from being in the *Top of the Pops* audience various weeks that summer.

'And who are *you*?' the blonde girl, Charlotte, asked me frankly, her squad of fellow groupies laughing in chorus at her bluntness.

'I'm... umm... Paul's friend, Malcolm. Well, I've known him a little while, just a few months really, from coming to *Top of the...*'

'It's fine, we don't need your life story!' Tasha, the stubby, bespectacled one, said, interrupting my bumbling introduction before they laughed again riotously. I smiled, my face glowing like an outdoor heater.

'Just ignore them, Malcolm. We're nice really! Hang out with us tonight, if you can stomach them. Be nice to have someone quiet around for once!' Steph said, reassuringly. She was the oldest of the group, a mother hen in dungarees, who quickly took me under her wing.

'Welcome to the nuthouse,' Gemma, the slightly whiny one, said.

Paul stood there, smiling throughout it all.

They made endless in-jokes about people I'd never met, but I still found them hilarious. They were brasher than the Luton Girls, constantly ripping the piss out of each other and even the security staff on the gate. I couldn't believe how much front they had. Inside, they continued their practical jokes: tapping cameramen on the shoulders while trying to set up shots, nicking a filming schedule from a runner boy's back pocket so we knew exactly when and where to wait, as well as standing where they shouldn't, but cracking jokes with production staff to get away with it.

Part terrified, part obsessed, I hovered behind them as they bounced around the studio. We stood at the front for performances by Monica (of 'Brandy and' fame) and Ace of Base, and skulked at the back with them during Bryan Adams, PJ Harvey, Eels and the Lighthouse Family. Like the Luton Girls, they too seemed to know the B*Witched girls well, and, as I stood next to them during their two effervescent performances, I became envious of how casually they chatted to the Irish pop babes in between takes. I tried to get in on the action but I knew none of their in-jokes or the band members, just hovering behind them.

With the recording complete, we were ushered offsite with all the other knackered audience members. Tasha announced they were heading to the legendary 'Back Gate' for one last chance to pester the stars after the show. I was enjoying myself too much, so quickly agreed to this deviation from my usual chips, station, home routine. What they'd forgotten to tell me was that it was a ten-minute sprint down endless concrete alleyways, behind some housing estates, in order to reach it before the acts drove home.

While waiting for B*Witched, we beckoned over Sweden's second-most famous mixed-gender quartet as they were putting their bags into their people carrier. Three members of Ace of Base ambled over to us, all bright and cheery. I made bland small talk with them, but Charlotte, one of the B*Witched groupies, got straight to the point.

'Where's the blonde woman? And why is she always blurry and standing at the back of your band photos these days?' She'd been tucked away at the back of the stage during their two pre-recorded performances that night, and never seemed to be in any interviews anymore.

'She does not seek the limelight anymore,' Jenny, the brunette, and now de facto lead singer, said.

'What? That's so weird!' Tasha said, as we all cackled in bemusement. 'Who wouldn't wanna do *this* job?'

So, the blonde lady was becoming a recluse. Jesus, they got more like ABBA every day!

When the B*Witched girls came over to chat they were the friendliest band I'd ever met, all surprisingly interested in who I was and my connection to this motley crew of their groupies. They said they hoped to see me again, which, naturally, I took as, 'Please follow us everywhere we go from now on'.

The band was going from strength to strength; 'Rollercoaster' was dead set to be their second Number 1. They just seemed like they were out to have a laugh. *Maybe I could get in on the fun?*

All this loitering with Swedish and Irish pop stars meant I missed the last train back. In the days before mobiles this was bad. I pleaded with Steph to let me use the last of her credit to call Mum way past her bedtime. She begrudgingly agreed to let me and Paul squeeze between the others in the back and give us a lift to Staines, from where my poor mother would have to pick me up.

When we pulled into the station car park I was pushed out of the car, like gang bosses returning a hostage. They hollered goodbye out the windows before racing away into the night, leaving me in the deathly silence of a hugely disapproving Mum. The only conversation she made was to ask me, *'Who the hell* are those people and *why* are you so late?' I smiled, gazing out the window, wide-eyed with delight. 'They're my new friends.' She made it quite clear this would never happen again. I, of course, had other ideas.

◆ ◆ ◆

I retained even less information than usual the next day during Physics and French. Not from lack of sleep, just excitement at my adventures the night before with these new friends: I wanted to worm my way into this gobby group and their brazen pop world antics.

That evening, I called Paul and asked when everyone was meeting up again. He said B*Witched had now basically finished promoting 'Rollercoaster', but that they were planning to hang outside *Live & Kicking* that coming Saturday, as the band were on the show. I casually said I'd probably be up for it, but inside I was desperate to get a slice of the action again.

After a few hours messing around outside Television Centre, B*Witched waved at us as their driver sped off, out of the gates, in their crimson people carrier. Annoyed, but not deflated, we went window shopping in Covent Garden while the most proactive of the group, Charlotte, used her massive mobile phone (a rare luxury in 1998) to call up every London rehearsal and recording studio stored in her contacts list to try and locate where the band might be working that afternoon. Using her professional blagging tactics she managed to bluff the studio where the girls were working into confirming they were there – this lot made it look so easy!

So, off we marched, that bright afternoon in late September, to an industrial estate in deepest Bermondsey. We trundled through housing estates and railway tunnels, past ramshackle corner shops, launderettes and football pubs. This place was so off the radar, I was promised, no other fans even knew about it. No Security. Just the band, off-duty.

I was commanded not to stop walking as we ambled past the main entrance, so no one would cotton on that we wanted to enter. 'Shit! There's a guy working on the gate today, just our luck,' Tasha moaned as the others cursed and sighed. I wondered if that was it – game over – but Steph led the way to the back of the big, brick industrial complex, where there was another locked gate, and a wire fence, ten feet high. There was no chance of scaling that, but the girls led me to an area of it in the corner that had previously been clipped. I asked no questions and followed the girls and Paul through the small gap in the fence. From here, we crouched behind parked cars, waiting for the rotating security camera's watchful eye to face the other way, before making a run for it towards the unmarked rehearsal studio on the other side of the car park. I was enthralled by this James Bond-style operation: all just to sit next to a skip and a parked people carrier on an industrial estate.

After three long hours of discussing other bands, groupies and lyrics, as the sunlight dimmed in the desolate car park, the B*Witched girls and their tour manager finally emerged at the studio doors, from whatever top-secret pop activities they'd been burrowed away doing, and we all got our own special moment with each member of the band. I foisted a couple of CD singles under their noses to get signed, but although I was desperate for a quick photo with them all, I knew Steph would be angry with me for not 'playing it cool'. Luckily, the Luton Girls weren't out again that day so I didn't have to play piggy in the middle, but that day would surely come. I knew most of this Lairy Lot wouldn't have taken kindly to them tagging along for the ride.

Following our success with the band, the Lairy Lot were off to score some alcohol and hang out somewhere, like normal teenagers. I used Steph's mobile to call Mum and tell her what time I'd be home and was met with a frosty reception down the end of the blower. Despite letting me get away with things my classmates could only dream about, she demanded I return home immediately for a family dinner. Fuck's sake! The others sniggered at my childish curfew and, once back at London Bridge Tube station, walked the other way into the night for more adolescent antics, leaving me heading home for a casserole and *Gladiators*, back in Ottershaw.

♦ ♦ ♦

Year Eleven wasn't such a success. I hadn't exactly taken Tony Blair's 'Education, Education, Education' mantra to heart. As the teachers piled us up with more and more coursework, I increasingly ignored it, devoting hours to studying the tour schedules of the latest manufactured acts to be spewed out by EMI or Sony.

The bullying I had continually hoped would end also turned out to be a perennial feature of my comprehensive days. I tried to ignore it, but invariably found myself responding with calm and elegant responses such as 'fuck off' or 'twat'. I even managed to get myself suspended for a day when a brawl broke out in a Maths class after a kid called me a 'dirty queer'.

Instead, I spent time thinking about all the people who actually liked me. But in classic teenage style there was politics there too. The Luton Girls hated the Lairy Lot for being brash and bitchy. In turn, the Lairy Lot hated the Luton Girls for being boring and stuck-up. Trapped between the two groups, I was just desperate for them all to like me. It was a fine line I had to tread and I just wished they could all play happy families, but when you're sixteen, it doesn't take much for things to get tribal.

A couple of weeks later an invitation fell onto the doormat one morning: it was for Laura's eighteenth birthday party at a village hall on the outskirts of Luton. That might sound lame as hell now, but back in those simpler times, this was magnificent. There would be alcohol, there would be friends, and, most importantly, there was minimal chance of anybody yelling 'poofter' at me across the room.

♦ ♦ ♦

The rusting double decker let out a plume of black smoke and a loud rumble as it deposited me by the side of a suburban road on the outskirts of Luton and drove off into the darkness. I scanned the deserted street, looking for the village hall where Laura's legendary eighteenth birthday party was being held. As

I approached a likely-looking 1950s hut, I noticed three slightly deflated balloons and made out the muffled bassline of a Five song. This *had* to be it. As I walked in, I noticed a distinctly familiar set-up to my Borehamwood outings, namely overly glammed-up girls and slightly awkward-looking men in cheap shirts, their spiked-up hair held in place with crispy hair gel, like mine.

'Malcolmmmmm! I'm so glad you made it!' Laura screamed, as I entered. Away from the baggage of my reputation back at school I felt strangely confident, chatting to a room full of strangers THREE YEARS OLDER THAN ME! They weren't judging me, and seemed genuinely impressed by our Friday night TV appearances. Mid-way through the evening, the local DJ announced an indecipherable message about the buffet being ready. We filed past a trestle table covered in beige delights with cash-and-carry paper plates that bent in two as soon as they were loaded up with chicken drumsticks and coleslaw. After that interlude the music was turned up even louder and I schmoozed my way around Laura's college friends and a smattering of middle-aged neighbours.

The room went wild when, Song of the Moment, 'Believe' by Cher came on. A whole village hall of Lutonians sang in unison to the auto-tuned chorus of the song that was dead set to be the new Number 1 that weekend. I ended up dancing with three girls with matching blonde highlights and Miss Selfridge vest tops. After impressing them with my dance moves to 'Horny '98' by Mousse T vs. Hot 'n' Juicy, I saw one of the three (the prettiest one) was looking my way with a facial expression I'd never seen before. She had a half smile on her face, and I noticed her huge brown eyes were looking directly at me. And then it crossed my mind... *I think she might fancy me?* Shocks of excitement hit me, followed by a wave of apprehension. I moved in her direction and we danced together, embodying every lyric of that summer's sexiest anthem, when suddenly, out of nowhere, a wiggly, wet tongue was being rammed down my throat. After a split second of confusion, I realised I should probably reciprocate. We gyrated with our mouths locked together for what felt like an eternity, until the next track came on. It was 'One for Sorrow', our song of the summer. *I might have just found the love of my life, but sod it*, I thought, *the DJ's playing Steps!* So, I ditched my Belle of the Ball and went straight into the perfectly drilled dance routine with my *Top of the Pops* friends. Apparently my 'first kiss' took one look at my rendition of H and slipped out the fire exit for a Silk Cut before disappearing into the night.

♦ ♦ ♦

The following Thursday, Madonna herself was making her first *Top of the Pops* appearance in years and *everyone* was talking about it. Well, they were in our world at least! Not usually one to make promotional appearances, she'd had a change of heart for this single and agreed to venture to Borehamwood to perform her haunting new song, 'The Power of Good-Bye'.

As I approached the studio that Thursday afternoon I saw exactly what I'd feared: Madonna fans. Dozens and dozens of them, pacing around in their oversized *Blond Ambition* Tour T-shirts, way older than us. Clare and I, plus one of her friends from Luton, sat on the wall outside, surveying the scene. 'Excuse me, have you got any spare tickets? I can pay good money.' 'No!' I barked back at the Madge fan who'd dared to approach me. 'Alright! Just asking, mate! If you do, I'll pay you. Hundreds!' replied the middle-aged woman.

'Fuck! We are *so* not getting in tonight. Look at this lot!' I moaned.

'We might,' said Clare, optimistically, 'We're gonna have to work *so* hard though.'

What we lacked in years and finance, we made up for in cunning: we spent two hours dashing up and down Borehamwood High Street, begging any likely looking people for spare tickets. We even resorted to manning the train platforms to catch *Top of the Pops* goers as they stepped off the carriages. We finally secured three free tickets from a couple in their twenties, who were no doubt pissed off when a manic Madge fan at the studio gates thrust dozens of notes in their face for every spare ticket. Laura's little brother, who'd joined us for the first time, decided to take the money and run when someone offered him £300 for his. The rest of us thought no amount of money could persuade us. It was a killer week, the rest of the line-up consisting of Robbie Williams, Five, Steps, Jay-Z, Boyzone and Stereophonics. *This was a no-brainer!*

Back then, Madonna hardly ever performed, so the prospect of seeing her in such an intimate setting made the atmosphere electric. Inside the waiting room none of these Madge diehards knew where they needed to wait to get into the studios. They were all looking around, on edge, trying to suss out which doors led the way. Very calmly, the three of us headed towards the double doors at the far-right end of the room. One or two observant megafans realised they were waiting in the wrong place and made a mad dash to queue behind us. Seconds later, it was a stampede. The BBC staff called in vain for order.

Once the last audience members filed into the waiting room, two enormous bodyguards marched in and scoured the place, clearly looking for someone. 'What the fuck is going on?' I murmured to the others. This was not your average week in Borehamwood. They didn't find who they were looking for by the cloakroom, and so barged past the queue of glammed-up girls waiting for the ladies' loos to continue their search. The whole room was muttering, trying to figure out what was happening.

Then screaming and shouting came from within the loos as two conspicuous women were marched out, distraught and crying into their hands with pound-shop wigs and thick-rimmed glasses. They refused to leave, pleading with the burly bodyguards in front of the open-mouthed audience. 'She saw you on the way in, she doesn't want you here!' one of the security guards boomed. 'Those disguises won't work, don't try doing that again.' It was like when they pull the rubber masks off the villains at the end of every *Scooby-Doo* episode, except this week the villains had come dressed as Velma.

Thanks to our prime spot in the queue, we were the first three in the studio and immediately bolted to the middle of the Main Stage, where we hoped she'd be on. To our delight, after the laborious warm-up, Danny announced that Madonna would be the first one on that evening, on the very stage we were pressed up against.

After a drawn-out introduction full of superlatives from Jamie Theakston, out she walked, standing silently and emotionless, directly in front of us. The rest of the crowd went wild, but the three of us were quite calm, taking in the gravitas of the moment, rather than losing our shit. They weren't just fans though, they were the most obsessively devoted followers I'd seen at *Top of the Pops*.

Aesthetically, Madonna had gone for an Andrea-Corr-meets-Mystic-Meg look: black dress, black trousers, dead-straight black wig. I kept thinking to myself, *she* really *looks like the villain from* Ducktales. There was a big orchestra crammed in behind her on the stage, but I could tell straight away that she was miming. I couldn't work out why she had bothered to wheel in some flautists, a bassoon and more fiddlers than the

Catholic Church, only to make them mime over the top of a backing track. A few years later I found out that she'd been lampooned in the press for singing 'off-key' at the MTV Europe Music Awards in Italy a week before. She could have wailed like a drunkard doing karaoke and the audience at *Top of the Pops* that night would still have sworn she gave an outstanding pitch-perfect performance.

Magnificently aloof, she stood there like an ice queen, gazing into the middle distance for the whole performance, apart from one dreamlike moment when she lunged forward, stared straight into my eyes, and sang a whole line of the song right to me. It was so surreal. Out of all the hordes of socially awkward and badly dressed people in the audience, I was the one she singled out for that brief moment. But what made it even odder was that she was really fucking close, like two inches from my nose, as though she had no concept of personal space. If I had eaten garlic for lunch she definitely would have smelt it! Maybe she thought I was a beautiful stranger, or maybe she just thought I looked like a virgin.

Afterwards, she shook the hands of a few of her adoring, cult-like followers and swept off stage as coolly as she'd come on. I, seemingly the chosen one that evening, then had fans crowding round and touching me for a few seconds, as though Her Holiness had rubbed off onto me.

I was buzzing all night during the other performances: Robbie did 'No Regrets' and 'Millennium', Boyzone sang their new cover, 'I Love the Way You Love Me', Jay-Z performed his rap song, 'Hard Knock Life' – containing a sample from the musical *Annie* (I know that sounds made up), Five, the boy band of the moment, sang their festive ballad, 'Until the Time is Through', Stereophonics woke us up with 'The Bartender and the Thief' and Steps entertained us with both of their double A-side new singles, 'Heartbeat' and their legendary school-disco-tastic cover of 'Tragedy'.

Dad was speechless when I told him about my brush with Her Madgesty. Kids at school just said I was bullshitting, so I told them to tune in that evening and they'd be proved wrong. When Monday arrived, after loads of them had watched it and saw that it really had happened, I just sat there in class embodying the painted nails emoji.

◆ ◆ ◆

No sooner had my rendezvous with Madge been aired than Mum and Dad made it clear they'd had enough. A laborious fortnight of mock GCSEs were about to start. No more gallivanting. 'They're MOCKS, Mum – bloody meaningless!' But my pleading didn't work. My wings were clipped and I was confined to my cage in the burbs until they were all over.

As we hit December 1998, the countdown to the Christmas Number 1 had begun – or, basically, a contest of who could finally knock Cher's 'Believe' off the top spot. Would anyone? *Ever*? After my fortnight of cramming in pointless answers to old science papers, I spent the next week cramming in as many visits to see the B*Witched girls at various appearances around town as I could, as they promoted their festive single, 'To You I Belong' – the sound of a magical wintery Christmas in Ireland.

At the end of the week of B*Witched's single release, rather than go and meet them with the Lairy Lot and Luton Girls for the twentieth time, I headed to The London Studios on the Southbank, after school, to see an old friend. Kelle (formerly of Eternal) had been given her first TV job, co-presenting a crap teatime ITV show, *Capital Christmas*, with Eamonn Holmes. TV gold it wasn't, but it did provide me with a place to see her, finally, a year on from that special night at my first *Top of the Pops*. How my life had changed since that phone call...

I was dying for her to remember me, and get the gossip on the band's breakup. I'd become ballsier in the couple of months I'd known the Lairy Lot, and thought, *Sod it, I'll blag waiting in reception*. My palms were sweating and my face flushed as I told myself, *look confident*. As I scanned the room for somewhere inconspicuous to lurk, I noticed the receptionist eyeing me up and down inquisitively through the mêlée of couriers, presenters and an ebbing tide of grey suits. When I saw a twenty-foot Christmas tree in the corner, decked in tinsel and oversized baubles, I made a dash for it, concealing myself between two cardboard boxes wrapped up like Christmas presents. I even briefly considered getting into one and pouncing out on Kelle like a jack-in-the-box. From my secret vantage point I saw the lift doors open and Kelle walk out. No longer caring about the beady-eyed receptionist, I ran over and, to my delight, she remembered me from our telephone call and *Top of the Pops* the year before, and was touched that I'd come down to see her after disappearing off the face of Planet Pop that summer! She was with her manager Wendy, who'd parted company with the Bennett sisters when they discharged Kelle from the group. Wendy was a legend: the real-life Patsy from *Ab Fab*, but with a heart of gold and always happy to answer my mundane questions when I rang her office. She said I'd be seeing a lot more of Kelle as she'd be releasing solo music the following year.

I returned to the same studios bright and early the next morning to see B*Witched at *CD:UK*, alongside the Honeyz and Aqua. But the main event that weekend was Sunday's Smash Hits Poll Winners' Party – an annual awards ceremony, aimed not at the industry bigwigs (like the BRITs), but purely at the teenage megafans. The categories were pretty questionable, like 'Best Boy Haircut', but the televised ceremony was still a high point in the musical calendar of every self-respecting pop fan.

To secure a decent spot at Poll Winners required dedication as you had to be one of the first in the queue when the tickets went on sale. Eager fans would arrive days early and camp out. 'Sleeping out' for concert tickets, as fans called it, was a bit like middle-aged *Times* readers at Wimbledon, but with more acne and less Pimm's.

Steph asked for volunteers to sleep out and I jumped at the chance to prove my worth to the Lairy Lot. Paul agreed to come along with me, so all I had to do was lie to Mum and Dad that I was staying at his that Friday after school. Little did they know their fifteen-year-old was spending an autumn night on the backstreets of East London, with only an Argos sleeping bag and some packets of Haribo.

The actual experience of sleeping out was surprisingly fun. One enterprising fan even had a portable TV that we huddled round and watched *Friends*. After sixteen chilly hours, and a numb bum from sitting on tarmac, I had the golden tickets in my hands.

Surely this would seal my place in the group.

When, a few weeks later, the night of Poll Winners arrived, I felt like I was going to the Oscars, except the entire audience was made up of adolescents and the bands had to dress in that year's 'theme'– *Titanic*. It featured the usual 1998 suspects: 911, Five, Another Level, Boyzone, B*Witched, Billie, Steps, The Corrs, Cleopatra, Louise, Shania, Aqua, East 17, A1, Westside (later rebranded as Westlife) and the Fresh Prince himself, Will Smith. Hit after hit after hit, and all with a Jack and Rose nautical vibe. This was my Christmas. As I'd camped out to secure us front-row seats, I was treated like a hero for the day. It was definitely worth risking hypothermia and violent crime to ingratiate myself with my new gang.

◆ ◆ ◆

As most kids at school were out panic-buying Body Shop gift sets I made the trek across London after school to join my whole crew at *Top of the Pops* for its big festive special. Now, when we were normally in attendance, we all looked pretty average. 'DRESS TO IMPRESS', the BBC tickets always stated in block capitals. (They also had the veiled threat '18–30ISH –NO WRINKLIES' printed on them, but we won't get into BBC ageism right now.) For once, we decided to go for it. The girls donned LBDs and I dug out a blazer of Dad's, as though this was our alternative Christmas prom.

Unwilling to break their run of Number 1s, B*Witched had released their festive track a week early, when the competition was much less fierce. Joining them in the yuletide line-up that evening were Billie Piper, Honeyz, The Lighthouse Family, Lutricia McNeal, Boyzone, Mousse T, Johnny Vaughan & Denise Van Outen (performing their novelty cover of Kylie and Jason's 'Especially for You'), plus Jane McDonald. The star of 1998's groundbreaking docusoap *The Cruise* was there, performing her Top 10 kitschfest, 'Cruise into Christmas'. Yes, Jane McDonald went salty balls to the wall, competing with Chef from *South Park* and the Spice Girls for the festive Number 1 slot. Oh, the past!

Lastly, the Ginger-less Spice Girls were also in attendance – hungry for a THIRD Christmas chart-topper with 'Goodbye'. I reckon, by that point, some of them would rather have named the single 'Bye, Bitch', but they wisely opted to give Geri the send-off that the fans all wanted. It was a rare performance from

Posh and Scary in their third trimesters, sitting on bar stools after waddling on stage in black maternity wear, looking fabulous, obviously.

As B*Witched were about to start their performance, Tasha boldly asked when they were flying home for Christmas.

'In the morning... Early,' Keavy Lynch murmured back from the glare of the stage lights.

'Heathrow?' she probed back.

The audience erupted into applause as the music started playing. Keavy nodded and winked at us, before getting back to the task in hand.

'We're going,' Tasha declared, turning to us.

That was all the tempting I needed. The Luton Girls weren't up for it, though. Like me, they'd never really done the airport groupie thing and didn't want to progress to 'actual stalker' level. After the show I headed off with Steph, Gemma, Charlotte and Tasha to lose my airport virginity. Less glamorous than the Mile High Club, this involved loitering for hours in the miniature city that is Heathrow. With no one around to keep us in line, we had high-speed trolley races, rehearsed routines while blaring out songs on my boombox, and nicked food from breakfast buffets being laid out by weary-eyed night-shifters.

When morning arrived, we made sure we were back in the right place to meet the stars. I was flagging by this point, wrapped only in a cheap coat on a hard plastic chair by the Aer Lingus check-in desks. I mean, where else are you going to meet B*Witched in an airport if not under the luminous signs with emerald clovers?

Just as our spirits and body temperatures were beginning to sink, by magic, the B*Witched girls emerged from a revolving door next to where we were huddled. We snatched half an hour with them as they checked in their luggage and listened to the banal goings-on in our teenage lives. They were flying to Dublin for Christmas, but then heading straight from there to America, to join boy band *NSYNC and a new artist called Britney Spears on tour all over the States, so we wouldn't see them for a couple of months.

♦ ♦ ♦

Christmas 1998 finally arrived. Santa didn't let me down, rewarding me with a portable minidisc player – the *future*! I spent the following month hanging out with my new groupie friends, drinking, bunking trains, and generally being teenagers. On a couple of occasions during tipsy sleepovers at Tasha's family home in Romford, when we were feeling desperate for a low-grade B*Witched fix, a bunch of us would visit the Tesco down the road, where the boy from the *C'est la Vie* music video worked nights on the bread counter. We'd harass the poor guy with our Irish jigging and he'd beg us to leave him alone.

By the time B*Witched returned from the States at the end of January, I was an integral member of the Lairy Lot. I was noticeably more confident and happy when we met them at Heathrow. We also managed to bump into Mel C, Boyzone and B*Witched's tour mates *NSYNC at the arrivals gate that same evening. My life had gone pop!

The other happy news at the start of 1999 was that I had successfully passed my mocks, with respectable grades for someone who'd spent more time learning the lyrics to Steps' new album than the periodic table. By no means had my first term of Year Eleven been easy. I daydreamed through it, obsessing over pop songs and the friends I'd made in the groupie world. Kids still called me 'batty boy' and tried to make my life hell, and the teachers still looked the other way; except our Maths teacher, who used to tell me to tuck my blouse in during class, for a few cheap laughs.

I didn't fit in there. Puberty had turned my school against me. My people were fellow pop addicts whose weekly worship was on Thursday nights in Borehamwood.

7

It's Not Right but It's Okay

With February 1999's half term a week away, the end of school seemed tantalisingly close. I no longer cared about what kids there thought, now that I had a real group of friends. I was finally part of a tribe, and having invested far too much time meeting B*Witched, I felt like they were 'my band'. We were on first name terms, darling! When kids at school were yelling at me, I yelled back; inside thinking how much more fun I was having in life than these yokels, destined to be trapped in Surrey for all eternity.

I'd ventured to Heathrow to see B*Witched twice in the past week, jetting off promoting their album. They'd been getting loads of airplay across Europe and looked set to bag their fourth successive UK Number 1. Their tour manager Tommy regularly roped Paul and I into helping him carry their luggage, us being the only guys in our gang of groupies. I didn't mind a bit of child labour when the trade-off was him letting us all sit at the band's table as they ate overpriced reheated airport dinners. We'd quietly talk between ourselves while not-so-secretly eavesdropping on the music world conversations at the other end of the table.

Every radio show we tuned into that week, while zooming around London in Steph's car, was discussing the upcoming BRIT Awards, in a week's time. The BRITs are the industry's self-congratulatory event, and in the nineties the likes of us couldn't buy tickets for love nor money. Back then, ten million tuned into ITV to see the biggest stars' legendary boozy antics: Chumbawamba throwing water over John Prescott, Jarvis Cocker mooning at Jacko, or *that* Union Jack dress. The big rumour going round in early 1999 was that a whole host of young stars would perform an ABBA medley. The seventies Swedes were enjoying something of a revival, and the prospect of seeing some of our favourite bands performing together sounded too good to be true.

'Are you *sure* you can't just get us tickets or passes? Just say we're part of your crew, we basically are!' Steph pleaded.

'No!' Edele shrieked, 'You know we can't! We don't have that kind of power, as much as we'd love our fans to come along.'

'Just enter the competitions on the radio loads of times,' Sinead added, semi-helpfully. 'Or bloody watch it on TV like everyone else!'

'We're *not* doing that. That's completely lame! We're going, mark my words!' Charlotte insisted.

'Okay, good luck wit' that! See yas round,' Keavy said, pulling the door of their people carrier shut as they laughed and sped off.

◆ ◆ ◆

Half term started a few days later. Revision was out and pop was in. That Saturday, the B*Witched girls kicked off the campaign for their new single: a bittersweet love song about Michael Fish,

'Blame It on the Weatherman', by performing at *The National Lottery Live*.

'I'm just going into London to watch B*Witched and then coming straight back,' I promised Mum that Saturday afternoon. She was still wary about who these friends were that I spent so much time with.

'Well, don't be back late, please – and I don't want you phoning me for a lift in the middle of the night again.'

I swore not to, but knew there was no chance I'd miss out on an adventure in favour of traipsing round DIY shops with Dad and Sophie. So, six of us went down to Television Centre and blagged tickets off the dull forty-somethings in the queue, none of whom exuded 'Irish girl group superfan' vibes.

We whooped and cheered during our Denim Clad Ladies' performance and tedious chat with Dale Winton. One of the girls then had the honour of releasing Set of Balls No. 4 into Guinevere. And THAT, kids, is what the entire nation watched on a Saturday night in the days before social media.

After the recording, Charlotte and Steph announced that we were all going into Central London as Steps were performing at G-A-Y, a club night at the legendary Astoria venue. They didn't have tickets but still wanted to meet them outside beforehand. I wasn't sure what to do – I'd promised to go home, and didn't want to be seen hanging out at the back of a *gay* club. But Steph was insistent, and lent me her phone to break the news to Mum that I wouldn't be coming home till later (I put the phone down before she had the chance to bollock me!). We piled into her metallic green Vauxhall Corsa and, after a night-time tour through Piccadilly Circus, pulled up in Soho.

I had barely seen a nightclub before, let alone loitered outside a gay one. The others brought me up to speed: apparently G-A-Y was the biggest gay night in the country, with weekly performances from music icons; a pop disco filled with glitter-doused twinks ('skinny young guys') and 'old pervs that want to sleep with the twinks'. 'Plus, loads of lezzas too.' They also told me that 'everyone's on poppers', a solvent that gives you a rush on the dance floor and loosens your anus. 'Right, got it,' I said, in glazed shock. In those two eye-opening minutes that was me schooled on the warts 'n' all of the London mainstream gay scene.

The excited clubbers snaked in a long queue from the club doors, all around Soho Square, many sporting angel wings or flashing devil horns, or tight tops boasting glittery toned torsos and bulging biceps. It took less than an hour to get here from the leafy cul-de-sacs of Surrey, yet this was another planet; one I had never visited. Kids like us weren't the only ones who loved pop bands, apparently.

Despite my initial nerves, we chatted to loads of tipsy clubbers in the queue. They said we should try to get in, but Charlotte said we were happier drinking White Lightning by the stage door, waiting for the band to arrive. I was relieved – I wasn't ready to step into that world.

We could hear the deep dance beat pulsating through the venue to the dark square outside. Then we heard Steps' set bring the house down and there was a crazy scrum afterwards, with paparazzi photographers and screaming drunken fans as they left the building.

After the buzzing atmosphere of Soho, and a couple of litres of low-grade cider, I couldn't face returning home to Mum and Dad, and I was too pissed to even think about how annoyed they'd be with me the next day. By this point most of our group had made their way home, leaving me and a couple of others on the mean streets of Soho. We decided we'd go over to the Docklands Arena in the morning to see the bands arriving for

BRITs rehearsals, and hopefully see if there was any evidence of that rumoured ABBA medley.

We trekked to Waterloo Station to get out of the cold and find somewhere to sleep. It was a Baltic February night, so we huddled together on a bench to stay warm. Every half an hour, the same security guard would ask us to get up and move on, and we would sit upright till he walked off, only to lie back down again in a heap once he'd left us alone.

◆ ◆ ◆

At first light we drifted over to the BRITs rehearsals, a little worse for wear and thoroughly underdressed for the weather. There was not much going on apart from some hungover-looking crew setting up. We were the only sad fuckers outside there on a Sunday morning, so we bought food and had a strip-wash in a nearby Asda.

After a couple of hours, more crew members, catering and equipment began arriving, before, finally, the artists. It was now clear that the rumoured ABBA medley consisted of the musical dream team that is B*Witched, Billie Piper, Cleopatra, Tina Cousins and Steps, as we met them all walking in by the dockside stage door.

Security were overbearing, although I think it was the presence of Cher and David Bowie rather than blessed Cleopatra that warranted the extra heavies, as well as the need to prevent show secrets being leaked to hungry journalists.

I phoned up Tasha, Steph and Gemma from a payphone and told them to come and join us. We loitered outside, discussing how we could possibly get to see the show in a couple of days' time and caught glimpses of the stars as they arrived to rehearse. As crew members left the now fenced-off stage door area to have cigarette breaks next to us, we joked with them about stealing their backstage passes so we could attend the show on Tuesday night.

When we made small talk with a young crew woman, Gemma looked preoccupied, writing furiously in a notepad. Upon closer inspection she wasn't writing at all, but sketching the design of her laminated pass, annotated with comments on colours and fonts. We all laughed at her ludicrous plan to forge one. However, the more we thought about the insane idea, the more genius it seemed. We got into a conversation with a sound guy for Placebo who didn't have the 'Crew' pass, but an 'Artist' one. In for a penny, in for a pound, Gemma thought, and made another rushed sketch. Crew seemed vaguely plausible, but it was doubtful us scruffy lot could pass as artists.

After an hour's gap with no sneaky fag breaks, someone came out and stood beside us, and we all spotted that he had the Holy Grail of passes – 'AAA' (Access *All* Areas). While we feigned interest in how the guy got into working in live events, Gemma jotted the pass down. Yes, our chance of success was low, but the rewards would be beyond our wildest dreams.

The more we spoke about the backstage passes in the car back to Central London, the more frenzied we became, plotting how to orchestrate it. With our extremely limited design skills we thought we could cobble something together, but had no idea how to create the swirly-blue design which formed the main background to the AAA pass – that would be tricky.

'Stop the car! Stop the car!' Charlotte wailed.

'What?!?' Steph shouted back, worried she'd driven over a cat or her car was falling apart.

'Pull over!' Charlotte bellowed. 'Look at that BRITs banner... On the DLR station. It's got the blue swirly background!'

We all screamed in disbelief. Steph swiftly changed lanes, to a chorus of car horns, and pulled onto the pavement.

'Hurry up, for fuck's sake!' she yelled as we all jumped out and darted across the traffic to the station. The canvas banner, advertising the BRIT Awards 1999, was taunting us, high above our heads.

There was only one way to get a piece – someone was going to have to climb onto the side of the escalators and somehow bring it down. Excelling at the high jump was one of the only benefits to being tall and gangly at school so I volunteered immediately and jumped up to grab it, hanging on for dear life, my legs dangling in the air. I shook about on the banner, while onlookers gawped at me, perplexed. Eventually, one end snapped off and swung me down a few feet, into the path of one of the escalators. Steph had now crossed the road to help and, being the practical lesbian she is, produced a Swiss army penknife from her pocket so I could hack off a section of the trailing banner. We cheered in delight as we ran back to the car and sped off, elated our plan was quickly falling into place.

The reception was frosty when I arrived home on Sunday evening, having left Saturday lunchtime. I cornered Dad on his own and asked if Gemma and I could come to his office the next day to use the scanner and printers. He reluctantly agreed, saying he didn't want to know what we were doing. He probably guessed it was something to do with the BRITs, as I'd spoken of nothing else for the past week, but I was happy to keep him in the dark.

♦ ♦ ♦

The next morning, Monday of half term, Gemma caught the train to Dad's work and we set up camp on a spare desk at the back of the open-plan office. They'd recently connected every machine to the World Wide Web, so we were able to pilfer the BRITs' logo from their very basic website. We scanned the swirly background from the destroyed banner and, using my well-honed Microsoft Paint skills, painstakingly assembled the 'AAA' pass, with only Gemma's sketch and accompanying notes as a guide.

All day Dad's inquisitive colleagues were peering over our shoulders, perplexed as to what we were doing. After hours of tweaking, test prints and debates about letter spacing, our masterpiece was complete. We'd convinced ourselves our homemade passes were so accurate, we'd definitely manage to get in. This time tomorrow, we would either be on the verge of hobnobbing with anyone who was anyone, having pulled off the greatest stunt imaginable; or sitting in the back of a police van charged with trespass, fraud, harassment, breaking and entering and who knows what else.

The final creative decision was to get them professionally laminated at the newsagent by the station. Everyone had agreed to provide their own lanyards, Charlotte and Gemma having one each from when All Saints had got them backstage at V Festival the summer before. I had nothing to use for my neck though, but Gemma saved the day by pinching the cord off her nan's reading glasses. Sorry, love!

◆ ◆ ◆

The next morning, we all woke up with a slight fear: the big day. The exhilaration of the last few days had given way to mild panic. If this didn't work, I'd be gutted, and if it did, the risks were huge.

B*Witched were appearing on Simon Mayo's Radio 1 show in the morning, so we arranged to meet at Richmond Station to drive to the studios. We neatly folded our 'smart clothes' in

Steph's boot, ready for the evening. In an attempt to blend in, I opted not to wear my lime-green Adidas jacket, but my one smart shirt, school trousers and a jacket of Dad's.

We noticed a people carrier with blacked-out windows also waiting outside Richmond Station. We knew immediately from the number plate that it belonged to the boy band Five (as a pop groupie, you absorb these things). We thought we'd go and say hello for a laugh. While Sean, the baby of the group, was getting cash out, we chatted to J, the band's 'hard man' figure, and let him in on our planned BRITs heist. He was clearly amused, but wasn't putting money on our success. 'See you in there!' we said, as the car pulled away. 'Err... yeah. Good luck!' J sniggered.

By the time we got to Radio 1's Fitzrovia studios, in the shadow of Telecom Tower, we were smug with cocky confidence: there was no going back. We met the B*Witched girls as they left and revealed our devious plan to see them perform that evening. 'Yer feckin' bonkers, yous lot!' was Edele's reaction. The good girls of pop did *not* approve of our actions, and, like Five, didn't fancy our chances of success – some people just had no faith in my Microsoft Paint skills.

We wandered Central London for a few hours, before finding some public toilets where we could change into our glad rags. I imagine most people going to awards ceremonies don't stand in a battered cubicle, an inch deep in piss, to get ready for the night ahead.

Steph's car was our limousine, transporting us to the Isle of Dogs, which, that evening, was like nothing I'd seen before. The streets were lined with limos, as far as the eye could see. A blinding spotlight shone into the night sky from the roof of the arena and an army of Security patrolled the roads and entrance to the venue.

Steph drove into the Asda car park opposite, the same nervous smile mirrored across all our faces. I could tell Paul was anxious, and even Gemma looked like she might be having second thoughts. Were we *really* going to do this? It was too late to run home to Surrey and watch it safely on TV now.

We walked up the driveway to the first line of stewards, Steph's mantra 'Play. It. Cool' on repeat in my head. A cursory glance from a guy in a black fleece and waft of the hand. Wow! We were over the first hurdle. I wanted to burst out laughing, but knew we weren't home and dry yet.

Stretching ahead of us was a never-ending sea of red carpet. An alluring storm of sporadic flashes and thunderous cheers. A gauntlet of screaming fans and paparazzi that seemed to go on forever. As we took our first steps on that hallowed carpet, a wave of confidence hit me. I soaked up the atmosphere as the echo of cameras clinked around us. We were somebodies, we could do this!

As we basked in the limelight a distant voice stood out in the crowd.

'Charlotte! GEMMA?! What the fuck?'

We winced at the sea of people through the flashes. Shit! It was a couple of boy-band groupies we knew from hanging around TV studios. Back down to earth with a bang. We'd been spotted.

'Fucking ignore them!!!' Steph roared. 'Get inside, NOW.'

As we reached the venue's doors we could hear them angrily yelling stuff still, but we couldn't hear what, and didn't really care.

Another wall of black-jacketed gatekeepers. This time they were looking at us a little closer, but the noise and lights were enough to distract them and once again we just got the response 'Enjoy the show, ladies and gentlemen!'

We stepped into the arena's foyer, all on cloud nine. Tuxedo-clad music execs and radio DJs wearing glittery numbers shuffled about, searching for bars, toilets and cloakrooms. For once, we weren't those fans outside – freezing cold and trapped behind the barriers in baggy combat trousers. We'd transitioned to something far greater – we were inside the BRIT Awards, and people all thought we had every right to be there! With the girls looking glam, and me and Paul looking half-decent, it felt like we'd left childish fandom behind us: we'd crossed the velvet rope.

We knew that so many industry people at the ceremony that night had no interest in seeing the performances or the winners in the flesh. They'd been given complimentary tickets and just wanted a free night out, slap-up dinner and booze. They couldn't even have selfies with soon-to-be-forgotten pop stars back then.

Our main problem, though, was that we had no plan whatsoever of what we were going to do if we managed to get in. We wanted to watch the show more than *anything*, but we got complacent once inside the building. Our fake passes were so believable we'd managed to fool not one but TWO big checkpoints already – we felt invincible.

After a quick perusal of the main arena, with its tiers of banqueting tables and banks of seats stretching up to the roof, Charlotte suggested we make full use of our 'AAA' status. She marched us off towards the backstage area. We entered a decidedly less glamorous corridor, only to be faced with door after door, Security after Security, like being trapped in a horrible nightmare. With every door we were let through our excitement and invincibility gave way to fear. And through each door the lights got brighter and our passes more visible. We finally reached the last stretch of corridor. *We've almost done it!* I thought, imagining myself sipping champagne with Whitney Houston in a matter of minutes.

We were ecstatic to get waved through by the final security guard after giving our passes a quick scan with his torch. *We were in!* No sooner had this junior guy let us through than a six-foot-tall woman with shoulders broader than a Russian weightlifter rushed towards us, shouting at him. She was head of security for the whole event and, honestly, just not the kind of woman you would ever want to mess with. Instantly, we were shit-scared of her. We must have looked so shifty – the six of us, mostly kids, just waltzing into the backstage area, laughing and joking.

She screamed at him, 'NO! NO! NO! You've GOT to check them properly.' She grabbed one of the girls' passes and shone her torch right onto it.

'Let me see this...' pulling it closer to her face for a better look. 'WHAT IS THIS??? WHERE DID YOU GET THIS? THIS IS A *FAKE*!' She was raging! 'Right, tell all the others down here we've got a problem. They need to be on high alert for counterfeit passes!'

She looked at the passes round all our necks – 'They're all fakes! This is unbelievable!'

We were kicking ourselves, our cockiness instantly changed to terror. What was going to happen to us? We had visions of being thrown into cells for the night and charged with fraud. The lines on the security woman's brow unfurled and her tone softened.

'Who gave these to you?' she quizzed.

'What?' we replied, baffled by her question.

'I'm sorry, guys. These are not genuine passes. We need to know where you got them from.'

Without hesitation, Charlotte piped up, 'This guy outside the arena. He sold them to us for fifty quid each.' We discretely glanced at each other at the next ridiculous turn in our evening's saga.

The woman continued her interrogation, 'I thought this might happen this year. What did he look like – was he mid-thirties, a bit scruffy?'

'Yeah,' Charlotte, said earnestly. 'With a big coat!'

I wanted to burst out laughing. Even I half-believed Charlotte's ad-libbing!

'Right, I think I know who it is,' the security boss told her colleagues. 'It must be that guy loitering outside the side entrance earlier. I need a group of you to go and find him immediately.' She turned back to us. 'I'm sorry, guys, but I'm going to have to ask you to leave. Your night's over, I'm afraid. I'll need to take these passes off you for evidence. I'm really sorry this has happened to you.' She clearly felt bad for ruining our evening.

'Can't we keep them as souvenirs even?' Steph brazenly asked.

'No, you can't. This is quite serious.' She collected up the passes and lanyards from our necks. 'Look! This one isn't even a proper cord, it's from a pair of glasses or something. Unbelievable!' she exclaimed at mine, letting out a loud tut. Charlotte and Gemma couldn't hold back their chuckles.

'Yeah, it may seem funny but this is all *extremely* serious stuff, guys,' she said, her tone growing sterner.

She marched off with our passes and a small harem of twenty-something security guards. One escorted us out via the fire exit – not quite as glam as our arrival – and along the dockside at the back of the arena. As we walked out, we saw a bunch of people bringing in barrows full of cheap champagne and helium balloons for an after-party somewhere within the labyrinthine corridors of the arena. We were shown out of a guarded side gate leading to the service road, where HGVs were parked up after dropping off speaker systems and banqueting tables. That was it; it was all over. The BRITs dream ruined, all because we got greedy and blew it. But at least for those few precious moments we'd done it, our plan had actually worked!

After the adrenaline wore off, and the reality of our situation sunk in, we bickered bitterly for a good ten minutes in the freezing cold about whose decision it was to go backstage. I can't remember who got the brunt of the blame – probably Steph, the eldest, and our self-appointed leader.

'I'm so pissed off. I haven't even got my bag or bloody coat!' Charlotte shouted.

At that point Gemma, with a devious grin, opened her blazer and slowly pulled out an Access All Areas pass.

'What the hell?! How have you got that?' I wailed. 'You didn't bring a spare?'

'No! I kept mine. Wasn't gonna let *her* take it,' Gemma answered, coyly. 'I took mine off straight away and put it inside my jacket really secretly.'

We all screamed in hysterics. If *anyone* was going to think of doing that, it just had to be 'sneaky Gemma'. That was her style to a tee – hide all evidence, so she could get away with murder time and time again.

Someone had to go back in to get our coats, but nobody had the guts to try their luck again (and alone). We were all in this together, so we'd all go back. We thought the security would recognise us straight away and we'd have to plead to get our bags and coats back from the cloakroom in the foyer, or stand around in the freezing cold till the end of the night to collect them.

After plucking up a bit of courage we strolled over *again* to the red carpet, just as supermodel Caprice was arriving and posing for pictures. There was so much commotion with all the flashing cameras and shouts from the paparazzi pit that the security just waved us through. Miraculously, none of them were the same people that threw us out the back a few minutes earlier, and clearly the word hadn't got round about fake passes.

We got back to the foyer, again disbelieving our luck. We'd all walked straight in – this time with one fake pass between SIX of us! We got our bags and coats from the cloakroom and tried to decide what to do next, all aware that we had to be on our best behaviour.

'Someone's going to recognise us, we'll get arrested this time,' I kept saying, my eyes darting around the room for the security boss.

'Who cares?! Let's just hang out and have a drink. We might get to meet some celebs arriving late if we stay here,' said Paul.

The announcement for the final call before the show blared out over the tannoy. Then we heard the magic words: 'Ladies and Gentleman, welcome to the 1999 Mastercard BRIT Awards...' The sound of piano blared out from the main hall of the arena and, as the room erupted, a voice began to sing, 'Hell is gone and heaven's here... there's nothing left for you to fear'. Robbie was right. We thought, *SOD IT, let's just go in. Hopefully, nobody will notice in all the commotion*. Boozed-up PR workers rushed past us in all directions with ice buckets enveloping overpriced bottles of crap Chardonnay, scrambling to reach their seats.

Paul flung open the door to the arena and the muffled tones of Robbie Williams gave way to the full deafening sound. The black tie-clad audience were all on their feet for the opening number.

A helpful young usher diligently sought out empty seats for us to fill, up in the balcony just to the left of the stage. Their rightful owners angrily prodded us after a couple of minutes, and the supportive usher found us some other spare seats, this time slightly closer to the action, ensuring we had an incredible view of the once omnipotent Johnny Vaughan, our host for the evening, and the mismatched duos of B- and C-list celebrities delivering their awkward scripted dialogues prior to introducing the nominees.

The pit at the front of the stage was reserved for pupils of South London's BRIT School, the performing arts academy that was to gift the world Amy Winehouse and Adele. They had the best spot in the arena, that was where we really wanted to be.

After a third-rate joke about the Battle of Waterloo, Johnny Vaughan introduced the much-anticipated 'ABBA All-Stars' medley, featuring the biggest names in bubblegum pop. And Tina Cousins. The collective's silhouettes took their positions on stage in front of us. We screamed our lungs out, the smartly dressed people around us gawping in bewilderment. I realised we six imposters were some of the only true pop fans that would get to witness this one-off in the flesh. The medley kicked off with a bit of 'Take a Chance on Me', then segued into 'Dancing Queen', with Steps and Cleopatra taking centre stage in white and gold lamé costumes, almost swallowed by a cloud of dry ice. The salesman for knee-high boots must have made a killing that week. Then the lights changed and it went into 'Mamma Mia', in which our girls B*Witched, with Billie Piper, moved to the front to perform their segment, kitted out in pound shop blue wigs and 'Waterloo'-esque body-length leotards.

It ended with 'Thank You for the Music', and, just in case the whole ensemble wasn't quite kitsch enough, the last line was changed to 'Thank ABBA for the music'. Together we witnessed something that, in hindsight, seems decidedly average, but at the time was the mother lode. To see all those acts miming along in choreographic unity was, for us, like witnessing Michael Jackson, The Rolling Stones and The Beatles do a rendition of Elvis's greatest hits... in dodgy fancy dress. Björn from *actual* ABBA then trotted on stage to present the next award, and revealed to a sceptical-looking Johnny that he was launching a musical based on the songs of ABBA, called *Mamma Mia!* Oh ye of little faith, Vaughan!

From that point on, we didn't really care if we got thrown out, as we'd seen what we came for. Anything else was a bonus. And what a bonus it was – David Bowie and Placebo, Whitney Houston, Cher, Manic Street Preachers, The Corrs, Boyzone, plus a closing set by the reunited Annie Lennox and Dave Stewart of Eurythmics. Of course none of these were quite in the same league as Cleopatra and Claire from Steps in platform boots miming to 'Dancing Queen'.

Fifty-two-year-old Cher was at the peak of her late nineties comeback, having achieved the biggest-selling single of 1998 with 'Believe' (cruelly snatching the accolade from Céline Dion in the final days of the year). She was dressed like a human glitter ball, with hordes of dancers in matching Cher wigs. *Amazing*, obviously. Whitney performed her new comeback track, 'It's Not Right but It's Okay', I think for the first time ever in Europe, the song already being massive on radio and music channels around the world. Whitney's performance, unlike Cher's, was sung live and pitch-perfect. I'd seen her the summer before when Dad had taken us on our late-night adventure to Manchester, but she'd sexed-up her look and sound since then, appearing in a leather basque-cum-ballgown. David Bowie was also performing, doing a duet of '20th Century Boy' with Placebo. Us basic bitches were too pop-obsessed to realise we were witnessing a bonafide legend – although I'd seen a couple of his LPs in Dad's record collection, so I knew he must be pretty old.

♦ ♦ ♦

The Eurythmics closed the show, and everyone sat around us in the upper balcony started shuffling along the rows to get to the front of the queue for cabs. But, for us, the party was only just beginning: we *needed* to make our way down to the floor of the arena where all the stars were milling around the tables. We managed to find our way to the lower balcony, but the security guarding access to the hallowed inner circle weren't satisfied with our one pass between the six of us and refused entry. The cheek of it!

If we could blag our way into the arena twice, we could definitely blag our way down from a balcony to the main floor. We scattered to find a way down. Paul and a bunch of the others got a group of pissed guys to catch them from below as they lowered themselves over the front of the balcony (fortunately, only about a ten-foot drop). These drunken men obviously thought it was hilarious, but judging by the look of terror on Charlotte's face she wasn't having quite as much fun.

Gemma and I were trying to get people's attention from our balcony but no one was looking, and the crowd was really thinning out now, making us much more visible to Security. Then the adrenaline took control and we decided to just go for it and climbed over the balcony railing together. The concrete wall was slightly sloped, so we knew we could probably slide down, although with a moderate chance of requiring surgery in the process.

One at a time, we hung onto the banner spanning the wall (God bless those bloody banners!) and jumped onto the tables and chairs of the people nearest us, giving the couple sitting at the table a massive shock as I landed just inches away from their screwed-up napkins and dreg-stained wine glasses. We apologised and ran away, laughing our heads off. The floor of the arena was arranged in tiers; each one towards the stage reserved for higher-status guests than the last and each guarded by beady-eyed Security to ensure that nobody tried to spike Whitney's drink or pester Bowie to sign their bra. We didn't have a pass between us by this point, so didn't want to risk the gauntlet of seven ranks of security guards. Instead, we went underground. We dived underneath table after table, scurrying between each row until eventually we found ourselves surrounded by the calves and ankles of the top dogs.

Here in the inner sanctum we managed to meet Boy George, Eagle-Eye Cherry, Sara Cox, Cornershop, Meat Loaf, Steps, and finally – B*Witched! I left Gemma talking to some of the girls from All Saints, and ran over to chat to B*Witched with the others. They all had gobsmacked looks on their faces. The ludicrous plan we'd told them about that morning had actually worked! They just kept tipsily shrieking, 'You guys are hilarious! You're terrible!'

We chatted for a few minutes before they said goodbye and left to go to a swanky nightspot on the other side of town. Most stars headed off to various after-parties at clubs across London. The official VIP after-party was just kicking off in the arena.

All six of us went over to the security guard. We wafted our shared fake AAA pass in his direction, but unsurprisingly he said we needed one each, or at least a couple more, to get down to this area. We insisted that we were the children of producers of the show and had access to go anywhere all evening with our one measly pass. It pays to be persistent (or at least annoying). He gave up arguing with us and astonishingly let us all through.

We entered a large room, just at one side of the stage. All I can say is this party was very 'fur coat and no knickers'. From the outside looking in, its fairground décor looked so enticing, and we imagined we'd be tete-a-tete'ing with incredibly famous people. The reality was all a bit shoddier. The homemade ghost train featured real-life 'ghosts'. Sadly, they all looked to be wearing Halloween costumes their mum had made by Sellotaping black bags together. We kept being handed plastic tokens for the casino, but it was definitely more Blackpool than Monte Carlo. Even the pop stars they had lured in were at the less than 'very' end of the VIP spectrum. The room was bustling with blokes in suits, and as the evening wore on, they thinned out and headed back to Buckinghamshire or Berkshire.

We sauntered over to the bar and casually asked for some drinks. Fortunately, the staff didn't care that we were clearly all about sixteen. Unfortunately, the drinks weren't free, as we'd assumed. When you're living on pocket money, you just can't afford absurdly overpriced drinks. Steph, the only one with a proper job, flatly refused to let us put an evening's booze onto her card. Paul wanted us all to get drunk though, and remembered seeing loads of half-drunk bottles scattered on the tables in the arena, so Charlotte, he and I agreed to go on a mission. We knew it was a risk, leaving and then trying to sneak back in again, only this time with armfuls of alcohol, but we'd got away with so much that day. This, in comparison, would be like taking candy from a baby. Or brandy from a bigwig.

After making some excuse to the security guy about leaving stuff on our table, we made a dash for anything that looked vaguely palatable. We managed to pilfer an unopened bottle of vodka and some orange juice, deciding not to risk the many half-full wine bottles. I hid the vodka bottle up the back of my dad's jacket and nervously walked past the security. Fortunately, he just gave us a nod and a smile as we passed.

Back inside the party we cracked it open and filled some empty glasses we'd pilfered with very generous portions of vodka. Steph – the eldest by far, at twenty-one – warned me in particular that I was only fifteen and that she couldn't drive me home if I was blind drunk. I was so overexcited though, and despite Steph always playing the 'sensible older sister' role of our group, she was never a mum or dad figure who actually had the power to stop us from being idiots, and so we all got pretty hammered.

Although Whitney and Placebo evidently had better offers, we did meet some celebs at the party – Billie Piper and a couple of members of Steps milled past us. Also J from Five. He initially looked at us blankly, but his face dropped when he realised we were the kids from outside Richmond Station, that same morning. 'You kids! Shit, you *actually* did it?!' he yelled, and then tried to explain the convoluted tale to his drunken mates.

After dancing for a while, my overly generous portion of vodka took effect and I ended up collapsing on the floor. Newbie radio DJ Chris Moyles and *Top of the Pops* presenters Jamie Theakston and Jayne Middlemiss were sitting right opposite and apparently looked on, unimpressed. My friends were still trying to scoop me up when Security bounded over and said I had to leave.

Steph and Paul begrudgingly marched me out and we ended up back in the main foyer area next to the no longer glitzy-looking red carpet, where we'd made our *two* entrances of the night. A woman with long, blonde dreadlocks stood next to us, chatting away on her phone. The others took their eyes off me for two seconds and I was behind her, running my hands up and down her thick Rapunzel dreads, while singing a chorus of church bells.

'DING DONG, DING DONG!' I chimed at the top of my lungs. Steph and Charlotte dragged me away, apologising profusely for their inebriated friend. The victim of my stunt turned round, snapping at me to go away.

'Oh my God, it's ALDA!' Steph bellowed. 'We love you!'

To our utter delight, the abused lady was quirky Icelandic pop star Alda.

She turned round again, smiling this time, and swiftly ended her phone call to soak up our praise and chat about her future music plans. Sadly, the bell tolled for Alda's pop career soon after that evening.

The others eventually got me back down the red carpet and over to the Asda car park across the road. I sat slumped on the floor while there was a heated debate about how to get me home. Paul agreed to take me back to his dad's flat, dragging me, nursing me or propping me up on night buses across to the other side of London.

A banging headache woke me early at Paul's on Wednesday morning, after two hours' sleep on the only mess-free area of his bedroom floor. As I walked home from Chertsey train station, like a bleary-eyed zombie, I knew that, even if we tried to repeat our BRITs antics, nothing would *ever* beat that heist. What a night!

8

We Like to Party

I spent the rest of the day comatose in my bedroom hovel, pinching myself every time I had another ridiculous recollection about our BRITs escapades the night before. I slept right through the afternoon, even with Anja and Sophie running around the house, only surfacing when Mum returned from work and I recounted to everyone in (too much) detail what madness had occurred the evening before. They were all dumbfounded that a bunch of kids could pull the wool over so many people's eyes at such a high-profile event, but said if anyone could find a way to make it happen, it would be me! They were just glad I didn't get arrested.

My half term adventures continued with *more* trips to the Big Smoke to meet B*Witched, still criss-crossing London, promoting upcoming single 'Blame It on the Weatherman' at full throttle in a bid to nab a fourth chart-topper. I was back in class on Monday with a bump, trading half term tales with my few friends, Zanna, Lucy and Kathi, telling them about the BRITs and all we'd got away with. Word got around the playground. Some kids were impressed, many just called me a fucking liar. But with my new-found confidence as a result of my London adventures, I no longer sought anyone's approval.

I headed to Borehamwood, that Thursday after school, to see B*Witched at *Top of the Pops*, as their promotional slog for 'Weatherman' drew to an end. Irish dreamboats The Corrs also played, as did chic Swedish indie-poppers The Cardigans and a bunch of other acts, with Jayne Middlemiss holding the presenting reins again. We were all out in force that night: the Lairy Lot, all the Luton Girls, plus local kid Arash. (Arash grew up in Borehamwood and, like us, had a taste for pop. We'd see him there most weeks and some of the older girls took him under their wings.) B*Witched performed in the middle of the studio, with the twelve of us lining the entire front row of the 200-strong audience swaying behind them. In a few rollercoaster months I'd somehow managed to bring the two rival fan groups together in harmony. We were having the time of our lives and the band were on top of the world. Could it please just stay like this forever?

♦ ♦ ♦

Steph, Tasha, Charlotte, plus Sarah of the Luton Girls and I left our houses bright and early that Saturday to head to West London's BBC Television Centre to catch the B*Witched girls. They were performing on *Live & Kicking*, but, sadly, we were all over their 'Under 15s' age limit. The irony of being *too old* for once! Instead, we contented ourselves by perching on the kerb outside and waiting for them to come out.

We were desperate to have one final catch-up with them before they disappeared off on another ten-week tour of the

States with *NSYNC. With hindsight, if we thought us fans had a ridiculously hectic schedule, those poor B*Witched girls, like so many young pop stars, were being worked *to the bone*! In reality, their America trip would be relentless TV appearances, performances in malls and arenas, rehearsals, signings and photo shoots, as the record label tried to extract every last penny out of them before the world moved onto the next disposable group.

Also on *Live & Kicking* that morning was the legendary Cher, still turning back time and *still* in the UK, promoting her new disco single, 'Strong Enough'. TV double-act Mel and Sue completed the line-up – there to publicise their cult daytime TV show *Light Lunch* being moved to a teatime slot. Pre-*Bake Off*, they were about as famous as that woman from *Homes Under the Hammer*. It's no wonder we all turned out gay, when kids' TV in the nineties was so goddamn camp!

Annoyingly, B*Witched left without stopping, so Charlotte made calls to transatlantic airlines to blag her way into finding out their impending US-bound flight.

Bored fans waiting outside TV, radio and recording studios had a habit of leaving their mark wherever they went, using the trusty marker pens they always kept handy for autographs to graffiti walls and paving slabs. Like dogs pissing up lampposts we, too, left blots all over the landscape to mark out our territory to other fans. Notes, messages and insults were left in prime spots. Television Centre was a social hub – basically, one big Facebook fan group.

After the show Mel and Sue were chauffeur-driven out of Television Centre with exactly the level of glam you'd expect from them: in the back of a messy Ford Mondeo. To their surprise we all cheered and waved as they were driven out of the security gate and, after a bit of persuasion, told their driver to pull over onto the pavement outside the studios so they could mingle with their adoring fans. They were belly-achingly funny, hanging out with us for about twenty minutes, asking who we were there to see and looking through our tragic photo albums in amazement. It turned into a sort of Louis Theroux documentary, with them asking us in detail why we stalked pop stars and what we got up to on cold Saturday mornings on street corners. We showed them the fan graffiti on the pavement slabs beneath their feet, including the scrawls we'd just added. Then we urged them to write on it themselves.

'Come on!' Tasha pleaded. 'You'll be the first-*ever* celebrities to sign the pavement outside Television Centre!' (Or anywhere, probably.)

'Don't be *ridiculous*!' said Sue. 'We're respectable D-listers and won't entertain the idea a second more.' After three more minutes of pleading and cheering, both Mel and Sue got down onto the floor and signed their autographs on the dirty street, mere inches from BBC property. We erupted in cheers, beside ourselves that we'd convinced them to do it. Sue even did a fist pump in jubilance at her own rebelliousness, just as a fancy blacked-out Mercedes crawled out of the studio gate a few metres away.

We glanced over, Mel and Sue included, wondering who could be inside it. The back window glided down and revealed a lady underneath a shimmering, bejewelled wig, shouting hello at us, her hand giving us a royal wave out the window.

'OH MY GOD, IT'S CHER!!!' Steph screamed. We all belted over to the car, ditching Perkins and Giedroyc on the freshly vandalised pavement, gawping inquisitively at the commotion.

'Okay, fine, you've deserted us for Cher,' Sue relented. 'Understandable, really.'

'Yep. We shan't even *attempt* to compete with Cher,' Mel agreed. 'We'll be off then!' she added, as we gave them a brief wave and farewell from the midst of the Cher scrum.

We chatted sycophantically to living legend Cher for ages, extolling how much we adored her songs, her films, her outfits. And of course, how we'd got into the BRITs. She was clearly flattered and intrigued, but with hindsight probably slightly sceptical about our claims to have faked our way into the biggest music event of the year.

After running out of things to talk about (I didn't think she'd be particularly interested to hear about my GCSE mocks results), Cher waved us goodbye, rolled the window up and glided away into the glamorous boulevards of Shepherd's Bush.

With our hearts still racing from the triple whammy of Mel, Sue and Cher, Charlotte announced that her persistent but pricey calls to every airline flying from Heathrow to Jacksonville, Florida, that day had paid off: she'd conned the airline into telling her which flight B*Witched were departing on. Next stop: Heathrow, Terminal 3. We spent an hour or so with them as they hung around the check-in desk, their suitcases filled with well-worn jeans and Levi's shirts.

◆ ◆ ◆

The band may have headed stateside for a relentless couple of months, but we still had their autumn tour to look forward to. Obviously in need of front-row seats, we coordinated our plans to sleep out before they went on sale. So, one cold Friday night in March, we all made our way up to Wembley Arena with our sleeping bags, ghetto blasters and bottles of low-grade alcohol.

My memory of it is hazy, mainly because of the ingestion of a toxic mixture of various spirits all VERY carefully stolen from

Mum and Dad's booze rack in the study, draining out only a tiny amount from every bottle so they wouldn't notice.

I lied to them that I was travelling with Paul, when in reality I was heading there alone. And I had already started swigging my stolen alcohol. By the time I got on the last train of the night up to North West London I was pretty hammered, and got some casual abuse from a gang of older teenagers, who got on the train in the depths of suburbia.

Drunkenly, I trekked through the back and beyond of Wembley: past parades of glum-looking shops and through concrete underpasses. The mile-long walk had sobered me up a bit, and the hangover was kicking in, which meant I was weary by the time I got there. The others – the Lairy Lot and the twins from Luton – were in high spirits when I found them, lifting my mood immediately. We were the only ones dedicated enough to be spending the night on the tarmac. We drank, we sang, we danced. We passed around cigarettes, chatted shit and took it in turns to do the fifteen-minute freezing walk to the public loos. The alcohol was mainly consumed for its medicinal properties, as it insulated our buttocks from the cold hard ground and made the prospect of sleeping in insalubrious surroundings less alarming.

Charlotte and I were quite close by now and, with our hormones all over the shop, ended up spending half an hour fondling each other in a sleeping bag, while our confused mates sang TLC songs around us. Gemma had brought with her a cassette copy of a CD she'd imported from the States, by upcoming teen artist Britney Spears, who she and Paul kept drilling into our heads about being 'the next big thing'. She was alright; nothing special. Half the album was catchy bops, the other half *utter* shit. One track that still sticks in my mind was a grotesquely sweet ballad called 'E-mail My Heart'. Britters provided more insight into this futuristic world masterpiece during an interview to promote the album, revealing how 'Everyone has been doing e-mails... so everyone can relate to that song.' Hmm... I was dubious about it catching on. (This 'Britney' girl, I mean.)

I managed an hour's sleep before dawn broke on the concrete paradise beside Wembley Arena. Some fans arrived at first light to stand behind us, and the mess we'd made, for the final painful hours. At 9 a.m. the little hatch opened, bank notes and coins were dumped through the kiosk and our Block A, Row A tickets were printed off and placed in our eager palms. We still had six months till the actual night, but we knew it would be worth it. Now, to go home and sleep off this hangover!

Other outings that month included a spontaneous Sunday night trip down to Brighton to see Steps' first arena tour and meeting them at their Brighton hotel afterwards (just 'cos we could, really) and a run-in with Westside (still not called Westlife) on the South Bank one late afternoon with Tasha and Steph, Like five Ken dolls in matching black attire, Westside were delighted that we recognised them despite not having released a single yet. We chatted to them about Ireland, our B*Witched obsession, and what they were doing for St Patrick's Day, before they giddily jumped in their car back to their hotel.

I took another trip up to the outskirts of Luton for a debauched party. My *Top of the Pops* friend Emma was turning eighteen. It was a similar affair to Laura's, except I got too drunk on Archers and Lemonade (such a lad!) and was looked after at the bar by Emma's lovely mum until I was fit enough to re-join the others on the dance floor. I got a snog from a random girl again as well. After a slow start I was becoming quite the lothario in my final weeks of school. It still wasn't really floating my boat, but the kissing was fun, as was getting a reputation for being a total stud muffin.

◆ ◆ ◆

My loyal paternal chauffeur picked me up that drizzly morning from outer Luton so I didn't have to catch three buses and two trains back to Ottershaw. After a Sunday spent disguising my hangover at home, and a gloomy Monday dodging footballs being kicked at my head back in the playground, I spent most of that evening at home on the phone to my new BFF, Gemma. She'd been hanging out with All Saints all day at Pineapple Studios (yeah, the Louie Spence place) while they rehearsed for their first-ever world tour, playing glamorous venues such as Plymouth Pavilions and Wolverhampton Civic Hall. Gemma, Charlotte and Paul had been following All Saints around since their early days in 1997 and I'd heard many stories about their times spent with them. I'd never met the band, but was curious about their no-nonsense ladette image.

Gemma and I would chat total crap for hours, back in the days when an hour-long call from a landline to a mobile cost about £87. Needless to say, Mr and Mrs McLean, who were paying the bills, were none too happy about my embracing the white heat of mobile technology. They'd get out the highlighter pens every time the dreaded BT bill arrived and spend an evening going through every line, striking off mine and Anja's calls in contrasting neon shades of shame.

Gemma was chatting on the phone to me when All Saints finally finished rehearsals, having perfected jiggling their hips in combat trousers.

'Who's on the phone, Gem?' I could hear Natalie Appleton asking in the background.

'It's my friend.'

'BOY OR GIRL?' one of them shouted.

'Boy,' Gemma answered, coyly.

'OOOOOOOOOH, Gemma's got a boyfriend! You little minx!' Mel Blatt bellowed.

By now, all the Saints were joining in and excited that Gemma, their superfan who they'd never once seen with or talk about a guy, had a stud in her life.

'What's his name, Gem?'

'Malcolm.'

'Oh God,' I muttered, secretly dreading what they would shout next, but loving living vicariously through a phone call.

'Oooooh, Malcolm! Gemma's loverboy!' All of them were hyper after a day spent dancing in a tiny room. 'Give me the phone, Gem.' (giggling and rustling noise) 'Hiiiiii Malcolm, this is Natalie!' I laughed nervously at her sultry voice whispering through the handset. Natalie, the band's bottle blonde, fielded questions from the other band members, before asking, 'Why aren't you here?!!'

'Ummm, Gemma didn't invite me,' I stammered.

'How fucking rude! Right – we wanna see you here tomorrow. No excuses, Malcolm!'

'Well, I've got school tomorrow. I can come after,' my teenage voice squeaked.

At that moment, my beloved mum entered my bedroom, holding a basket of clean pants, declaring she was about to serve dinner. I responded with a stern 'PISS OFF' expression. I did *not* want her ruining this moment!

'How old are you? Fifteen?! Oh my God, Malcolm's Gemma's toy boy!' I could hear Gemma laughing in the background. 'Okay, well, get here tomorrow. We want to meet you. We're all going for drinks now, talk to you later!'

The phone cut dead.

I could already tell that the Appleton sisters and I were destined to share Nokia ringtones.

I packed my bag, ready to head into town after school the next day, and wondered if they'd even remember anything about me then.

After a relatively routine day at school (bullying punctuated by French and RE), I headed to London, hanging out with Gemma and co. on the pavement outside Pineapple Studios, looking like Adidas-clad extras from *Oliver Twist*.

When they eventually appeared at the top of the studio steps, I was really excited. All Saints weren't my favourite band, but hanging out with them was a damn sight more exciting than sitting at home in Ottershaw while Mum and Anja watched *Ricki Lake*.

The band tottered precariously down the stone steps, their trademark combats impeding their footing. Familiar hellos were given to the others around me. A couple of the Saints were grinning, their eyes cautiously giving me a once-over, checking out my own fabulous camouflage combat ensemble, no doubt. 'So, this is Malcolm?' Shaznay giggled. 'Gemma's toy boy. Oh my God, you're so cute! And skinny!' Natalie chimed. They were clearly delighted to meet an Adonis such as myself.

The Saints were forthright with everyone:

'Charlotte, I've told you before, I fucking love those patchwork jeans!'

'Paul, you look tired. Been up all night, babe?'

'Yeah, wanking probably!!!'

Poor Paul... even All Saints were ripping the shit out of him. They just said whatever they felt like, unlike the more polite and restrained members of Eternal and B*Witched. All Saints were the Mean Girls of pop – in a good way.

At one point Natalie quipped, 'Are you sure you're not gay, Malcolm? You're a bit too *nice*. Are you man enough for Gem?'

I responded with an awkward laugh and an embarrassed 'of course not!'

I was far more concerned about all these rumours that I was Gemma's boyfriend. Charlotte and Paul were obviously green with envy that our 'relationship status' was the hottest gossip that day.

As the band lugged their own equipment into the back of their people carrier, Mel Blatt made a jibe about Gemma and Charlotte 'always cheating on them with the Spice Girls'. Little did she know we were spreading it about with anyone who'd had a Top 40 hit in the past six months.

◆ ◆ ◆

The Easter holidays usually brought a welcome relief from school, but I now spent so many evenings in London anyway that being off school didn't give me the same elation it used to. I was entering the final stretch. It was a matter of weeks till it was all over (after the final, inconvenient matter of GCSE exams). My pocket money was running low too, so I'd started bunking trains to economise. I'd hide in the toilet, paranoid every time someone knocked on the door.

Conor was flying over for a week during the Easter break. But our interests were leading us in different directions: he was into politics, I was still into pop stars. He was into Tony Blair, I was into Toni Braxton. He'd chat about Gerry Adams, I thought he'd just got Ginger and Posh Spice mixed up – he certainly wouldn't fit in with my new crew.

Other than the usual trips to the cinema in Woking, and shopping for posters in Athena and crap that we didn't need in The Gadget Shop, we found common ground by attending the Capital FM London Awards that Wednesday afternoon at a swanky hotel in a posh part of town where you felt like an extra in a Richard Curtis film.

Well, I say we went to the awards, we actually waited outside the entrance, behind the barriers, along with a hundred or so pop fans and paparazzi. It was less exciting than most of my *Top of the Pops* exploits – I really wasn't used to waiting *outside* awards shows now – it felt like a step back after the BRITs, but it was something to do.

We saw some members of Boyzone, Another Level, an Eternal-esque new girl band called Fierce, and Kate Winslet – still riding the post-*Titanic* wave. I was ecstatic when Easther and Vernie of Eternal arrived and Conor and I got to chat to them briefly on the red carpet, despite having booted my beloved Kelle out the group – first loves run deep. It was Conor's first experience of meeting pop stars and, although enjoying the moment as a one-time Eternal fan, I could tell it wasn't quite his cup of tea.

A ubiquitous blacked-out Mercedes pulled up, and, as we prepared ourselves for another D-lister milking their red carpet moment, a strawberry blonde woman stepped out. The lady was wearing the shit out of a powder blue power suit, with a sizeable grin sitting beneath oversized sunglasses. That grin... It was definitely lacking some lippy, but the smile was simply unmistakable. 'GERIIIIII!' The crowd erupted into mass hysteria.

The Artist Formerly Known As Ginger had been almost completely off-radar since walking out on the band ten months ago, despite still being one of the most talked-about women on the planet. She had a bizarre cult status. Everyone was screaming, begging her to prove that she was still here, still alive. I was thrilled to see Geri taking her first steps out of her ginger cocoon. She was bundled inside and didn't surface again that day.

Conor and I trundled home, still buzzing, on the train back to Surrey. I left him playing with Sophie for a bit while I called up Gemma and Paul to report back on the Geri sighting, knowing that the news would spread through our friendship group like wildfire. In the first half of 1999, Spice Girl sightings were really quite rare (none of them had even attended the BRIT Awards we'd sneaked into a few weeks earlier) and, at that point, seeing Geri was the *ultimate* spot. The Lairy Lot were buzzing that she was back from obscurity and, with speculation rife in the tabloids, we wondered if she was preparing to make an attack on the pop charts once more.

The next day I forced Conor out the house for a day of trekking around Surrey. Not in my neck of the woods; after a disagreement (with me agreeing to go shopping with him all day in Guildford the next day and revisiting some of his favourite old Surrey hangouts), Conor reluctantly promised to accompany me to Purley, south of Croydon, to traipse round suburban houses on the hunt for Easther and Vernie from Eternal. We knocked on the doors of several addresses, given to me by some Boyzone fans, but none of the leads led us to the Bennetts. Conor was not impressed. I conceded and spent the rest of his trip being a better friend.

♦ ♦ ♦

After Conor left, I skulked back into school on Monday, dragging my feet every step of the way to registration. I had already coordinated my return to the world of All Saints, meeting Paul, Gemma and Charlotte after work to see their beloved baggy-trousered babes. I spent three evenings that week up at studios in Covent Garden and bleak Bermondsey industrial estates with my best friends (and the sassy Saints). We larked around with them and their crew, going shopping or trading gossip from the pop world whenever they'd come out and chat to us. I loved their hilarious, catty energy. Each day I was surprised at their openness and willingness to let us kid fans into their gang.

One afternoon, after rehearsals, we accompanied them to a small Covent Garden pharmacy, where the All Saints girls tried on make-up while Mel, their joint-lead singer, was pushed by the others to ask the glamorous lady behind the counter for a big box of tampons.

'We're going on tour and we need a big box – no, the *entire* box, pleasssse!' We hovered behind, squirming with the other Saints, during this unusual transaction, which seemed to go on forever. 'No, not these. I need HEAVY FLOW.'

'*Stop it*. You're doing this on purpose!' Shaznay howled.

'What kind of bus are you gonna have for your tour?' Gemma asked Nicole, as we walked back from the chemist's.

'I dunno, Gem!' Nicole quipped, 'A really fucking great one.'

'The Spice Girls had an enormous silver one for their tour. Omigod, it was sooooo cool!' Gemma continued in a high-pitched tone.

'Well, *obviously*, we're gonna have a better one than them,' Mel snapped.

We all laughed. 'Even Steps had a flashy gold one,' I teased.

'Look, Malcolm,' Natalie barked in her sultry Canadian twang, 'we're going to have an all-singing, all-dancing, state-of-the-art fucking bus, alright? Definitely better than Steps!'

After the band headed home, as it was a Thursday and we'd forked out for day travelcards anyway, we jumped on the train to *Top of the Pops* for some more complimentary entertainment. We managed to get in, despite the sea of hormonal Backstreet

Boys fans scrounging for tickets as well. Inside, Gemma and I positioned ourselves directly behind the US boy band titans during their premiere performance of new track 'I Want It That Way' on the Floor Stage. That song has stood the test of time in a way that their backwards caps and bandanas thankfully haven't. Catatonia, Busta Rhymes, Kula Shaker and Reef brought an edgier touch to the line-up, and, looking back, that shows just how diverse the charts used to be, week in, week out.

With All Saints' final rehearsals now finished, Gemma and Charlotte decided we should all wave them off on their tour bus. The problem was, we didn't know where they were leaving from. So, Charlotte did what she does best, and made some phone calls (in her best grown-up voice) to London Records to extract information on the departure location. 'Kings Cross Train Station, York Way. Sunday 9 a.m.,' said a naïve and overly helpful young secretary on the other end of the line.

When Charlotte, Gemma and I rendezvoused at a dirty but peaceful King's Cross that Sunday morning there were some tourist bus tours unloading – fanny packs aplenty – but no flashy coach, as assured. Still the epicentre of the London club scene back then, bleary-eyed ravers stumbled past us on their way back from grimy superclubs up the road. The three of us sat on the pavement by the side of the station, bored out of our minds, playing I Spy. Charlotte rang the number of the restaurant opposite, making ridiculous enquiries, her huge handset put on speakerphone, to provide a few minutes of entertainment.

Eventually we walked up and down the road to enquire with the drivers of the coaches. Some of them, although pretty fancy, were clearly from continental Europe and not about to drive All Saints on a provincial theatre tour of the UK. Charlotte suggested we approach a particularly scummy one. 'Don't be ridiculous!' Gemma scorned. 'Yes, I'm driving All Saints,' the mulletted driver politely replied. A two-minute laughing fit followed before we could even string a sentence together. *This?* This dingy rail replacement coach? It was too good. '*Wait* till they see it!!!' we squealed, oozing schadenfreude.

After denting the poor man's ego, we tapped on the door again and told the driver we were dancers for the band. 'Oh right, okay – hop on!' We climbed aboard the hunk of junk, enthusiastically acting out to the driver our supposed routines for their hit songs, while we christened the toilet and even tucked into the free Pringles and soft drinks from the 'snack area'. Teenagers have *no* shame.

The girls' burly, bald tour manager was, unfortunately, the first to arrive on the bus. After ten seconds of stunned shock (and us starting to wonder if we'd gone too far) he did see the funny side, but told us to piss off and take our rubbish with us. We stepped off as the band was arriving, suitcases of tampons in hand. The All Saints girls thought it a great prank, although they were shaken by the clapped-out tin on wheels parked before them.

'What the fuck is THAT?' Nicole asked, peering over her sunglasses.

'That's your tour bus,' replied Charlotte.

'Are you *kidding* me?' wailed Natalie. 'Even STEPS had a big bloody gold one!!!'

They left for the tour on their Bus of Dreams. I'd be seeing them again in a few weeks when they rolled back into town for their final dates in Shepherd's Bush. I definitely didn't need another band to obsess over, but was happy they filled a void left by my favourite pop stars, and their matey behaviour came closer to breaking down the fan/star dichotomy than I'd ever experienced before.

◆ ◆ ◆

In the fickle world of late-nineties pop the record labels were petrified that, if a band wasn't getting column inches or drip-feeding fans with singles and tours, they'd quickly turn into tomorrow's charity shop fodder. Even the Spice Girls. That spring, their management arranged a couple of Christmas tour dates for their loyal fans to look forward to. The fact they announced the select few dates just a couple of days before Geri unveiled her much-anticipated debut solo single, 'Look at Me', was probably just a coincidence.

Gemma worked out a way of us experiencing both: we would have to sleep out at Earl's Court for front-row Spice tickets the night before they went on sale. We'd take a portable radio with us so that we could hear Geri's single's world exclusive first play at 8.20 a.m., then jump on the rush-hour Tube across London to see the ginger one herself as she departed Radio 1's studios. Phew! The plan worked wonderfully. We obviously omitted to tell Geri where we were when we heard 'Look at Me' come over the airwaves.

The Shirley Bassey-esque single was a bold request for attention from someone who knew that this, her debut single, was a make-or-break moment. Geri's fans wanted her to prove she could go it alone; the tabloids were desperate for a flop. It was a bit too 'out there' to get much airplay, and peaked at Number 2. Geri admitted she was devastated. It clearly meant everything to her. Personally, I think that's a pretty impressive feat for a camp-as-tits narcissists' anthem. Well done, Ginge!

♦ ♦ ♦

May – the final month of school – finally arrived, and not a moment too soon. I'd outgrown the playground. Get ready, world! Mum and Dad let me out of solitary revision confinement for a day of fun at Shepherd's Bush Empire, seeing the raucous All Saints girls. We were first in line on the steps of the venue for the standing gig, where we remained all day, whiling away the hours listening to my boombox and recounting sketches from our current obsession, TV show *Smack the Pony*.

We only left the queue for toilet breaks and to run over and chat to All Saints as they arrived throughout the day. Nicole from the band was still letting off steam about the false start to their first-ever tour. Turned out their shoddy tour bus broke down barely an hour after leaving us for North Wales, and they were stranded on the hard shoulder of the M1 for hours, waiting for a replacement! We couldn't hold back the laughter. 'We knew you bastards would find that funny,' she said, her smile returning.

There were celebrity boyfriends and showbiz pals galore inside the little theatre and we met a beaming Baby Spice on the balcony, buzzing to see her mates (and faux rivals) on stage. The day had been perfect: random pop adventures in some far-flung corner of London with my best friends.

For the next few weeks I had to spend every hour after school holed up in my bedroom, buried under a pile of textbooks, as well as filling up sketchbooks for my final art project. I was on the home straight now, but I hated missing out on fun.

It was during this time that a great split divided our group: Paul, Gemma and I on one side, Charlotte, Tasha and Steph on the other. From what I can remember, a trivial disagreement over who'd be getting a lift to Heathrow one Saturday morning escalated into a full-blown slanging match. No more adventures in Steph's car or laughs with us all. Overnight, my gang was torn apart.

9

I Quit

There was only one present I wanted for my sixteenth birthday. After weeks of desperately pleading with Mum and Dad they finally agreed to buy me the one thing I wanted more than anything else in the world: a mobile phone. With a contract. In Dad's name.

It was, with hindsight, a *grave* mistake on their part and would trigger two years of fiery family rows and hundreds of pounds' worth of calls, but at the time, thanks to my persuasive arguments, they thought it a reasonable gift. I also had to agree to getting a summer job. Only four of my friends had mobile phones, and only Steph, who was *loads* older and in full-time boring office work, could afford the luxurious Nokia 5110 Dad agreed to buy me – the late-nineties equivalent of a sports car with a pretty bow on it for my Sweet Sixteen.

We had to drive down two motorways to glamorous Hounslow to acquire it, as that was the nearest Carphone Warehouse, and the only place I could get it on Vodafone: the same network as Dad. (As if I'd actually be calling him, other than to ask 'Can you pick me up from *Top of the Pops*?') In Ye Olden Days of telecommunications if you weren't on the same mobile network as someone, and you called them for a chat (even off-peak), you then had to re-mortgage your house when the bill arrived, making sure you *never* made that error again. He allowed me to get one official Nokia cover (for the obscene sum of fifteen quid), so I picked the Irish flag design, in tribute to my favourite girl band.

Having someone splash out on a mobile phone the size and weight of a concrete brick, with a massive aerial sticking out the top, doesn't sound like a huge indulgence, but believe me, in May 1999 I was the luckiest teenager in all of Surrey to be given such a stylish portable communications device. Not only was this the most beautiful handset money could buy, it was my lifeline to the outer-world. The pop world. It changed *everything*.

That night, Zanna and I were hitting the town. A girl from school's parents were away, and half our school year saw it as an opportunity for some debauchery in Walton-on-Thames. It wasn't what either of us wanted to be doing, but we had no other offers and I was gagging to show off my new phone. Someone even shouted, 'Ooh, look at you! Wow, is that a Nokia? *Fancy*!' I felt so flash. I was nervous about going because I wasn't actually invited and had never been to a proper house party with school people before.

The party was out of hand by the time we arrived. Kate – the geeky, not particularly popular girl whose parents' house was being wrecked by hundreds of adolescents – was clearly freaking out, and in front of what felt like *everyone* from our year, screamed, 'Why are YOU here, Malcolm?? I didn't even invite you. Fuck *off*, out of my house!'

Time stood still for a brief moment and, just before the ground swallowed me up entirely, Zanna grabbed my arm, snapping, 'Come on, let's go. This is the shittest party ever! I hope you get grounded for getting your house trashed.'

This tense standoff was interrupted by a knock on the door: it was two policemen, shouting to everyone that they were breaking up the party and searching for underage drinkers. Zanna and I looked at each other and bolted in the other direction, out the patio doors, scaling a number of garden fences, before making it out to the street, unscathed. After the excitement died down, and we were sure no coppers were chasing us, we cracked open the drinks we'd bought for the party and got drunk on a street corner in Walton-on-Thames, before getting picked up and both of us doing the desperately pointless act of trying to act sober in my dad's car after a party. He was just pleased I hadn't lost my phone already. Slurring, I promised to keep my side of the bargain and get a job after my birthday.

◆ ◆ ◆

I turned sixteen on my last ever day of school: 14 May 1999. I'd made it out alive, and with only slight mental scarring.

Zanna and I spent much of the day avoiding girls bugging everyone with crappy notebooks, where you have to write fake nice things about their owner. Overemotional outpourings in coloured gel pens about how you'll keep in touch until you're grey and old (then immediately ghost them until they try and add you on Facebook a decade later). And getting messages scrawled on your white shirt by all the hot people you fancied for five years and want to keep a piece of them in your parents loft forever? No, that wasn't our style.

Zanna and I were the Romy and Michele of our school. The Muriel and Rhonda. The cast-aside misfits who are actually way cooler than the popular kids. At least we thought so. In reality, we were probably more like Tom and Linda from *Gimme Gimme Gimme*. With no desire to be sentimental, we fled as soon as the last bell rang, getting the bus into Woking to get my ears pierced and buy some Goth clothes for Zanna. We were extremely rebellious like that. And we'd transitioned to proper grown-ups now.

And just like real adults, there we were – drinking milkshakes in the cafeteria of the Peacocks Shopping Centre with a group of pensioners and some nasty kids throwing food at each other, feeling on top of the world! My ear lobes were stinging from the savage firearm they'd used in the Italian barber's to pierce them, but at least it was only £3 per ear. As my holes were brand new, I was told to wear the big ugly starter studs for the first few weeks, although Zanna made it perfectly clear she wouldn't be seen dead with me at any social event if I didn't risk infection by changing them to some small Elizabeth Duke hoops from Argos. That was the look I wanted anyway – generic Home Counties rebel bad boy and possible member of Five – so I changed them that evening, as well as my first-ever 'Sun-In' session in the bathroom at home. After only twenty-eight bleaches and severe burns under the hairdryer, I was almost strawberry blonde! *Screw you, Mum and Dad, I can do what I like now and you can't stop me!* I just needed a job now to fund my continued makeovers and pop-stalker habit.

◆ ◆ ◆

As part of the deal for my mobile phone I had to miss the B*Witched book signing in London the day after my birthday, in favour of revising for my exams. I would have been annoyed about this at *any* time, but with the band back for only a few days before touring the US *again* for three months, this was probably my only chance of seeing them.

At the exact time of the signing I was hurling piles of books around my room and having a cry, if I remember correctly. The amount of revision I got done that weekend was practically non-existent too, making it all the more painful that I missed seeing the girls just to sit, holed up in my room for two days, miserably staring in a trance at the same two pages of a science textbook as if it were a Magic Eye picture.

Gemma rang me that afternoon to update me on the signing, and to confirm that she'd managed to get the details of their flight from Heathrow to the US. Having been locked away in my bedroom all weekend, I'd convinced Dad I'd worked hard enough to earn a little reward. He drove me to the terminal, where I had a hug with all four B*Witched girls, before mooching round the shops, discussing neck pillows and Accessorize scarves. We waved them off, promised we'd fax them every day, and assured them we'd be waiting when they jetted back, a couple of months later.

True to my word, I went onto 'Ask Jeeves' every day to get the fax number of that night's venue and sent them a detailed description of our groupie antics. They never replied, so I didn't know if they ever got them. Just to be sure, I'd send the same fax several days in a row.

After waving B*Witched off at the airport, I decided to ignore my promise to Dad that I'd go straight home and revise. Instead, Gemma, Paul and I headed to Elstree to watch that evening's *Top of the Pops*.

Jamiroquai were playing their funk-inspired hit, 'Canned Heat'. I wasn't usually into pop music sung by stubbly blokes who loved sports cars, but this guy sang like a diva from the seventies, so we loved it (even though he performed in a beige fleece). Tatyana Ali (recent B*Witched tour-mate and Will Smith's baby sister in *Fresh Prince*) was also performing, along with comedy pop act Cartoons (a low-rent version of Aqua, in more ridiculous outfits) and a washed-up Gary Barlow. It was a run-of-the-mill line-up that Thursday.

Post-Take That, poor Gazza was on his way down by 1999. After massive success with his first solo album a couple of years earlier, his current reinvention, with snoozy elevator dance music, was pretty ill-advised. The tinny single 'Stronger' limped in at Number 16, and the album didn't even make the Top 30. He looked like a broken man on stage that night. Robbie Williams, now on top of the world, had pulled the rug from under him, blaming Gary for his departure, and the public had taken Rob's side. Perhaps he'd bounce back into pop one day...

◆ ◆ ◆

A few days after my sixteenth birthday I was elated to score an interview at Woking's premier American diner, McDonald's. I felt like things were really starting to happen for me: I had a career.

Upon arrival at the interview the depressed-looking shift manager ran me through a bunch of mundane questions, at a table next to the ball pit area full of screaming kids. We whizzed through them, with me throwing cringeworthy business jargon at him every few sentences that even David Brent would flinch at.

Reaching the end of the interview, he asked, 'So, do you have any questions for me?'

'Yes, actually!' I said, feeling high on life. 'When do I start?!'

'Umm. Well, you haven't got the job yet.' (I immediately wished the earth had swallowed me up.) 'But, we haven't had any applications in weeks and we're desperate for staff, so you start tomorrow, in the kitchen.'

'THANK YOU!' I screeched. 'You won't regret it!'

The next day, he regretted it – but probably not as much as I did. I turned up for work and, after filling out a bunch of forms, got changed downstairs, spending ten minutes covering up my magnificent new earrings with bright blue plasters. Turns out it's actually quite hard to stick tape successfully over hoops in ear lobes. I felt like a total dick, but I'd cleared it with the manager the day before so this was just going to be my working look for the foreseeable future. I also wasn't happy about the hair net they forced me to wear. Or having to clean out the inside of the scalding hot fryers and flip greasy burgers, particularly as a faddy teenage vegetarian.

It's a means to an end, I convinced myself. Money meant train tickets to London.

The manager that day paced up and down, scowling at me. After just twenty-five totally-hellish minutes flipping bubbling pink cow patties I was summoned to her office by the kitchen supervisor. *Okay, this isn't great*, I thought to myself.

I sheepishly made my way to a dingy back room full of ring binders and a computer running MS-DOS. She condescendingly told me that I had to remove my earrings or I wouldn't be allowed to stay working there. *How dare she!* I stared angrily back at her.

'I'm sorry, these earrings are a *part of me*. I'll find somewhere else to work where I *can* wear them, thanks!'

So I yanked off my already-greasy apron and released my luscious locks from that ugly hair net in the middle of her office and threw them in the bin. I marched downstairs and gleefully ripped off my plasters, only to find that one had already dropped off in my extremely brief stint in the kitchen. It looked like my career was over when it had only just begun.

'Hi, Mum? Can you pick me up?'

◆ ◆ ◆

I got home from McDonald's and turned on the radio defiantly. Dr Fox announced that Geri would be doing her first-ever live show at G-A-Y in Soho. The gig, at the Astoria, would also be the launch party for her debut album, *Schizophonic*. The world would be watching... the Spice Girls were the biggest band on the planet, and by ditching them, Geri had become the most talked about woman in showbiz. I knew I had to go. Sixteen-year-old me would be witnessing history. Ginger Spice had always been my favourite anyway, and now she no longer had the others to temper her overblown campness, she'd be *even* better!

This would be the start of something mega – a long, glittering career as a world-class solo artist (well, what were we to know at the time?). Out the way, Madonna! Shift over, Cher! Miss Halliwell was about to take over the *world*... again. I phoned Gemma to divulge the exciting news.

'Oh my Godddd! Whennnn?!' she shrieked.

'A week on Saturday – 5 June.'

'Oh... I'm busy that night, got a family party I have to go to. Well, we'll just have to miss it and see her soon,' Gemma said, laying down the law.

'Erm... well, I can still go,' I replied, wincing at the handset.

'With who?' she mocked. 'You don't have anyone else! You're gonna have to miss it. And it's at a gay club.'

'I'll ask someone at school, one of the girls will come with me,' I retorted, not wanting to rock the boat, but deadly serious about not missing this.

'Fine. Whatever. I have to go. Bye.'

There was fear in my mind though. For years everyone at school had called me gay, but I'd shrugged off their slurs and told myself I wasn't. Now I would be actually stepping *inside* a gay club. What would happen? What if it opened up a Pandora's box? What if someone from school saw me?

My imminent GCSEs were also posing a bit of a problem. Geri really hadn't thought about my revision when she planned all this. I'd still not forgiven Mum and Dad for the unimaginable trauma of missing the B*Witched book signing a few weeks before. I'd have to come up with a really convincing alibi so they would think I'd been diligently studying.

I also needed to find a substitute for Gemma, one willing to join me on a massive bender in London, in the middle of our exams, at a gay club. Luckily I knew one friend who had a similarly blasé attitude towards qualifications and a penchant for the glamorous nightspots of Guildford.

Lucy had been in my class since Year Seven. She had seen me transition from prepubescent schoolboy to the fully grown man I thought I had become, with my newly pierced ears and recently home-bleached hair. Along with a couple of the other girls from our class, we'd done all the usual exotic teenage excursions: cinema dates and shopping trips to River Island. Lucy was always up for a laugh, so was bound to relish the opportunity to literally smell Geri Halliwell's sweat.

We both had to tell white lies to our parents in order to be able to go. She told hers she was at my house having a video night and revising. I told mine I was going to a Geri concert in the afternoon (a matinee? I obviously thought my parents lived under a rock), then staying at Lucy's to do some revision. As long as we said the word 'revision' enough times they were bound to believe us.

♦ ♦ ♦

I stuck my head out of the train as we pulled into Hersham. 'Lucy, where are you?' I yelled, desperate for her to see me so that we could get this party started. Lucy ran down the platform and jumped aboard, just as it was about to leave, slamming the clanging door behind her. The excitement of seeing Geri was diluted each time I remembered it was at a gay club – I was anxious about entering a world I desperately told myself I wasn't part of. We walked through the scummy train carriages into First Class, thinking we were so rebellious. Lucy lit a fag and we took alternate swigs on a bottle of Smirnoff Ice, getting high on a heady mix of sugar and 4 per cent alcohol. I read out the letter I had lovingly composed for Geri. It was an introduction to everything about me – basically, 'You don't know me yet, but this is a polite heads-up, you're going to be seeing me *everywhere*. Love Mal.' Gripping stuff! What I didn't realise at that point was that there would be a couple of thousand other effeminate teenage boys also desperate for her attention that night.

We hopped on the Tube to Tottenham Court Road, the landing point for the Astoria on Charing Cross Road. As we emerged from the station, that sunny Saturday afternoon in 1999, we were faced with a barrage of shoppers ambling around, totally unaware that in a few minutes' time I would be face to face with one of the world's most famous women. Towering over us were the huge white letters spelling 'CENTRE POINT'. In that moment, it felt to Lucy and me like the centre of the universe.

The Astoria was a faded old beauty. Her once-ornate 1920s façade was grimy and crumbling, and I would soon discover that the interior of the once grand ballroom had been given several coats of thick black paint. The floor was sticky, the toilets left a lot to be desired, but she had soul. Squashed between a Soho sex shop and a road junction at the wrong end of Oxford Street, the home of G-A-Y was later demolished to make way for Crossrail.

As we approached the venue what did we see? Bloody fans! All over the pavement, the steps of the venue, the alleyways around it. They couldn't all be waiting for Geri as well, could they? These bitches weren't real fans like me, actually hoping to meet her and be best friends, were they? They all were. Damn! I was going to have to scream pretty loud to make sure my voice was heard.

Nervously, Lucy asked one of them if 'She' was inside. Apparently she was sound-checking. I couldn't believe it, Geri was actually inside this very building. We had to wait twenty minutes for her to come out. I'd been waiting for this moment for over a year, since the day she hung up her Union Jack dress and stormed out of the band. But those twenty minutes felt like FOREVER.

Finally, a blacked-out Mercedes pulled up. Her black-suited driver opened the rear door and waited for his hallowed passenger to turn up. The front doors of the Astoria burst open and, like a *Stars in Their Eyes* reveal, out strolled Geri. Entourage: check. PA: check. Harry the Shih Tzu: check. This was a woman who knew how to be an international superstar cliché. She glided down the stairs while a bunch of stunned shoppers gawped with their M&S carrier bags, unable to believe their eyes. Along with all the other superfans, I screamed and waved my arms, desperate to catch her eye and shove mementos into her hand to sign.

She pushed her way through the scrum of fans, accepting letters and gifts with smiles and pleasantries, eventually making it down to me. I thrust my letter in her face, and she responded with a husky smoker's 'Thank you'. And she was gone. It was a brief moment, but I had actually made contact with Geri.

The fans let out one final cheer as she slid into the car and disappeared into the Saturday afternoon traffic on Charing Cross Road.

◆ ◆ ◆

Back to reality with a bump: there were still hours till the gig even started. We didn't even have tickets. We were under eighteen too, so entry was by no means guaranteed. Luckily, we got squished up against a suave Italian guy in his twenties and his sarcastic British boyfriend, who'd clearly been dragged along kicking and screaming. We struck up conversation and quickly all bonded over cigarettes and Geri.

They shed some light on the mysterious ticketing situation too. Apparently, if you wanted to get into the venue in the first half-hour you had to have a special queue jump ticket. Shit! This was news to us. And apparently only three gay bars in Soho sold them. 'A man with a special envelope will drop off a limited number of tickets at each bar and if you're very lucky, you'll get to buy one,' they told us. What the hell was this secret underworld of the gay pop scene? If we didn't get one we'd be nowhere near the front and that would be catastrophic to my plan of waving my banner inches away from Geri's face.

We decided we'd leave Lucy and Suave Italian on the steps outside The Astoria, and Sarcastic Brit would escort me to one of the bars, where we'd pick up these elusive queue-jump tickets. Even with all the time I'd spent in London I had no idea where we were going. I felt strangely nervous as he marched me down Old Compton Street, the epicentre of Gay London, for the first time ever, laughing and telling me to 'just relax'. *Hello! I'm about to walk into a bar, where gay men will be undressing me with their eyes – of course I can't relax!* Old Compton Street had a strange atmosphere. It was only a few weeks since one of the gay bars on the street, the Admiral Duncan, had been the scene of a horrific nail bomb attack. I suddenly felt apprehensive and out of my depth, as the reality of my situation struck home.

The first bar we tried was so busy we could barely get in the door. He said it wasn't even worth trying, so we headed to Ku-Bar on Charing Cross Road instead. It was so dark when we stepped inside, my eyes took an eternity to adjust. It reeked of Silk Cut and stale Carling, and was also heaving.

At the time I felt like every man would be eyeing me up and down, trying to mate with me or any young man with a pulse. In reality, I think they were just having a few pints on a Saturday afternoon and didn't notice the awkward-looking, badly dressed teenager.

Sarcastic Brit could sense I was shit scared so he grabbed my hand. I didn't try and let go. I suddenly felt much more at ease. We waited in line, snaking up a pitch-black staircase to the dingy toilets and back, with pumping generic Europop blasting out the speakers above all the chatter around us. After a long thirty minutes, we got the four tickets we desperately needed. We excitedly ran back to the Astoria, *still* hand-in-hand to reassure me that I was safe. I might have felt like an adult when I boarded the train in Surrey, but making my way through crowds of gay guys in Soho I realised I was still just a kid, not ready for this new grown-up world yet. The others laughed about it when we got back to the queue for the club – 'What?!! I would've got lost if he'd let go of my hand in there!'

◆ ◆ ◆

Just before the club opened we were accosted by a drag queen clutching a clipboard, asking clubbers to sign a petition to repeal

'Section 28'. I had absolutely no idea what they were talking about (and how it had anything to do with us). Lucy and I responded with gormless expressions, our eyes darting from side to side. In a Babs-Cabs-esque *League of Gentlemen* voice, the drag queen growled at us, 'If you don't know what it is yet, darlins', you *will*. Just sign it.'

'I think it's something to do with gay rights,' I whispered to Lucy – a groundbreaking statement if ever there was one. Years later, I would realise just how enormously this bastard law DID affect me. We nervously signed their petition, worrying if doing so could somehow be traced back to us in leafy Surrey.

We had our IDs (dog-eared fake birth certificates) as emergency backup in case we were asked our ages by the bouncers. However, when the doors flung open, after only a frisk and bag-check, a flirty woman called Karen that I can only describe as a Home Counties Lolo Ferrari ripped off our ticket stubs and ushered us in with a wink and a warm 'Welcome, kids!' Next, some flirty young twinks, caked in a can of glitter each, placed glow sticks and cheap whistles around our necks with all the fanfare of an Olympic medal ceremony. We belted down the grimy stairs and across the dance floor like Sally Gunnell on speed, just in time to grab a place centre stage. *The ultimate position!* We were actually inside Geri's first gig at the very front. This was the stuff that pop dreams were made of.

The biggest shocker for Lucy came in the first half-hour. 'I can't believe it,' she yelled, shaking her head, her eyes agog, 'The men are the *first* ones on the dance floor? I have *never* seen this in Guildford! If only the stupid straight boys back home were as confident as this lot. It'd be *way* more fun!'

I'd never seen so many grown men looking like they'd raided Emma Bunton's shoe cupboard. We stayed there at the front, bopping to the pulsating music in the packed sea of people all night. The chorus of whistles grew louder with every floor filler. The music was a never-ending mix of tinny nineties pop remixes and huge camp classics. 'Like a Prayer', 'Love in the First Degree', 'It's Raining Men' – all the old clichés, along with more current camp anthems like Cher's 'Believe' and Ultra Naté's 'Free', which nearly brought the roof down. Hands were in the air, vocal chords stretched. The whistles seemed to act as a vote of approval. If the next song up was shit, you'd know it was a stinker by the silence. If it hit the spot, you'd have to plug up your ears to avoid tinnitus for a week.

Charlotte, my former best friend-turned-arch nemesis, was there with a gay friend of hers. They pushed their way right up behind us. 'Ugh! That's her,' I shouted to Lucy over the deafening music. We tried to ignore them in the packed crowd and have a laugh but the tension was *severe*. At one point her mate tried to stick his water bottle up my bum. I had no clue if she'd asked him to do it, or if this was just how gay guys always hit on each other. Either way, I retrieved the vessel from my rectum and pushed his hands away, not wanting to show my distress at the thought of losing my virginity to a warm bottle of Volvic.

♦ ♦ ♦

At exactly midnight a nasally camp man made an announcement over the intro to Kylie's 'Better the Devil You Know': 'LADIES AND GENTLEMEN, THERE'S JUST ONE HOUR REMAINING... UNTIL THE FIRST-*EVER* LIVE SHOW FROM MISS... GERI... HALLIWELL!' At that moment, Kylie's iconic dance anthem kicked in. High above us, six-foot wide balloons were dropped from the ceiling in their dozens. Two thousand pop-worshippers danced for their lives while the gargantuan balloons sluggishly zig-zagged over rhythmically

Me and Conor outside Rosefield Gardens in 1995, aged 12.

Waiting outside Elstree Studios, for Top of the Pops, with Kathi and Sarah in May 1998. Despite my face, and the bleak surroundings, I'm in my 'happy place'!

My homage to Eternal: a leopard print radiator in my bedroom, spring 1997.

Dad, Mum, me, Anja and Sophie in Kefalonia, summer 1998. Mum obviously wasn't following her own advice about applying suncream.

Reunited with Kelle at The London Studios, November 1998.

B*Witched twins Keavy and Edele reading our magazines for pop gossip (cheapskates) at Heathrow Airport in January 1999.

The London Astoria, Charing Cross Road, in all her faded glory, April 1999.

My Emerald Queens: Keavy during the campaign for their final single 'Jump Down'; Sinead at Heathrow in 1999, between USA tour stints; Lindsay at Capital FM's studios in Leicester Square, December 1998; Edele at Heathrow, on my first trip to meet pop stars at the airport.

Me and Tasha giving Louise a giant cookie to celebrate '2 Faced' reaching Number 3 in July 2000.

Meeting Geri properly for the first time, at Heathrow, after returning from the 'Mi Chico Latino' video shoot in Sardinia, July 1999.

With Emma and Mel on the last day of recording Forever at Abbey Road, summer 1999.

*With VB at Heathrow, during **that** chart battle with Sophie Ellis-Bextor in August 2000. David's shaved head is making a cameo appearance in the background.*

Mel and Arash bitching about Girl Thing outside The Big Breakfast in July 2000.

A brief glimpse into Britney's life. London, December 1999.
Her mum, Lynne, is in the background in the Yoko Ono sunglasses.

Chilling with JT and the guys at their tour date in Washington,
after Tasha won the competition in summer 2000.

A bright-eyed and happy Hear'Say outside a Heat Magazine party,
in the week that 'Pure and Simple' was released, February 2001.

Me with The Luton Girls: Emma, Clare and Laura (minus Sarah) at an 18th birthday party, 1999.

Me and Zanna at school, aged 15, flouting the strict 'blazers on, ties out' rule. Early 1999.

With Dad and Sophie at Euro Disney in 1999.

Trying to pass the hours on a Bermondsey industrial estate with Tasha, in May 2000, waiting for B*Witched.

Me and Charlotte in our getaway rickshaw at the BRITs! February 2001.

Cramming two years of college work into three weeks, June 2001. Wearing the baggy old T-shirt Geri donated to me.

thrusting heads with bad highlights (me included). At that moment I realised that this place was pretty amazing. Despite my preconceptions, these glittery, happy club kids were just friendly, up for a laugh and living for pop anthems.

Just before the show kicked off, the electric crowd started screaming at the VIP balcony. Who was it? An unmistakable man flashed us all a bearded smile and a wave: it was George frigging Michael! Then Geri's mum made an appearance from the same balcony, giving a regal wave to us peasants below, to further roars of adulation. Once they had taken their seats the evening's first act took to the stage. It was new girl group Precious – our entry at Eurovision a couple of weeks back. Despite finishing twelfth in the Jerusalem contest, and with some shaky live vocals and dodgy silk outfits, the G-A-Y crowd loved their Butlins-esque performance at the Astoria. It was catchy and inoffensive, but their cliché-ridden pop was definitely more cubic zirconia than precious gem.

By one thirty, I was starting to flag. Dehydrated, overheated and ready for Geri. She finally appeared, opening with recent debut smash, 'Look at Me', being spun around on a chaise longue by topless male dancers to rapturous applause. THIS is why I came. She threw on a red and black floral skirt and the castanets came out for upcoming single 'Mi Chico Latino'. The crowd quietened briefly for her heartfelt OTT ballad 'Walk Away', a song about her tearful and heroic resignation from her previous job. She picked a man out of the crowd (not me, outrageously), straddling and serenading him at the same time to some bizarre a capella number. After a costume change into a peculiar purple top and pink flares combo, with a pink feather boa for an extra statement piece, she sang another future mega-hit, 'Bag It Up'. There was more straddling as Geri spread her legs just inches from the audience, and gay men reached forward to get a piece of the ginger one, although luckily for her, she was just out of reach.

This was not Wembley Stadium, it was a VERY intimate show. The male dancers sprayed us all with silly string, before a final encore of 'Look at Me' for a second time. She was presented with an enormous bouquet of flowers, waved at the crowd and left the stage, safe in the knowledge that she was still loved.

And then, just like that, it was all over. Except, this wasn't your average gig. As Geri tottered off, the opening bars of the Spice Girls' 'Who Do You Think You Are' blared out and more mammoth balloons fell from the roof onto the screaming crowd. The stage became overrun.

'Let's go. I can't handle any more fun,' Lucy said.

We made a hasty exit with the other diehards to the backstreet behind the Astoria, affectionately known as 'Piss Alley' to try to snatch one last moment with Geri (and hopefully, her GBF George) on their way home. As they appeared to a flurry of flashing cameras, the crowd went apeshit once more. They jumped into Geri's Mercedes and sped off, to the final cheers of adoring fans.

Lucy and I went to sit by the fountain opposite the club to cool down; a grubby oasis in a sweltering urban jungle. We were on cloud nine, trekking back blearily through Soho and over the river to Waterloo as the sun came up, replaying every event from the night over and over. We huddled together on the concourse floor, sharing a hot tea, until the first train back at 7 a.m., where the tiredness really kicked in. We were dirty, shimmery and dead behind the eyes, but it was so worth it.

◆ ◆ ◆

The high of our wild night kind of got me through my GCSEs over the coming days, and I even managed nearly a full hour of revision for my Maths exam. I bragged to the girls in my class about how wild we were, running away to the Big Smoke for a night of clubbing with randoms when everyone else was sitting at home revising. I'm pretty sure people thought we were reckless idiots rather than the fuck-the-system punks we were styling ourselves as.

With exams over, I was truly free. *Later, losers! I'm out of here.*

10

Summertime of Our Lives

With school and exams behind me, Mum and Dad bugged me almost daily to make some decisions on my future but, like most sixteen-year-olds, I just wanted to stay out all night and buy big bottles of gut-churning cider without being ID'd.

Ever since seeing Geri together at G-A-Y, Lucy from school became my new partner in crime. She had a proper career, a huge step up from McDonald's. Lucy worked at the esteemed 'Zenith Windows' (pronounced 'Zeniff' by everyone unfortunate enough to work there), selling uPVC glazing solutions to households across Surrey and South West London. She said she'd even help me to get a job there.

The reality was not as glamorous as I'd imagined. Instead of the chic glass-and-steel edifice I had in my head, the office was packed into the extension of a suburban semi in a shit bit of Walton-on-Thames. The poky, drab 'call centre' (the converted lounge) consisted of seven teenagers, a thirty-something mum and a pensioner sitting at a semi-circle of MFI desks. Buried under a mangled mass of phone wires and headsets, we'd cold call people for hours on end. Inside the semi-circle sat a supervisor – a girl from Anja's class at school – filing her nails, stopping sporadically to make vague encouraging statements.

The 'call centre' was separated from the manager's office by a double-glazed window, like you'd find on the front of a house, as if there was nothing else imaginable to divide the two rooms. The wide-eyed manager sat on the other side of the glass in a shiny Matalan suit. He emerged occasionally by pulling his blind up and opening the window, to shout at us like sub-humans, then disappear again, like a cuckoo lurking in a clock – 'OI, YOU – I've watched you sip that cup of tea for the last thirty seconds! That's another call you could have made!' In his mind he was a powerful executive but was actually just sitting in a uPVC box, shouting at teenagers.

Poundland Lord Sugar took umbrage with me one day for apparently 'staring at him funny' and 'looking like *I'm* on drugs'. One of his minions took me into the double-glazed boardroom to tell me that my career in telesales was over, four weeks after it began. I was genuinely sad, but only that he'd deprived me of my dramatic 'You're Fired' moment in person.

Despite being a high-powered career bitch for a short while, Mum and Dad had promised not to stop my pocket money until the end of the summer. So I had just enough cash for pop stalking on a child travelcard five days a week, pinching crisps and Trio bars from the kitchen cupboards to get me through each day on a shoestring. Realising I had enough resources to get through the summer in this way, I decided to take a sabbatical, put my feet up, and enjoy a few months of hanging out with my friends and A-listers, instead of being trapped in an office or greasy kitchen. Yes, I was spoilt. But the sun-kissed, carefree days of Mum and Dad paying my Bills, Bills, Bills were numbered.

When I wasn't up in town doing that, the glamorous flipside was hanging out in the park with Zanna, drinking rancid spirits stolen from my parents' drinks cabinet.

◆ ◆ ◆

Gemma and I arranged to go to *Top of the Pops* at the end of June and blagged tickets with local boy Arash. He was camp, Iranian and always wore a beaming smile. We stood bored through Blur and Suede, but our mood improved when human Ken doll Adam Rickitt appeared on stage with his pumped-up tits, to – the greatest and gayest late-nineties pop song of them all (quite an accolade) – 'I Breathe Again'. Oddly, this man, touching his body in a crop top and shiny combats to a soundtrack of male climax and a tinny dance beat, would later be selected by David Cameron as a Conservative MP candidate.

Some new singer from America (and star of the recent highly respected movie *Anaconda*) named Jennifer Lopez was also there to sing her debut single, 'If You Had My Love'. Despite being Number 1 in the States that entire month, in a world before YouTube, hardly anyone knew the song over here.

J-Lo was quiet as a mouse that night, barely muttering a word to the staff, let alone the crowd. Wearing what looked like a sparkly bin-bag LBD, she admittedly looked incredible while her less-glam backing dancers sported Croydon facelifts and black pleather netball skirts. She came back out later that evening to do a pre-record of her hands-in-the-air, bongos-galore future smash, 'Waiting for Tonight', so that she wouldn't have to grace our shores again to do promo for a good while. For this number, Jen was decked out in pearl necklaces around her collar and armpits, with her dancers stomping around her in sun hats and white versions of the netball skirt.

Just before the song started, the crowd pin-drop quiet, Arash nudged me and muttered, 'Oh my God! Have you ever *seen* such a big bum?!' I winced, positive that J-Lo, just inches away, must have heard. She subsequently decided to build her entire empire around one bum joke between two teenage boys in Borehamwood.

Most of the journey home that night was spent, phones to ears, calling every airline that flew between London and Dublin. Gemma and I were desperately trying to find out which flights the big name guests would be taking to the wedding of the century that was happening that weekend...

Victoria and David would be tying the knot on giant red and gold thrones in a castle somewhere in the middle of Ireland. The world's media were *desperate* for photos of the event and, as a precaution, the future Mr and Mrs Beckham had Ireland's answer to the Berlin Wall erected. Behind 17-foot barriers, away from the paparazzi's lenses was an event so lacking in subtlety, it makes Jordan and Peter's nuptials look decidedly low-key.

Meanwhile, back in London, two other huge events in 1999's pop calendar were also happening that weekend. Sultry divas All Saints were headlining G-A-Y's Pride event on the Saturday night, while Geri was performing at Party in the Park on the Sunday with 100,000 screaming teenagers in glorious thirty-four-degree heat. Yes, Geri would be lapping up the attention on Posh and Becks' wedding day – the shade of it all!

We had a tight schedule, but we were pros. Heathrow, Piccadilly line, Old Compton Street to get G-A-Y tickets, up to the Astoria; no sleep, wander the streets of the West End in the small hours before fourteen hours of solid pop! And to top it all off, going back to Heathrow on Monday for the post-wedding analysis with Sporty, Scary and Baby.

Since my groupie friends had acrimoniously split into two factions, I was spending a lot more time with Gemma. She was an old hand at this stalking malarkey, and co-opted me as her assistant. As I had no job to go to, I agreed to dedicate the rest of the summer to seeing the Spice Girls wherever they happened to be, but by 1999 they were pretty much on hiatus. After Geri left the summer before, the four remaining girls were either forging solo careers, enjoying their millions or going into labour – some were doing all three.

With David and Victoria's upcoming wedding on all the front pages, we knew the rest of the Spices would be flying to Dublin for the big day and we *had* to see them before they boarded the Aer Lingus party jet. We perched on the kerb outside Heathrow Terminal 1, me in camouflage combats, Gemma in Buffalo platforms. Basking in the evening sun, we sat surrounded by black cabs and BMWs, breathing in the sweet smell of kerosene and carbon monoxide. From this prime spot we could see everyone arriving. First up was Sporty, with spiky bleached hair and gold tooth, looking like a Scouse Long John Silver. We made friendly small talk, keeping one eye out for the other two's grand arrivals. Then we bade her farewell, as she struggled through the revolving doors with a trolley loaded up with Adidas and confetti.

Minutes later, another taxi turned up and two girls in their early twenties stepped out: one with voluminous curly hair, the other with long blonde locks. As Scary turned round we saw she had a baby over one shoulder, drooling down her Gucci top. 'A'RIGHHHT, YOU TWO!' Her thick Yorkshire accent greeted us against a backdrop of clucking luggage trolleys. 'Double trouble,' Emma added with a big grin. 'God, not you two!' Gemma shouted back. In that moment, we felt like their best mates in the world. Obviously if we were real mates we would have got a wedding invite. Maybe they both got lost in the post.

No PAs with them that evening; we had them ALL to ourselves! They were clearly already in party mode, ready to knock back a couple of Baileys in the First Class Lounge before getting on it at their mate's wedding. It just happened to be Posh and Becks', and half the world had been scrambling for details of the event. Here we were, asking them what they were going to wear and guest list gossip. We helped the struggling Mel and Emma with their luggage, which mainly consisted of breast pumps, a Burberry pram and enough other baby-related crap to set up a branch of Mothercare. It was the first time we'd seen Phoenix, Mel's four-month-old baby, and, albeit a little cranky, her jet-black hair slicked up on end was *ridiculously* cute.

We let them check-in in peace (how kind!), but Phoenix immediately started throwing a tantrum, livid that her mum had had the audacity to talk to some Irish woman with a green hat and polyester neckerchief. Mel apologised profusely to the mildly star-struck staff about her screaming tot, then turned to Gemma and I and beckoned us over.

'EH, you two – can y'entertain 'er a min while we do this?'

'Erm... okay?' we said, having little experience with babies, other than the Bunton kind. I stood there blowing raspberries and giggling, praying she wouldn't puke down my C&A vest.

'Ta, guys. Yer the best,' said Mel after, as we walked them to the security gate. We said our goodbyes and wished them both a fun time.

'It's gonna be A-MAZING!' Emma squealed, as they headed off to their gate, waving back at us. My vest, thankfully, was vomit-free.

'Big fans?' the airport woman asked us with a grin.

'Err, obviously!' Gemma replied conceitedly, before we skipped off to the Tube station to make our way to All Saints' G-A-Y performance.

Upon arrival in Soho, that Gay Pride weekend, we were greeted by the vision of a parallel universe in which everyone was gay. And drunk. There was a sea of leather and/or hot pant-clad homosexuals standing proud on Old Compton Street. And men kissing men in broad daylight. I wasn't sure whether to watch or turn away. We fought our way through the crowds to reach Ku-Bar so we could buy our tickets. I pretended that I was an old hand at this clubbing lark, and kept telling myself I was straight.

I'm sure All Saints were marvellous but twenty years after the event, I can't remember a single thing about their performance. So, I'm guessing it wasn't that memorable (or we were really pissed!). We danced till the very end when the lights came on. In an instant we were transported from the halcyon world of pop tunes and disco balls to a grim, sweaty reality of fluorescent strip lighting and crusty, old glitter trodden into the beer-soaked floor.

◆ ◆ ◆

At 5 a.m. I left the Astoria and trundled over to Hyde Park to meet Lucy and some other girls from school. We'd all agreed to queue up early to guarantee a decent spot. After failing to reach the 'front barrier' the previous summer (and thereby not getting on TV or the front page of the papers), I was determined to succeed that year. Geri would definitely remember me then, my face etched into her mind every time she watched the footage back. If you wanted to get to the hallowed front row, though, you had to sprint *all* the way there when the gates opened. And Hyde Park is pretty damn big.

Despite being a bone-idle asthmatic I was still fitter than a lot of other diehard groupies and whizzed past tons of people, like Linford Christie, without the lunchbox. I was looking around so much, though, that I missed a hole in the field. My foot went straight in, sending me flying and crashing to the ground, almost triggering a pile-up. Kids running behind me had to leap out the way to avoid the same peril. I sprained my ankle and had a few grazes. My black and white camouflage combats were covered in grass stains – *That's alright!* I thought. I just looked *more* concealed among nature now. Upon closer inspection I had ripped my combats all the way, from cock to arse. 'Okay, this is bad.' I muttered in mild panic. I continued hobbling as well as I could with my bad ankle and fumbled around desperately in my bag to find my jumper. I tied it around my waist to hide my pants, which were showing through the camouflage crotchless chaps I was now sporting – this wasn't how it was meant to go!

I managed to make the front barrier though, limping the final stretch and looking like a wild cat in Hyde Park had mauled me. Crisis averted! We watched all the acts, from the sublime to the ridiculous. From Blondie to Martine McCutcheon. Boyzone headlined, just two weeks after Stephen Gately had been forced to come out by a tabloid paper. The media were hungry to know whether fans would accept him now they knew he was gay. The reaction was beautifully rambunctious, and he looked overwhelmed when he received the biggest applause of the day.

When Geri came on for her set, I whipped my subtle 'WE LOVE YOU GERI' banner out and a cameraman spent a good minute or so filming me for the massive screens and the live feed on new channel ITV2. Job done! I could have gone home then, but we stayed till the very end, soaking up the baking sun and singing along to all our favourite hits.

Being a typical sixteen-year-old, I was so high on life I didn't put on a drop of the sun cream Mum had lovingly packed in my rucksack, and woke up tired and red raw the next day. UGH! My face?! 'MUM – I have to go to the airport in ten minutes to see the Spice Girls!' I wailed from the bathroom mirror. I was desperate to get first-hand gossip about the big wedding, but couldn't go looking like that! In order to look less like a burnt backside I slapped on a thick paste of after sun and talcum powder. 'That'll have to do,' I sulked, before setting off on the half-hour trek to the nearest station.

When I got to Heathrow, Gemma agreed that I looked horrendous. 'Okay, well, I'm here now. I'm not going home!' I said, embarrassed, but for once my blushes masked by my crimson tones. 'I'm sure they won't even notice.'

'What happened to *you*?' tell-it-like-it-is-Sporty said when she strolled through Arrivals. I told her I'd been out all day, seeing Geri at Party in the Park. 'Fair enough!' she laughed. Gemma rolled her eyes, shooting me her 'DON'T MENTION THE BLOODY G-WORD' look. Baby didn't seem to notice when she bumbled through in a daze. I'm not surprised – these days, after my friends' weddings I basically stare into space and eat fried food in the recovery position all day. I can't *imagine* having to make small talk with teenage fans on a monstrous hangover. What utter hell!

♦ ♦ ♦

Back in Surrey, Dad and I had started going for late-night drives around the suburbs. It was the only time I felt able to overcome my teenage angst and have actual conversations with him. That week, on one of our drives, I asked if we could venture towards Slough.

'Okay. Any reason why?' he asked, slightly baffled.

'Not really... maybe. Let's just drive over there tonight?' We headed towards Berkshire on the M25, then I directed him onto some back roads. Dad used the time to ask me about my friends, my fears, what I might want to do now school had ended... This was all rare quality time together where no one could disturb us, even if I mostly just bored him with stories of the pop industry.

When we got close to Langley, Dad again asked, 'Why are we here, Mal? There's something you're hiding. Just tell me.'

'Okay. Don't get angry though... Geri lives round here.'

Dad sighed and banged his head against the wheel. 'How did I *bloody* know it would be something like that?'

'Just hear me out! Gemma and I are *so* close to finding it, but I can't quite tell from this aerial photo of the area which house it is. It's one of these—' I said, flicking the interior light on, casually pulling out his *A–Z*. 'Once we find it, I can finally get to know her and fulfil my dream!'

'Give me strength...' Dad whispered, followed by a hesitant pause. 'Okay, just let me have a look. I know some of these roads.'

Fortunately, I'd tricked Dad into being my accomplice. I knew we were really close! We drove around pitch-black lanes, not seeing anything that resembled the photo.

'Mal, we're gonna have to go home soon. I've got meetings in the morning.'

'Fine,' I snapped.

'Let's go this way. I don't think we've gone down this road anyway. I can't tell, they all look the flippin' same,' Dad said, turning down a winding lane to head home. By this point I'd switched off and was falling into a deep pit of teenage self-pity.

He slowed the car to a crawl. 'Mal – that's not it, is it? St. Paul's?'

'OHMYGODYES! STOPTHECAR!'

We drove past a couple of times, not wanting to look like the utter weirdos I'd turned us both into. 'Once Gemma and I have met her a few times at the airport, she won't mind us coming here from time to time,' I said, confidently. 'You're the best, Dad!'

♦ ♦ ♦

Some of the 'lesser' stars would happily tell us their flight details to guarantee we'd be there to wave them off. With the Spice Girls though, they were less forthcoming. We knew that the following weekend Geri was flying back from Sardinia, where she'd been filming her new music video. But we didn't know which flight she would be on. I'd suggested to Gemma that we just camp out for days, but she had a better idea. Assuming she would definitely be flying BA, we rang their call centre and, putting on the most 'mature' voices we could muster, insisted to the poor temp on the other end of the line that we were from her record label. After reciting security details (mother's maiden names, dates of birth and any other trivia), we managed to get them to reel off a list of upcoming trips. We struggled to keep up the pretence as we desperately jotted down flight details.

'That's insane!' I wailed as Gemma put the phone down. *We'd done it!* So long as the press didn't find out too, we were finally going to get our own special moment with her.

Gemma had just won a new mobile phone in a Capital FM competition. BT Cellnet were sponsoring All Saints' upcoming tour, so DJs were giving away phones as prizes, with £50 of credit. She wanted, as we all did, to have her favourite celebrity voice her answerphone message, so I agreed to go with her to Emma Bunton's house in Hertfordshire for the 'recording session'.

We chatted to Emma and played with her adorable dogs, Candy and Floss, in the front garden. She was more than happy for us to hang out by her driveway, but under no circumstances was she going to let us set foot in her mum's house! She seemed genuinely flattered to be asked to record the answerphone greeting. 'I wanna hear it now!' Emma demanded excitedly afterwards. I read out Gemma's new number from a scrap of paper while Emma dialled it. When it went to voicemail, she was pretty chuffed: 'Yeah, I like it!' she grinned. She even divulged where she was rehearsing for her first solo show and the fact she was doing a secret duet with Ronan Keating. When Emma drove off, I grabbed Gemma's phone and fumbled my way through to the Received Calls screen. Oh my frigging God! 'We've got a Spice Girl's phone numberrrrrr!!!' we wailed, still stood on the driveway of Chez Bunton.

Still buzzing, Gemma announced she wanted to kill two birds with one stone and visit Victoria at *her* mum's house, where she lived with David (pre-Beckingham Palace), as it was quite close to Emma's. Annoyingly, after trekking down country lanes, past endless smelly paddocks, Victoria wasn't in when we got there. Instead, we chatted with her parents, who remembered Gemma from a few events in the past. Victoria's mum Jackie was really apologetic, saying, 'I'm so sorry you've come all the way here for nothing – they're in tomorrow afternoon though. Come again then!' We knew we could probably fit it in after seeing Geri, so long as her flight was on time. 'Okay, we'll see you tomorrow!'

Sunday morning arrived. We were off to meet Geri! I sprang giddily out of bed to another scorching day. Unlike everyone else making the most of the heatwave, we were off to sit in an air-conditioned Arrivals lounge, like the happy freaks we were. I decided to wear my new statement piece, a lime-green Nike vest, to impress the Ginger one. We got there early to scope the place out. No paps: great! We saw a weird little man carrying one of those signs written in marker pen, spelling out 'G. HALLIWELL': she was definitely coming!

When she appeared through the double doors, in a sea of other passengers, my initial thought was, *Jesus, she is so small!* Geri was glowing after her break in the Med. Sun-kissed locks tousled around her shoulders and a gargantuan pair of sunglasses hid half her face. No one else recognised her, but to us she was unmistakable. She removed her shades and we chatted in Arrivals, surrounded by families awaiting their own dear loved ones, introducing ourselves with an exquisite bouquet from that well-known airport florist, Whistlestop Food & Wine. 'Ahhh, you *shouldn't* have!' said Geri, staring into the £3 wilting carnations. 'You know what? You bought these yourselves, and that means so much to me.'

Ah, sweet, if a little patronising.

We escorted her to the lift, the three of us yapping away. We all crammed in and silently waited for the doors to shut. They kept closing and opening, without going anywhere. At first it was amusing, but after a minute it was just downright awkward. Geri, being Geri, spoke up to diffuse the agitated atmosphere in the packed lift. 'Maybe, it's because we're all so overweight!' she joked, letting out her trademark cackle. Gemma and I giggled at the situation's absurdity, before Gemma's laughter turned to rage when she saw the obstruction in the door, snapping at me, 'It's your FUCKING BAG in the way, dumb arse!' I went a deep shade of crimson, but Geri just chuckled.

We walked out into the sunshine to her car, had a photo each, then Geri scrawled down the number of her main contact at the record label. 'Just ring Rebecca up and say I told her to tell you all the things I'm doing.' We laughed, 'Ermmm, yeah, it probably won't be that easy, Geri. But thanks anyway!' 'Honestly – just call her! I'll tell her to expect you.' We got one last hug and kiss and she was driven away. My dreams had come true. 'She was *everything* I'd hoped for and *more*!' I shrieked, bouncing around the road in ecstasy.

We raced straight to Victoria's house on the opposite side of London and arrived shortly before she and David were leaving for a friend's barbecue. Jackie and Tony Adams were excited to see us strolling down the lane again and chatted to us as they gardened. 'I told her you were coming!' Jackie said, smiling, repeating what a special weekend the wedding had been. 'You look thirsty – I'll fetch you some drinks.' Five minutes later, she ran out with some squash. 'We don't like having paparazzi here, but we love it when her fans make the effort.'

We laid Gemma's selection of CDs and tour programmes out on Tony's freshly cut lawn, ready for Victoria to scrawl on. They'd all been autographed by the others, and just needed hers to complete the set.

A short while later, the new Mr and Mrs Beckham emerged, still tanned from their honeymoon. Posh and Becks were just a few metres away, clutching a bottle of Blossom Hill and bowl of coleslaw, like mere mortals heading to a barbecue. David jumped in their convertible while Victoria tottered over to us two, sitting on their front lawn. 'Hi guys! How's it going?' she said, in the sort of tone you'd use with a six-year-old. 'Mum said you came yesterday? That's SOOO sweet of you to come back!' I glanced at Gemma, who shot me a sly grin. Every comment was answered with a pleasant but robotic 'that's nice' or 'ooooh, lovely'. This wasn't the sultry Posh Spice I knew from interviews. I wanted her to moan about having to traipse through the flowerbeds, but I felt like I'd been taken to meet one of the Tweenies in a shopping centre, being spoken to in baby babble.

After Victoria signed her Spice merch, Gemma asked if David could come and sign her *OK! Magazine* wedding 'souvenir edition' too. 'I'm not sure that'll be possible,' Victoria said, with dramatically woeful face. 'Umm, well... he's just over there?' Gemma giggled, pointing at a clearly bored David, playing Snake on his Nokia in the car. 'I'll see what I can do!' Victoria said valiantly, as if we were asking her to get Geri back in the band and perform in our living rooms.

When David trudged over, he was even more beautiful in the flesh than you can imagine; an angel with heavenly highlights and cheekbones carved by God himself. I didn't *think* I was attracted to him, but the guy was a work of art. After signing the magazine for Gemma, one of the most famous men in the world asked me if I wanted him to sign something. Looking down at Gemma's fully-signed Spice merch I panicked, thinking, *You can't write on any of this, mate!* Sophie *adored* David Beckham. If I returned home after turning down his autograph, she would *kill* me.

'Umm, no, thanks,' I said, his perfect smile crumpling.

'Okay, no problem. Lovely to meet you,' he squeaked, before returning to Victoria, who was touching up her lippy in the passenger seat.

'That was weird,' I murmured.

♦ ♦ ♦

The next week Gemma and I met up in North London to drop in on Emma rehearsing with Ronan Keating on an industrial estate off Caledonian Road. Their duet was top secret and the Boyzone frontman looked shocked to see us when they finished their practice and opened the big doors to let some air into the studio. 'Hi guys! Oh, don't worry – these are *my* fans! They're here to see *me*!' Emma boasted proudly. 'Thanks so much for coming – I'm SO nervous about this first gig. My stomach's been all over the bloody place!' (TMI Emma.)

After giving Baby a pep talk, Gemma asked her the golden question we hadn't managed to answer ourselves: 'Em... where are you recording the new Spice Girls' album?'

Emma hesitated for a moment, 'Well, I'm really not meant to tell any – *oh, sod it!* Abbey Road, a week on Monday. I don't mind you guys coming, but *please* don't tell the other girls I'm the leak – we're supposed to be keeping it top secret!'

I was having palpitations.

We left, feeling very special. 'Oh my God! We are like, SO in the Spice Girls' secret inner circle!' we squealed on the Piccadilly line home.

◆ ◆ ◆

Things were moving fast in Spiceworld. The next day, Gemma and I made the pilgrimage to Geri's mansion for the first time. We took our home-drawn map, and some flowers and chocolates, and started the trek from Langley station in Berkshire, past railway lines, industrial estates and farms. Forty-five minutes later (it would have been less, but Gemma walks like a tortoise), we finally arrived. Peeking out from behind tall trees and forbidding iron gates was the old monastery: Geri's hideaway home since the start of the year. It was humongous. Even her housekeeper had a three-bedroom cottage!

We rang the buzzer and the housekeeper answered, telling us Geri wasn't in. But we had a feeling she was, so we stood in front of the intercom camera in case she walked past and saw us. After a half-hour wait, we heard footsteps crunching on the gravelled driveway, getting louder. *Was it her, or just the grouchy housekeeper urging us to leave?* The footsteps stopped. A humming noise rang out as the gates slowly creaked open. The anticipation was killing us! A scruffy Shih Tzu ran through the gap. 'Harry!' a husky voice yelled. Out stepped off-duty Geri, in jogging bottoms and a figure-hugging T-shirt. 'Hello, you two!' she said, her wide smile telling us she was pleased to see us. 'How are you doing? Thanks for coming!'

We chatted on her driveway for ages, as Harry ran around, playing and pissing on things. She was so welcoming. Our adventures in popworld left little room for much else at that point, and feeling hesitant about bringing up our encounters with other Spice Girls, we mostly talked about her. Despite being an international superstar, out here in her *real* life, she seemed lonely. Geri later admitted to us she often felt isolated out there on her own and loved having visitors.

'I met some friends of yours here the other day,' Geri smirked.

Gemma and I shot each other alarmed side-eye glances. 'What? Who?!'

'I've forgotten their names. One blonde girl and another with thick glasses, dark hair.'

'Charlotte and Tasha!' we seethed with sharp intakes of breath.

'Yes! That's them. I told them I met you both at the airport last week and they had the same reaction!' Geri said, chuckling. 'I'm sensing some bad blood there...' she added, merrily pulling out a giant spoon to stir up our petty fan wars. 'I don't care, I love each and every fan the same. I'll definitely get Rebecca at my label to phone you about the promo we're doing for the new single. I can't remember all the details, I just show up!'

We gave her one final hug before starting the long slog home, recounting every banal sentence and minor body language reaction all the way back to Paddington.

♦ ♦ ♦

We saw Geri at Heathrow a couple of times the next week, flying to America and back on Concorde, if my memory serves me right, and having a nice chat with her each time. She was buoyant about her impending birthday, as well as promoting her new single around the UK.

I got an early night that Sunday, so I could be up bright and early for my Monday morning shift. No, not a job! For the Spice Girls' recording sessions at Abbey Road Studios! The spiritual home of The Beatles was about to house another Fab Four for the next two weeks. Gemma and I met them most days that fortnight. We kept our word to Baby, keeping schtum about her giving away their secrets. I reckon it's safe to let the cat out of the bag now. Not that the other girls seemed to mind us being there. It was a really fun couple of weeks. Sometimes we'd just put in a morning or an afternoon shift, depending on what else was happening on the pop radar.

Incredibly, there were no press, Security or other fans there, bar a couple of girls in the final two days, once the recording sessions had been announced in the papers. The girls mostly drove themselves every day, leaving us free to chat away to them about the album and upcoming tour. One highlight was watching Posh attempt a three-point turn in heels, having minor road rage and honking rush-hour traffic to let her out of the car park while waving us goodbye as she drove home one evening.

Another afternoon we were gassing to Sporty and, behind her, I watched as four lads stripped naked (apart from socks covering their junk) and posed on the famous zebra crossing (like the Red Hot Chili Peppers' *Abbey Road EP* photo). I told her to look behind her, to which she turned around, yelling, 'What the *fuck*?!' in her soothing Scouse tones. 'They're quite fit though!' she cackled, the boys unaware that Sporty Spice was judging their arses from the other side of the street.

Halfway through that fortnight we headed off to Geri's again. It had been widely publicised that the famous former redhead was holding a huge birthday party in her garden – giant Ferris wheel, street entertainers, candy floss, the works – all to celebrate the milestone age of... twenty-seven. So, off Gem and I went, on the day after the big Halliwell Carnival, cards and gifts in hand for the birthday girl, ready to pounce on her with a hangover.

We did our usual – rang the buzzer and waited for Gezza to come out, open-armed, once she'd seen us batting our Bambi eyelashes on the intercom. Unfortunately for us, the heavens opened while we were stood there waiting, dropping a biblical downpour onto us both. Believe me when I tell you there was *nowhere* to shelter from the elements outside Geri's, bar the nunnery down the road. I was less prepared than Gemma, in a flimsy T-shirt and shorts; she at least had a coat. Once it passed, I was left shivering like a drowned rat, wondering how long the sun would take to evaporate the liquid out of my outfit and pants.

I heard the sweet sound of footsteps on stones from beyond the black gates. 'For fuck's sake!' I cursed, looking over at giggling Gemma, as water dripped from my clothes onto my trainers, like a recently watered hanging basket. The gates opened and Geri stepped out.

'Hello!'

'Happy birthday!' we responded in cheery, bedraggled unison.

'Oh my God, you're soaked! That's *never* going to dry. Haven't you got anything else?'

I shook my head. 'It's fine, it'll dry.'

She squeezed my sopping T-shirt. 'No, it won't, you'll get ill. And your mum will kill me. I'm going to get you something to change into! Wait in here,' Geri said, ushering us onto her driveway. There were various people in the garden dismantling all the fun stuff from the previous day's party, all grinning, having avoided the monsoon themselves.

Geri returned, carrying some items from her house. 'Here you go – take this towel and dry yourself properly. In fact, just keep it. You can have this T-shirt too.'

'Thanks,' I said, grinning.

'*No* – take the T-shirt off and *then* dry yourself. You can't pat it dry.'

'What? Now?' I asked, with the pure panic of a weedy teenage boy being told to take his top off by a Spice Girl.

Geri and Gemma started laughing. 'Yes, now! I don't care what you look like under there, you just need to get dry.' I peeled off my T-shirt, flexing the area where my biceps should be, *mortified* at stripping in front of my friend, let alone FUCKING GINGER SPICE. I finished dabbing myself and put on the T-shirt from Geri.

'There – that's better, isn't it?' Geri declared, with a smile.

'Erm, yeah,' I said, awkwardly.

We chatted as she thumbed through and signed some of our photos, then we said we'd leave her in peace. 'Wait – take some party bags. And cake and balloons, please!' Geri dashed back indoors and presented us with four party bags, full of the usual (kids) birthday treats – party poppers, bubble kits and wedges of jammy Victoria sponge. Tied on with metallic ribbon were four giant helium balloons, each with a cartoon rendition of her on one side and 'HAPPY BIRTHDAY GERI' sprawled across the other. We trudged back to the station looking like overgrown seven-year-olds on their way back from a bouncy castle party. Gemma told me she was keeping the bath towel, as it wasn't fair that I go home with two random objects from Geri's house.

I carefully folded up the T-shirt when I got home as a memento of the best summer ever.

♦ ♦ ♦

Geri had the thrilling task of being a guest on *Des O'Connor Tonight,* down at Teddington Studios, to promote her new single, 'Mi Chico Latino', so we hung around on the leafy streets of South West London to meet her. We also saw her pre-record a performance at *Top of the Pops* that week. It was Geri's first performance in the legendary Elstree Studios as a solo artist, although a building she knew extremely well. It must have been pretty weird for her, returning alone. Also there were the lovely Travis (one of the only indie bands that didn't repulse me at sixteen), singing their surprise summer smash, 'Why Does It Always Rain on Me?'; Phats & Small, plus the man vying with Ricky Martin for the Best Bum In Leather Trousers crown, Enrique Iglesias – there to sing his worldwide hit 'Bailamos' – or as nine-year-old Sophie used to sing, 'BY THE MOLE... let the rhythm take you over BY THE MOLE.' I'm *still* unable to sing any other words to that song!

The next day, being the Spice Girls' final day at Abbey Road, we saw Geri do a pre-record performance at *CD:UK* in the afternoon, then legged it back to St Johns Wood to see the girls leave. Baby willingly told us the studio they were at the next week in Fitzrovia, but we decided not to go: they'd surely seen enough of us for a while! That final evening, Baby and Scary were the last to leave, tottering down the famous steps in their glad rags, to us and a waiting driver, ready for a big night out.

'We've finished! Well... the first sessions anyway,' Emma hollered in glee.

'And now we're goin' for a night out on the tiles! Man, there's gonna be trouble tonight, I can feel it!' Scary boasted, as if either of us doubted it in the slightest.

Scary was in favour of a group photo to capture the moment, but Baby was faffing around in her handbag. She kept calling to her, 'Oi, Bunton! Get over 'ere now! BUNTON!' as Gemma and I cracked up beside her. After a couple of weeks of hanging out with these icons I realised they weren't the distant goddesses I'd imagined, they were just ordinary girls up for a laugh.

◆ ◆ ◆

My old mate Kelle from Eternal did a BBC Radio 1 Roadshow on the outskirts of Portsmouth the following week. Paul and I bunked the last train down there from Woking, getting in at 1 a.m. We ended up spending the first half of the night chatting on the beach while pissed-up uni students went skinny-dipping next to us, then the second half sitting in a security guy's caravan at the roadshow site. He made us tea and talked to us intensely about UK Garage for three hours, and about how you could pour milk onto Nutrigrain bars in a bowl and eat them as a snack that way – we always managed to gravitate to the oddballs.

It was the first time I'd seen Kelle since I jumped out from behind a Christmas tree at The London Studios last November. She thought we were 'bloody crazy' for spending the night in a field to see her, but so appreciative, as her career was finally picking up again, thanks to an (over)generous million-pound deal with a major label.

Travis, along with Eternal wannabes Fierce, were also playing the roadshow, and we met them around the back afterwards. There were two other upcoming girl groups on the bill, as warm-up: failed late-nineties Pete Waterman project Toutes Les Filles – a rubbish Atomic Kitten prototype, who sang recycled Stock Aitken Waterman flops, and religious duo David's Daughters, who were like the sisters from Eternal but without raunchiness, catchy songs or any ounce of fun. No, I'm not sure why these musical dead ducks didn't become the next Spice Girls either.

After the Spices' success, every record label was desperate to find the next 'big thing', ploughing huge sums into cobbled-together acts. I'd love to say I could spot a stinker a mile off, but I think my CD collection tells a different story.

The following week, the Radio 1 Roadshow rolled into sunny Brighton, so Gemma and I packed our buckets and spades and headed down to see B*Witched headline the bill. We met them between soundchecks for the first time since their US tour. The first thing Keavy said was thank you for all the faxes. As we didn't know if any of them were being passed on, we'd send the same fax each day for a week before writing a new one for the following week, giving them updates on all the gossip from the pop industry back home. Unbeknownst to us, the venues had been giving them most of the faxes, and the girls would cheer when a new one finally came through. She promised they made them feel less homesick and they were all interested to read about our antics, but Gemma and I wondered whether they were just laughing at how dull our lives were compared with jetting round the States.

Another new girl band, Hepburn, were also performing, to promote their debut single, 'I Quit' – the *best* song to listen to after handing in your notice. We got past Security and hung out in the hotel bar the night before with both girl bands, along with a bunch of boy bands, of varying fame, including Westlife and Next of Kin (Essex's answer to Hanson. I know, that sounds worse than the real thing!). They all stayed at The Grand – the posh one that the IRA tried to blow up Thatcher in. What better setting to watch a half-cut Brian McFadden from Westlife serenade the staff and guests on the piano in the bar until 3 a.m., with various other members of the boy band and B*Witched wailing Irish songs on the piano stool by his side?

After Brian literally got carried upstairs to bed we reluctantly got up from our sofa to wander the streets till morning. We could no longer realistically pretend we were staying there, with the entire bar now empty, us having nursed the same warm Cokes since nine o'clock and only three pounds left between us.

◆ ◆ ◆

The next few weeks were spent gallivanting all over town to see B*Witched and Kelle, both promoting their respective new singles, 'Jesse Hold On' and 'Higher Than Heaven'. Handily, they were doing a lot of the same shows together. Also promoting a new single that month were the last remaining members of Eternal: sisters Easther and Vernie.

By this point, the Bennett sisters from Eternal were about as popular as foie gras at a vegan buffet. They'd suffered massive damage to their popularity since allegedly firing Kelle by fax, twelve months earlier. She was the smiley, personable one; they'd been the serious sisters, famous for *years* in the industry for being 'difficult'. Perhaps things had been so icy in the group that they just couldn't switch it on for the cameras like Kelle could. That month, Kelle spent every press and TV spot reiterating the treatment she'd received from them, whereas they just carried on with the awkward, angry responses to interviewers' questions about the sacking.

And while Kelle was out there, flogging her debut single, 'Higher Than Heaven' – a pop-gospel song, bright enough to lift even the Bennett sisters' moods – they thought it a good idea to release a dark, moody R&B track about what to do when God comes searching for you at the end of the world. It was well-produced and the video their most stylish yet, but the song choice was all wrong. It didn't help that in the two years they'd been absent, a girl group from across the pond, with a ton more sass and punchy songs (and a love for my mint-green shirt), had released one of the best R&B albums of the *decade*. Things had moved on.

I went to meet the sisters at the MTV Studios, after they'd finished recording an interview one Sunday, and it was one of my most bizarre experiences of meeting pop stars ever. I arranged to go with my friend Lisa, one of the Eternal Groupie Girls I'd met at my first-ever *Top of the Pops*. She was resolutely on Team Bennett, whereas I was *always* going to be Team Kelle in the ugly divorce.

When they strolled out, they knew who I was immediately, as bloody Lisa had been stirring the pot, telling them I'd been seeing Kelle loads. *Thanks*, Lis!

'So! *This* is Malcolm,' Easther said, looking me up and down, like a Wild West standoff. 'I hear you've been seeing a lot of Kelle.'

'Yeah, I have. *Actually*,' I replied.

'Give her our love, won't you?' Easther said with a wry smile.

Their hostility to me was bizarre, but I know I was being frosty to them too. Through my blinkered eyes they'd fired and bullied Kelle, and broken up my favourite band.

Vernie was quieter, but moaned when Easther passed her the CDs I wanted signing. 'You want *three* things done?' she asked, with a face like I'd asked her to gift me a family heirloom.

'Yes, *please*,' I smiled, through gritted teeth.

♦ ♦ ♦

With summer drawing to a close, Mum and Dad sat me down and had a little chat. I'd somehow managed to pass my exams with remarkably good grades considering my total lack of revision. I still needed a future though, or at least a job. Deciding that work didn't seem much fun, I opted instead to enrol at the local college, hoping a nice, easy qualification would buy me some time to hone my skills for a career in the pop biz.

11

You're My Number One

My epic summer was over. I'd got closer than I ever thought possible to some of the most famous people on the planet. And their mums. I was begrudgingly driven to Brooklands College in Weybridge by Dad, who threatened that if I didn't sign up for a course he would drive me straight to the Jobcentre. After much deliberation with the college's careers adviser, I decided that a Media Studies BTEC offered a useful balance of skills for the music industry, and adequate time between lectures to hop on the train to London. The college was only two train stops away from Chertsey, but that was far away enough for me to escape my old enemies at school. Kathi was joining me there, so there'd be one familiar friendly face at least.

Our class very quickly divided into *Clueless*-esque cliques: there were the Metallers – grungy kids with long, smelly hair and the baggiest trousers of the class (quite a feat, in 1999); the Elders – a bunch of twenty-one-year-old fuckups who'd still not yet managed to complete a further education course; the Drum

& Bass louts – a mostly agreeable bunch of weed-smoking wrong'uns, who spent every break time piled into a pimped-out Ford Fiesta in the car park, a powerful subwoofer and menacing cloud of smoke encircling them; and the Misfits – the oddball dregs, with a love of dyeing their hair, getting drunk and obsessing over Britney Spears, Christina Aguilera, and all other Swedish-produced pop pap. No prizes for guessing which clique I fell into! For the first time since primary school I was – dare I say it – popular with my classmates: I was king of my castle.

There were, sadly, a few boys in the class who spoke out about me being different – my campness and assumed sexuality. One ringleader, a good five years older than me, passed notes around class about me being a possible faggot, which I secretly cried about in the loos, heartbroken that history was repeating itself. To my surprise, most of the class called him a prick and he ended up dropping out soon after, flunking his umpteenth attempt at college.

I was overjoyed at the class's reaction, but inside I was struggling: I knew I had some attraction to guys, but also felt like I had feelings for girls too. Either way, I didn't bloody know, but thankfully, my college friends just let me be me, in a way that the kids at school never would.

♦ ♦ ♦

Despite loving my new peers, a month in I was fast becoming like that famous high school quote about Mariah Carey – her being nicknamed 'Mirage' because she was simply never there. It wasn't that I was *never* there, I just rarely attended lessons that clashed with important events on the pop scene.

One weekday morning, late that September, Gemma and I hauled ourselves over to Geri's Berkshire mansion. As always,

Geri chatted to us on her driveway for a good twenty minutes, despite her cantankerous PA coming out intermittently to try and coax her back inside to do some work. Relaxed and chatty, Geri said she was bracing herself before launching into the campaign for her third single, 'Lift Me Up', in a few days' time. I now see why she was mentally preparing: it being less of a promotional campaign, more a full-on nuclear assault.

We also had to allocate time to acquiring tickets for that year's Smash Hits Poll Winners' Party. Geri and B*Witched were playing, alongside other pop heavyweights of 1999. To get front-row tickets, you had to be early – like, three days early. Gemma, Paul and I had agreed to wait in the queue in shifts. For three drizzly October days and nights we lived outside the arena on the Isle of Dogs – definitely one of the less glamorous episodes in my groupie escapades. Also in the queue for tickets were three mouthy Geordie girls, who made the ordeal much more fun. One evening, the Geordies invited me into their tent for a 'heart to heart' and, without warning, launched themselves on me, ripping off my clothes and trying to get in my BHS underpants. I was tall but very feeble, and when three big Geordie lasses sit on you, it's *extremely* hard to escape! It was similar to the scene from the film *Almost Famous*, where the 1970s groupies decide to 'deflower' the young boy in their boudoir, except in a smelly tent full of grey bras and empty WKD bottles, with some *Byker Grove* rejects, while the DLR rumbled overhead. After ten harrowing minutes, and my chastity belt still intact, they eventually got tired and sparked up. A lot of sixteen-year-olds would have jumped at the chance of a foursome in a tent, but I was petrified. *What if they could tell I wasn't really into it?*

After three nights we got the tickets. Most people would then go home, wash and get some kip. Gemma had other ideas, insisting we head up to Hertfordshire to visit Emma Bunton at her mum Pauline's house. When Gemma pressed her on what her upcoming appearances were, Emma willingly got out her Filofax and leafed through the pages, giving us a rundown of promotional TV performances and radio interviews she was doing over the coming weeks. Gemma meticulously noted down the dates while I started to doze off behind her.

A couple of weeks later, Gemma made me escort her on another trip up to Chez Bunton. When Pauline discovered we didn't have tickets for the Spice Girls' upcoming dates in Manchester, she promptly scuttled off and returned with two tickets to sit *with the Spice Girls' families* at one of the shows. The equivalent of a royal box! We could have kissed her (I think we did).

We thanked her profusely as she drove us to the train station in her convertible, covertly playing us Emma's top-secret studio recordings. We promised we wouldn't tell Emma about the preview of all her demos and couldn't believe our luck as we rode the train back into London. What kind, loving families the girls came from.

I was still on top of the world when I got back to Ottershaw and told Mum about the tickets for the Thursday night show. She, for once, put her foot down and absolutely forbade me to miss any more college. Our pensioner neighbours were definitely grabbing their popcorn that night, as I did my best Kevin The Teenager impression, 'THAT IS *SO* UNFAIR! BABY SPICE'S *MUM* HAS GIVEN US TICKETS TO SIT WITH HER! IF I DON'T GO, SHE'LL BE *SO* OFFENDED!' [slams door off its hinges]

I usually got my way, but Mum rightly stuck to her guns. I *had* missed too much college (more than they even knew) and they *were* incredibly good to me, letting their teenage son do things that other parents would never allow. When Gemma rocked up at Manchester Arena with another friend who'd taken my ticket the adorable Pauline said she was pleased that I was such a hardworking student.

♦ ♦ ♦

With all these upcoming concerts and train fares into London (even at child prices), my piggy bank was running dry. My parents had been paying me to do chores around the house, but it wasn't enough to fund my pop stalking lifestyle: I needed a proper job. I also wanted to prove to myself that I could stick one out for more than a month. One day after college, I ventured to the Harvester restaurant up the road and managed to score a job as shit-on-shoe – sorry – chief salad cart replenisher at Ottershaw's finest bistro.

It wasn't ideal; the restaurant's boss was even more menacing than the BRIT Awards' head of security. A cross between Mrs Doyle and The Trunchbull. And, as I couldn't earn tips myself, I was instructed to beg the waitresses at the end of every night for a couple of quid, earned by helping to wipe down and reset their tables. Some were lovely, but there were many battle-axes who, at the end of every night, gave me nothing but a sad head tilt and a 'Sorry, Hun! I've barely earned a couple of quid myself tonight,' before waddling off, saddled with fat pockets jangling. Anja was also a waitress there. Although, like every classic big sister, she was always horrified when I spoke to her in public and warned me *not* to embarrass her.

After four weeks at my job I had to make an incredibly tough decision: show up for a Saturday night shift of restocking potato salad and bacon bits on the cart and wiping ice cream from greasy tables, or go see Geri perform at the *Lottery*. Never wanting to miss an opportunity to stick two fingers up to my big sister, I jacked in my job. I didn't even feign illness, I just switched off my

Nokia brick and ignored the voicemails from Irish Trunchbull (who'd had to listen, three times a day, to my pre-recorded message by Edele from B*Witched, telling her I wasn't available, every time she left me a voicemail) until my P45 eventually landed on the doormat. Anja was rightfully mortified, and had the ignominy of being interrogated about me every evening at work.

I craved my independence and thought I was grown-up, but like so many spoilt teenagers, I couldn't face actually working to pay for my lifestyle. It looked like I'd be dependent on the Bank of Mum and Dad (again).

♦ ♦ ♦

The same week I jacked in my glittering Harvester career I went with Gemma to *Top of the Pops.* B*Witched were still on their interminable promo tour for banjo-infused single 'Jesse Hold On' – a cross between *Deliverance* and *Ballykissangel*, but with more denim.

Among others, the line-up also included boy band Five, performing another sure-fire Number 1, 'Keep On Movin', Honeyz, living up to their name with a new sickly-sweet ballad, 'Never Let You Down' and a diva called Tina (not her from S Club 7). The legendary Ms Turner was attempting a comeback via dance music. And she wasn't alone. The global triumph of Cher's 'Believe', a year earlier, had coaxed numerous middle-aged divas out of retirement, all desperate for a club kid rebirth of their own: Diana Ross, Belinda Carlisle, they were all trying it! Watching fifty-nine-year-old Tina stomp her iconic legs in a sassy red dress a couple of feet away from me was amazing. Unfortunately, the song, and her mediocre miming, wasn't, and the single limped in at Number 19.

Also performing that night were the remnants of Eternal: the indestructible Bennett sisters with their single, 'What'cha Gonna Do'. It was surreal for me, seeing them perform for the first time as a duo. I thought back to the time, aged twelve, when I got that CD for Christmas from Anja and was captivated. Four years later, I was within touching distance, yet felt unmoved. Desperate to show that I was on Team Kelle, I stood behind them during their performance with a face that could curdle milk.

Unlike so many pop stars back then, they were really talented singers, but their refusal to 'play the game' meant the sisters were treated like villains by the press. Their single only reached Number 16. That was the last time I saw Eternal perform; it was all over for the band that had launched my love of pop.

◆ ◆ ◆

That autumn, the London skyline was being transformed as the Millennium Dome finally took shape on former mudflats in Greenwich, South East London. As the nation pondered the coming of a new century, two former friends-turned-archenemies were set to go head-to-head in a battle that would expose the cold, harsh realities of nineties pop.

I was sat reading the music news on Ceefax, getting ready to go to Heathrow with Gemma to see Geri, and nearly choked on my toast when I read that Emma Bunton's debut single would be released... ON THE SAME DAY AS GERI'S! We questioned Gezza about this remarkable coincidence, as we strolled through Terminal 4 Departures with her. 'It's just bad timing, Malcolm, it had nothing to do with me.'

Of course not, Geri.

The tabloids couldn't get enough of this War of the Spices. It looked set to be the biggest chart battle since the legendary

Blur v. Oasis shitstorm, back in 1995. The world was guaranteed countless TV appearances and column inches. Being on good terms with both of the challengers, I was looking forward to a front-row seat. *This is going to be amazing!* I thought to myself.

In one corner stood the Watford Warrior, aka Ginger: buxom, brash and brazen in her glam get-up and flowing locks of Titian hair. She didn't just want this win, she *needed* it, and wasn't going down without a fight. In the other corner, meek and timid, stood blonde Baby, the Potters Bar Princess. One time bosom buddies, these two were now desperate to watch the other one fail.

Baby's weapon was the single 'What I Am', a mediocre anthem for the naïve and innocent. Ginger responded with 'Lift Me Up', a song but also a request. With an orchestral B-side of 'Live and Let Die', this was a CD single middle finger if ever there was one.

Gemma's favourite was Baby. 'Geri's had a Number 1, let Emma have a chance,' she pleaded, but I preferred Geri's ballsy attitude.

Nine days before release. From the comfort of our living room I watched Geri's appearance on Chris Evans' show *TFI Friday*, where she dared fellow vertically challenged pop diva Kylie Minogue to an arm-wrestle. This somehow ended in a passionate lesbian kiss on live television, causing me to watch in amazement and generating countless headlines. After the show, Geri told the press it was all Kylie's idea – it definitely got the boys at college's tongues wagging.

Emma wasn't without her appeal though, receiving heavy rotation on Radio 2. Even Mum and Dad were talking about her single over the dinner table. Broad appeal versus Geri's teenybopper niche?

The following Thursday, just four days prior to release, Gemma and I were back in Borehamwood. Geri was pre-recording her *Top of the Pops* appearance for the following week.

Both camps scheduled their movements meticulously so that they *never* mistakenly crossed paths during this battle. Sharing the bill with Geri was Catatonia, timid rock act Semisonic, Shola Ama, Tori Amos and the offensively inoffensive Westlife. Brian was certainly looking more sober than last time we'd seen him in Brighton.

Eager to maximise sales, Geri's team organised a mammoth signing in Central London on the evening of release. At the same moment, another former colleague, Sporty, was at the other end of Oxford Street, performing her first headline show at the Astoria. I missed the show, and Sporty, but did bump into Emma while loitering at the back of the Astoria beforehand. We chatted about what a big week it was going to be, but I somehow forgot to tell her that I was about to leg it up Oxford Street for a rendezvous with her newfound nemesis.

As I approached HMV I saw thousands of fans queuing for their queen, through every aisle and out the door. Towering above the crowd in a black leather catsuit, poised atop a table in the centre of the shop, was Geri. She had fire in her eyes.

The shop tried to cut-off the queue but Geri soldiered on right up until closing time. For hours she signed CD after CD. By the time I'd crawled my way to the front her hands were raw, her face looked drained, and her eyes had a maniacal glint in them. She was so tired, she barely recognised me as she scrawled her name across my single. Despite her efforts, Geri was only 600 copies ahead the next day. The papers, loving every moment, were onto her, declaring her 'desperate'.

But by Wednesday evening, it looked to be working: Geri was now 5000 copies ahead in the midweek charts. But was it enough? Baby was chasing her tail every step of the way. That evening, as I lay awake listening to the radio in bed, a story was leaked to the media that would change *everything*. Geri was apparently dating TV presenter and fellow ginge Chris Evans. The fact the two shared a PR agent was *obviously* pure coincidence. This would put her on the front of every paper in the land!

On Thursday, the four Spice Girls put on a united front at a press conference for their new book, *Forever Spice*. But the reporters were only interested in one story. Sporty snapped at the crowd, 'We're here to talk about the book, not about the Gingers!' Gemma was there while I stayed at home, surfing the Net to devour any news on the battle I could. Emma made another blow as she declared to the media that, just a few weeks previously, Evans had been bombarding *her* with texts. Miaow!

The next morning I woke up early to hear Geri's guest appearance on her new lover's radio show. 'Hopefully it will go on forever,' said Evans when asked about their blossoming romance. A Shih Tzu dog was chauffeur-driven alone to the Virgin Radio studios, where the UK tabloid press were camped outside, reporting on every minor development of the story. The show ended with a spoof marriage ceremony, followed by Evans playing Joe Jackson's seventies hit, 'Is She Really Going Out with Him?' I shook my head in disbelief.

By that evening the gap had narrowed to only 4000 copies.

Sunday arrived: Judgement Day. Never mind Emma and Geri, I was flagging too. The excitement of the early days of the campaign had turned, for me, into something quite ugly. The desperation from both parties left a sour taste. At 6.47 p.m. the world would know who was Number 1, and who would be the also-ran in the annals of pop history. As the Top 40 were ritually played, there were only two songs I cared about on 7 November 1999. As Number 3 faded out, the world heard the opening bars of strumming guitars. Emma was Number 2, Geri had clinched it with a whopping *33,000* more sales! As a staunch Team Ginger member, I erupted into a frenzy of delight, while Gemma and other loyal Team Baby supporters sank back into their seats, tears in their eyes.

When the chart show DJ asked Geri if she had anything to say to Emma, she replied, 'I'd like to congratulate everyone. It was a fantastic week and it's been a hard one.' Emma was slightly more gracious, saying she was glad the 'silly' media battle was over and congratulating Geri on her success. That evening, Geri blew tens of thousands of pounds on a victory party at a glitzy Soho club for her showbiz pals, and all in her team (including Chris Evans), who'd helped beat poor Emma.

Gemma rang me later that night for some post-match analysis. I was still on cloud nine, and felt it proved Geri was right to walk out of the band. Gemma, though, thought she'd taken it too far and that her cheap tactics were below the belt. *Friendship never ends?*

One online blogger summed it up perfectly: '[Geri's behaviour] seemed to typify the depths to which her crass desperation would plumb. At this stage of her career Geri is winning all the important battles, but she's also planting the seeds for her own destruction.'

♦ ♦ ♦

In the days that followed, a hungover Geri was plastered all over the tabloids. The press was admiring her success, but also cynical about her behaviour. Gemma and I had seen photos of her being carried from her car to her house by her driver after too much Cristal at her victory do, but not yet in person.

We knew she was appearing at the MTV Europe Music Awards in Dublin that Thursday evening, along with *all* the biggest names in Planet Pop. So on the day of the ceremony,

Gemma, Paul and I found a comfy spot at Heathrow Terminal 1 and made ourselves at home while we waited for the stars to turn up for their various flights. We chatted to the Honeyz, Steps and a few other B- and C-list bands as they arrived for check-in, most of the ladies all wrapped up in big Jackie Stallone coats, with sunglasses attempting to hide their weary 6 a.m. eyes. Gemma disappeared for a while to look round the Virgin Megastore with Paul, while I kept watch out the front of the terminal in case B*Witched or Geri arrived early.

I stood patiently watching taxis and Mercedes arrive, half in a daydream, imagining each one might have a famous passenger. Eventually, a tiny figure with huge curly blonde hair emerged. 'Is *that*? No, that's not her hair.' But as the figure moved closer, I realised it *was* Ms Halliwell, albeit with new massive hairdo. I loved it, although the cynic in me thought the new look was an attempt to guarantee more column inches the day after the awards. Alongside Geri was Tor, her PA, who was always angry with us fans for tracking down Geri at the most unexpected places. She could never understand how it was that we knew what flights she'd be on, when she'd be home, or at which TV studios she would be doing an interview.

'Congratulations on your Number 1!!!' I gushed.

'Ahhh, thank you so much. I'm a very happy girl. Although the last few weeks have been a bit mad, *as you know*', Geri said with a flash of her smile. We continued chatting as we walked inside to the check-in desks, where grouchy Tor turned around and bellowed in my face.

'*Right*, you've had your lot! Now leave us alone and go home.'

I'd had enough of her shit for once and calmly asked her, with a coy smile, 'Why do you have to be so rude? I'm a *kid*! I'm only here to show support and say hello. It's us that buy the CDs – you know, *the fans*?' I glanced at Geri stood a couple of metres away, who was watching and grinning beneath her monster sunglasses. My life on the distant fringes of the pop world gave me a lot of confidence. Since leaving school I felt older and wiser. Without the constant bullying I felt happier to be myself and speak my mind. Gemma soon ran over and after a brief chat, we wished Geri good luck at the awards and left her in peace to check-in.

B*Witched showed up mid-morning, before we unexpectedly saw Mel C on her way home from somewhere. We chatted as we walked through the terminal, all of us stopping to peruse the day's papers in WHSmith on the way. Mel was most interested in reading about a certain old friend of hers, still splashed across every front page. Relations between the Spice camps had been frosty since Geri walked, but Gemma and I thought we'd take this chance to discuss the G word.

'We saw Geri here a couple of hours ago,' I said, as Mel scanned the tabloids.

'Oh, yeah?' she answered, pretending to read the paper but with a growing smile. 'How is she?'

'She's really good! We told her we were seeing you today. She said to send her love,' Gemma added. (A barefaced lie.)

Mel let out a small burst of laughter, still looking down at the *Daily Mirror* article in front of her. 'Oh *really*, did she now?!' she replied in an extremely sarcastic tone. 'Seriously, it's not gonna work, guys.'

'I don't know what you mean!' Gemma shrugged innocently – her best Baby Spice impression – the both of us now in a fit of giggles. We felt like Switzerland, acting as the neutral negotiators for high-level peace talks.

Those of us with the luxury of cable TV watched the awards live at our respective homes that evening. As Boyzone collected their award, Shane (brother of B*Witched's Edele and Keavy, husband of Easther from Eternal) stunned the audience, and his bandmates, with an expletive-filled rant. He was clearly going through some harder times, having been chewed up and spat out by the music industry. At the tender age of twenty-three he'd already witnessed the giddy heights and precipitous drops of the music world over the course of six years, and by 1999 Boyzone were on the brink of collapse. He and Easther apparently ended the night in a scuffle with Puff Daddy at an aftershow party. The media reaction was overwhelmingly negative, with no attempt to look at the causes, or acknowledge their part in his predicament.

At college the next morning I was greeted by classmates gathered round a copy of the *Mirror*. 'Have you seen the papers yet, Malcolm? Your pop princess has been dumped!' Geri, looking magnificent at the awards the night before, was splashed across every front page, with headlines like 'DUMPED!' and 'IF YOU'VE CHEATED ON THIS, CHRIS, YOU'RE A GINGER NUTCASE'. After two conveniently timed weeks, their love affair was over.

Easy come, easy go, Geri.

◆ ◆ ◆

By autumn 1999, after an incredible run of four Number 1s, the fact that 'Jesse Hold On' only made it to a respectable Number 4 no doubt gave B*Witched (and their label) some cause for concern. They were still huge, but there was fierce competition in the industry, and a fickle record-buying public increasingly weary of over-hyped pop acts. Fans already seemed to be moving on to the plethora of young groups desperate to be the next big thing: S Club 7, A1 and Atomic Kitten.

So, I was nervous when B*Witched told us their next single was a slightly leftfield choice. They'd teamed up with South Africa's biggest musical export – male choral group Ladysmith

Black Mambazo. I'm so gutted I wasn't in that brainstorming meeting.

The result was less cringeworthy than it first sounds. Sickly-sweet vocals actually work quite well with African percussion, chanting and bizarre tropical birdsong. Good money had been ploughed into the song and accompanying video, and the label obviously had high hopes for this groundbreaking offering. But would twelve-year-olds from Plymouth to Preston be forking out their pocket money for it?

In the middle of their big autumn arena tour B*Witched rushed down one Thursday to perform it at *Top of the Pops*, for the first time with Ladysmith Black Mambazo. The stage was crammed to bursting with the four girls and a dozen Mambazo guys trying to shuffle about doing their own moves behind them.

In the end it stalled at Number 13. Back when chart positions were the be-all and end-all, it was clearly a shock for B*Witched. When I saw them in the following weeks they were disheartened, not knowing what move to make next, after a whirlwind eighteen months at the top. I genuinely cared about them on a personal level too – they had worked so hard and I really didn't want it all to end.

On the same *Top of the Pops* as B*Witched that evening were the Wamdue Project, with their mahoosive club hit, 'King of My Castle', The Charlatans, Canadian one-hit wonders, Len, performing crowd-pleaser 'Steal My Sunshine', and your nan's favourite, Cliff Richard, with his charity single, 'The Millennium Prayer': a song, not about sitting in your Millennium Bug shelter, waiting for a technology apocalypse with tinned peaches and bottled water, but a fusion of celebrated bangers, The Lord's Prayer and 'Auld Lang Syne'.

Gemma and I were at the front of Cliff's stage, sniggering through his performance. He was surrounded by a wall of backing singers, dressed head to toe in black, looking like the cast of *Riverdance*. One of those singers standing right in front of me was a struggling young West End actress by the name of Myleene Klass. Little did I know that our paths would cross again, eighteen months later.

'The Millennium Prayer' topped the singles chart for three weeks, despite radio stations utterly shunning it, but was knocked off just in time for Christmas and the new Millennium by Westlife, with their double A-side of dire tinny covers: 'I Have a Dream' and 'Seasons in the Sun'.

◆ ◆ ◆

Two days later, just as we were excitedly preparing for the next day's mega Poll Winners' Party concert (yes, it had *finally* come around), we heard via Teletext that Geri had pulled out because of a virus. Gutted, I sat on the kitchen bench, remote in hand, wailing at the announcement displayed in coloured blocky text in front of my eyes.

Gemma was less bothered, as she was buzzed about seeing her beloved Britney. Just turned eighteen, she was the new darling of pop, having conquered the world with '...Baby One More Time' six months previously.

Eager to check on the health of my favourite pop queen, we decided that, before Poll Winners', we would head over to Geri's house with yet another cheap bunch of flowers and cards. We waited in the freezing cold for *hours*. The lights were on in the house but, for the first time, Geri didn't venture out to say hello, and the housekeeper insisted we just left the flowers by the gate.

Three years later I read in her second autobiography that she had got really depressed after the 'Lift Me Up' campaign, and didn't want to see anyone. What makes this even sadder is that back then no one ever saw behind the pop star veneer. We never had a hint that they might be going through real troubles. There was much less discussion about mental health, and no doubt quite a few stars whose antics were denounced by the press were, in reality, just incredibly young people struggling with the trappings of fame and fortune, constantly surrounded by adoring fans, but aware that obscurity and unemployment could be just around the corner. Geri in particular seemed so lonely at times. Back then we thought she had everything, but now I see that there's more to life than appearing on *Noel's House Party*.

♦ ♦ ♦

Paul, Gemma and I went to the Poll Winners' Party the next day, and saw all the acts from the front row: Britney Spears, B*Witched, Westlife, Five, Steps, Billie – everyone on the lips of every mainstream teenager. We snuck into the after-show party afterwards, held in a faux 'swanky' club in Leicester Square, by blagging a press pass from a tipsy journalist on her way out. Despite the scores of fans and paps outside it wasn't all that: we hung out at the bar with A1, Daphne & Celeste and Scooch. I even bought Celeste a drink (on Paul's credit card) to chat her up and get a snog. After cosying up to her for a long, heart-to-heart chat, I left with only a polite peck on the cheek.

As I lay bleary-eyed in bed the next morning, Mum knocked on my door with the phone in hand.

'It's Gemma. DON'T be long, I'm expecting a call,' she said, irritated I was blocking the phone line in the mornings as well as evenings now.

'I need you to come to the airport,' Gemma demanded. 'Paul's phone is off. I'm leaving now. Meet me at Terminal 3 Departures in two hours.'

'To see who? Britney?' I asked, feeling honoured and privileged at being allowed to go near Gemma's precious superstar.

'Yes! Duh? Stop fooling around, just be there.'

Having spent a whirlwind two days on our shores to promote her new single, 'Born to Make You Happy', Britney was jetting home. After an hour of anticipation on the pavement outside Terminal 3 that freezing Monday morning, our hawk-eyes clocking every car, a procession of blacked-out, pimped-up vehicles zoomed into view and stopped next to us. This was it! What would she be like? Would we have a nice chinwag about her favourite London landmarks?

Out stepped a cheery Britney Spears, followed by two man-mountain bodyguards, who I was sure could both pick me up and crush me to a pulp with little effort. Gemma had met Britney a few times before, so her security were surprisingly relaxed about our presence. She said 'Hello' and 'How are you?' before taking a gift from Gemma, uttering her trademark 'You're so sweeeeeeet', then being nudged inside by her nagging team. We walked through the terminal behind her, chatting to her lovely PA, Felicia, although there was no getting in the lift with *this* pop star – Gemma and I were forced to ungracefully scramble up the stairs. As we walked and chatted to smiley Britney through the terminal, she was enticed by something colourful in a shop window and starting veering towards the display.

'Oh my Goddd, I love that! Can I just...?'

'NO,' came the forceful response from her 'people'.

'Oh, okay. Never mind,' Britters said, looking deflated.

Crikey, they won't even let Britney spend her earnings in Tie Rack, I thought. This is one scenario I hadn't anticipated. She bade us goodbye at the gate and Felicia blew us some big kisses, then they slipped through the Fast Track gate. 'Bye, Britney! Bye, Felicia!' I yelled as she disappeared through the automatic doors.

'Wowww!' I gasped to Gemma, taking in our brush with pop royalty. 'They won't let her do *anything*!' I added in shock.

I'd never seen anyone so disappointed at being deprived of browsing gaudy pashminas in Tie Rack. We were used to seeing pop stars being told what they could or couldn't do by their 'people' but this was next level. Sure, she was only young, but they were treating her like a mollycoddled toddler.

And, sadly, we all know how that turned out.

♦ ♦ ♦

Regretfully, I turned down an invite from the Luton Girls of spending Millennium Eve at Laura's mum's house for the 'party of a lifetime' with vodka jellies, party games and a smoke machine (they really went all out), instead spending it with Gemma and a friend of hers on a dangerously crowded stretch of the Thames, near Tower Bridge. Mum, Dad and Sophie had also come into London to watch the fireworks by the riverside, but I'd ditched them in favour of a more 'grown-up' affair: cheap vodka and warm, flat cider.

As the clock struck twelve we all stood around, waiting to see if the predicted chaos would materialise. Would planes fall out of the sky and computers self-destruct? The answer, clearly, was no. When the alcohol wore off, we shuffled back to Waterloo Station, only to discover that the huge volumes of people attempting to get back to Guildford, Basingstoke and Southampton meant we'd have to wait hours for a train home. A new era was upon us and I stood thinking about what the Year 2000 would bring. Which pop bands would we still be following in a year's time? Would the Millennium Dome be a roaring success? Would I ever get out of fucking Waterloo Station?

12

Oops...! I Did It Again

I woke up late on 1 January 2000. Bleary-eyed, I rolled over in bed and switched on my radio, dozing through my hangover to the familiar tones of Britney and Christina. Maybe nothing had changed?

The pop landscape *was* changing though. The bubblegum pop of B*Witched and Aqua seemed to be falling out of favour, as pop acts went for an 'edgier' R&B sound (led by US acts like Destiny's Child and Kelis), and random DJs from Ibiza would appear out of nowhere and score a huge trance hit before disappearing without a trace. Even All Saints were bouncing back from a gap year with a mature, electronic sound. The hottest news in town was Craig David, with his trademark facial hair and plastic kestrel. B*Witched, seeing their happy-go-lucky image was now a turn-off, and desperate to move on from 'I Shall Be There', ditched the denim in favour of a sexed-up look, pleasing droves of hormonal, young *Smash Hits* readers, no doubt.

Geri was battling again, though not in the charts this time. At the start of the New Millennium she was literally in the dock with her old bandmates, although still not even on speaking terms with them. All five original Spices were in the midst of a court case with Italian scooter firm Aprilia – suing Ginger and co. for disclosing that she had mentioned her plan to leave *before* signing their half-a-million-pound sponsorship deal, back in 1998. Both camps were summoned to give evidence in court and forced to relive the messy split in front of the world's press. After many appeals the girls lost the case and were ordered to pay back around £1 million. Clearly, even Geri couldn't win that fight.

Never one to miss an opportunity for self-promotion, though, she stepped out of the courtroom, into the press scrum, clutching a clear plastic handbag with a box of pink 'Girl Powder' washing detergent bagged up inside it. This set tongues wagging in the press, and across Internet forums the world over. A few days later, this witty take on her former band's slogan was revealed as the idea behind her gleaming new single, 'Bag It Up'. You've got to hand it to her, there's a reason why Geri was heading for a third solo Number 1 and the less-shameless Spices were left in the starting blocks. The four-piece Spice Girls were still on hiatus. Their long-awaited third album was gathering dust at Abbey Road while the girls prioritised solo projects to prove their clout individually like Geri had done so fantastically in recent months. The quartet had agreed to perform at the upcoming BRIT Awards in a couple of months' time though – where they would receive an 'Outstanding Contribution to Music' award.

I, meanwhile (a bit like the Spice Girls, though not quite in the same league), had money issues again. My groupie needs were outstretching my means, so I went on the hunt for employment, scoring a weekend job at Waitrose in

Weybridge – in a glamorous dual role of trolley boy/checkout assistant. It looked like I too would be bagging up washing powder for the foreseeable future.

♦ ♦ ♦

I was eager to get home to share the news about my exciting new job with Mum and Dad, but realised there was someone who would be even more proud of me – my surrogate mum, Geri. Gemma and I headed off to Berkshire to stand diligently outside the seven-foot-high black gates. As we waited, we saw a silver Mercedes, exactly the same as Geri's, driving back and forth along the leafy lane. Gemma shot me a suspicious look as it slowed to a crawl and the window was wound down.

'Are you kids looking for Geri? She's just around the corner. I'll give you a lift, if you like...'

'We're *fine*, thanks,' Gemma asserted.

I felt very uncomfortable. Who was this weirdo?

He sped off, just as we heard scurrying footsteps crunching along the gravel drive. 'Hey, guys!' Geri beamed, as she popped her head around the gates. While we didn't want to frighten her, we *had* to warn her about this suspicious creep. A startled-looking Geri immediately ushered us into the garden and gave her housekeeper a knowing look as she asked her to phone the police again. People used to say we were stalkers, but we were just fans. Renting the same model car as a pop star and driving repeatedly past their house is *actual* stalking!

We discussed her upcoming BRITs performance in a few weeks' time, which was top secret, but she promised it would be *very* memorable, and talked about how she felt about the Spice Girls performing at the same ceremony. 'I doubt our paths will cross,' she insisted.

Geri was always reflective when we brought up her old colleagues. We both thought she probably missed the company she had in the band – she seemed to have so few friends and so much time for fans. We told her how we'd made fake passes the year before and that we intended on doing the same thing again to gain entry. During our long chats Geri always flitted between being fully engaged in conversation one minute, and being completely away with the fairies the next. She didn't even seem that excited for me when I told her about Waitrose.

Other than rushing to finish overdue college assignments, the next few weeks were filled with seeing lots of our pop favourites. Geri and B*Witched were both releasing new singles, so their promotional appearances matched up a fair bit, which was great, while Gemma was also seeing Mel C, who was out and about promoting her third single, 'Never Be the Same Again'. It was taken from her debut solo album, *Northern Star*, which received glowing reviews and the sales to match.

The first place we saw B*Witched officially promoting their chirpy new single, 'Jump Down' was at the current vile incarnation of *The National Lottery Live* (now called *Red Alert*). It was a bizarre mixture of celebrity interviews and songs, in front of an intimate studio audience, interspersed with comedy sketches and live performances of cover versions by the show's host, Lulu. Yes, *Lulu*. It didn't quite work and it was awkward to be standing in the audience, pretending to laugh at the many pre-recorded takes of Lulu's jokes. Like some sort of bizarre hell for people with bad music taste, like us.

Throughout these excursions, Gemma and I were constantly thinking about the upcoming BRITs. Would we be able to blag it again and recreate the magic of that fateful night last spring? I was dying to see Geri's much-hyped performance and Gemma wanted to witness the Spice Girls perform their end-of-show medley and bag their award. Although the BRITs were still huge, various other music awards had sprung up, and no doubt the promoters were eager to draw in more viewers with the possibility of a spicy reunion. Geri was more interested in making her own way though, and had no desire to squeeze back into her Union Jack dress.

◆ ◆ ◆

After seeing B*Witched at *The Big Breakfast* studios, two days before the awards, Gemma and I headed west to Earl's Court, where the ceremony had moved to from Docklands Arena. We met Geri, Macy Gray and the Spice Girls outside the venue as they came and went for rehearsals. Endless hours of waiting and chatting to crew members paid off; we had what we wanted: a cheeky photo of the 'AAA' pass, visible around someone's neck. No sketches on the back of fag packets this year. We split the hefty price for one-hour film developing at the nearby Snappy Snaps. They came back great! We had everything we needed to craft our passes again. Using our home PC and new scanner, I meticulously pieced together the recreated pass on Microsoft Paint, working well into the night. I packed my bag for college with my 'smart' outfit for the big night ahead, before finally bedding down for the night. I bounced round college all day with excitement, but there were no nerves this year. My confidence had bloomed in the past twelve months. Still only sixteen, I was fearless when it came to pop; *nothing* could stop me getting my way. I just *knew* we'd get in.

After college I walked giddily to the train station with a couple of classmates who were heading home. One of the boys asked, 'Why are you going to the fucking BRITs, man? You shouldn't even be into that music. You're definitely a fag, bro,' to which I smiled and shrugged, replying, 'Why not? What are you doing tonight? Hanging out with your mum in Woking?'

Mum and Dad both sent texts, encouraging me (surprisingly, with hindsight) but also warning me not to get drunk or arrested. I met Gemma under the cloak of darkness outside Earl's Court Tube station. The streets were clogged with limos inching sluggishly along, their passengers preparing for their grand entrance at the arena in front of a sea of flashing cameras.

Upon arrival at the first checkpoint outside the arena, Gemma and I linked arms, smiling cockily at the security guards as we were waved past. Every guard we encountered gave our passes a brief glance and wished us a pleasant evening. Once more, for one night only, we were somebodies! With these magic laminates around our necks we had the clearance to go anywhere. We reached the red carpet at the top of the ramp and waltzed along it in front of the press, with the same poise and confidence of the A-listers.

'Oh my God! Did you see who that is?' sniggered Gemma, among the commotion. 'CAPRICE! That was her arriving! It's a sign!' The memory came flooding back: the late-nineties model had been slinking down the red carpet, in her Jimmy Choos, with us the year before. What were the chances? She was our lucky mascot!

Once inside the main foyer, Gemma and I let out a sigh of relief and squeezed each other with elation. She snatched a seating plan from an information desk, making a note of exactly where Geri's and the Spice Girls' tables were. Stephen Gately and his boyfriend, a Dutch pop star called Eloy, milled past us in the entrance hall, followed by much-hyped new girl band Atomic Kitten, who had so far released only one single, 'Right Now'. One of them – 'the blonde one' – teenager Kerry Katona, had guys gawping at her in red leather trousers and a tight T-shirt revealing her atomic assets. That one definitely had a touch of Geri's attitude and a knack for grabbing headlines.

As they walked past I saw two faces I did *not* want to see: Tasha and Steph! They were hovering around in the foyer like us, but had two legit tickets in their hands. 'Shit! They're *so* gonna have us thrown out,' Gemma whimpered. It didn't look good. They must have blagged seats through Tasha's mum, who worked for the show's sponsor, Mastercard. Gemma turned away in despair, and Tasha looked me up and down, sternly. They didn't grab Security, though. Nothing. I was so grateful to Tasha for that. However hostile our friendships might have turned, she didn't use her power to deny us our night of adventure. I later found out that she only had one real ticket – the other was a butchered photocopy – and she didn't want to cause a scene and get us all thrown out, which is a slightly less touching anecdote.

We found some seats inside the arena halfway through Five and Queen's show opener: a Home Counties rap debasement of 'We Will Rock You'. The bohemian crapsody we witnessed still managed to become another massive Number 1 for the Five boys that summer.

Next up, Geri proved she was the queen of the genre by pole dancing out of a giant, inflatable vagina. This was the Spice Girls' special night of celebration and Ms Halliwell was clearly not going to let them have it (later, the press was split between those congratulating her attention-grabbing behaviour, and those calling her crass and obscene). I was beside myself – I don't think anyone knew how to put on a show-stopping, tongue-in-cheek spectacle quite like Geri did. A young Gaga was taking notes, across the pond, I'm sure.

After predictable award winners and badly scripted 'banter' between presenters, the Spices closed the show with a medley of live hits and graciously accepted their pre-arranged awards in front of a room full of people who at one point were shouting 'Ge-ri! Ge-ri!' so loud you couldn't hear the speeches. The girls were slick and great fun, but there was no denying it: they were missing something. Geri's performance had trounced theirs and everyone in the room, or watching at home, knew it.

After the show, Gemma and I barged into the seated floor area and shimmied over to where the Spice Girls' families were seated. Four big, circular candlelit tables, one for each Spice Girl, had their nearest and dearest sat around. Hailing from up north, we didn't know the two Mels' relatives, and they looked left out when the Buntons and Adams families stood up to give us excited, tipsy hugs as we approached.

'How did you two get in here? Did you love the show?' proud mum Jackie Adams asked us with great enthusiasm, as Pauline Bunton chimed in, 'You two are up to something, I can tell!' We cackled, showing Posh and Baby's clans the fake passes around our necks, and told them we'd created them in desperation to see the show. They howled with laughter and wonderment, then Jackie shouted across to clans Sporty and Scary to let them in on the joke. To our delight, the southern mums said they were going to tell their girls when they got home, before Jackie ended our chat abruptly to answer a call from her daughter on her buzzing flip phone.

Gemma and I ended up hanging out on the dodgems, bumper to bumper with tanked-up low-grade pop stars and industry folk at the official after-party for the second year running. Waiting alone at Waterloo for the first train home, putting on my work uniform in the train toilet and heading straight to the tills at Waitrose was a bit of a dismal way to end the night. I spent the day on the checkout opposite the newspapers, occasionally glancing over at them, while scanning the barcodes of frozen peas and loo rolls. Jubilant Geri graced the front page of every newspaper, stealing the night from her old colleagues. But I'd been there again, in the middle of the action!

After work, and still sleepless (how did I even function?), I headed straight to Wembley's Fountain Studios – Geri and Steps were appearing on that Saturday night Lulu tripe again, but I was happy to tolerate it to see them perform. Geri was relentlessly promoting 'Bag It Up', buoyant and fresh-faced at every appearance. I was struggling to keep up with her. It was just another bizarre evening in popworld, with me chatting to Geri on the side of the stage while Lulu sang a shouty mum's karaoke interpretation of the New Radicals' 'You Get What You Give'.

♦ ♦ ♦

Two days later, I was back at college after the highest highs of the BRITs, recounting tales to my friends. I walked into Weybridge town centre at lunch to get my camera films developed. Hardly anyone from school had gone on to attend my college but unfortunately, there was one bully who had. He and his new menacing mates had been taunting me around campus for a couple of months for being, in their eyes, clearly gay. Barely anyone else at college seemed to have a problem with me, and I really thought I'd left all that behind. That day when I left the campus alone, like a lamb getting separated from the flock, Paolo and his tracksuited cronies followed me out. My heart was pounding as they slowly closed in on me, shouting homophobic slurs, but I was *not* going to run. If I stayed calm, I'd surely be fine once I reached the main street.

Once on the leafy road the hunting wolves charged faster, about six of them, until I had to accept that I wouldn't escape unscathed this time. They went for my legs, trying to trip me up, to get me down on the ground. After twenty metres of dodging their kicks I crashed to the dry mud by the roadside. They kicked me from every direction, calling me the worst names they could beat me with, and then finished by spitting all over me. When they left, I was bleeding, aching and drenched in their saliva – by far the worst, most degrading part. Cars continued to drive past without stopping, just as they had done throughout the beating, as I lay there for a bit, taking in the humiliation. A few minutes later, I called Dad in tears, unable to really speak. I just needed to be safe at home. I wiped off all the blood, spit and mud I could – I didn't want him seeing me like that. Without even knowing what had happened, Dad was there in a flash. I didn't say much and he didn't push me for an explanation: I knew he was there for me if I needed him.

I still didn't know what was going on with my sexuality, but I thought that I could never come out, or even experiment, without risking attacks like this – the kind I'd been promised by boys at school for years. Denial was my *only* defence. Back home I lay on my bed, listening to my stereo, inspecting my wounds with tears in my eyes. I liked who I was, and loved the fun life I'd created for myself, I'd be damned if I was going to let some low-life jerks bring me down.

◆ ◆ ◆

Putting my bruised ribs and shaken confidence behind me, my Geri antics with Gemma continued. We saw her at *Top of the Pops*: sharing the bill with Destiny's Child, promoting their new single 'Say My Name', hairless dance hero Moby and the Honeyz – there to perform their current feisty hit, 'Won't Take It Lying Down'. It's possibly one of my favourite *Top of the Pops* performances of all the ones I ever witnessed. After being told to sex up their act for this song, the three Honeyz girls came on stage wearing raunchy PVC outfits. One member, Naima, took an 'in for a penny, in for a pound' attitude, and topped off her outfit with a full-on rubber gimp hood, looking like she'd got lost on her way to film *Eurotrash*. The performance was sassy as fuck, but she looked ridiculous, grinning like H from Steps while strutting her stuff in wipe-clean S&M gear. Some handcuffs and a can of whipped cream might have been a nice touch, but I guess she didn't want to shock the teatime family audience BBC1 were going for. I didn't think it was possible to upstage Geri, but Naima pulled it out the bag that night.

Two days later was another biggie: Geri was returning to her spiritual home, London's G-A-Y nightclub, where, with Lucy from school, I'd seen her bring the house down at her first-ever gig the previous summer. A lot had changed since then – we were now on first name terms for a start. Geri didn't disappoint, putting on the most OTT hour-long pop show I'd ever witnessed: costume changes galore, performing that Nancy Sinatra classic, 'These Boots Are Made for Walkin', while simultaneously recreating her mate George Michael's LAPD 'Outside' routine, and closing with a subtle song she wrote for her most loyal fans, literally titled 'G-A-Y'. She may not have lived on this planet a lot of the time, but the girl was definitely tuned into her fan base. Another sleepy shift on tills and trolley duty at Waitrose awaited me the next day, but I threw myself into the madness of it all.

After a few more shows that Geri and B*Witched did together the following week in last-ditch attempts to flog their now-released singles, the final appearance Geri did for this song's campaign was on footballer Ian Wright's chat show, *Friday Night's All Wright*. No, I'm not making these shows up! Gemma and I were the only Geri fans to find out about the recording, although we still had no tickets. Of course we'd try our luck when the audience arrived in a few hours' time, but Geri had a penchant for getting her biggest fans on the guest list for shows when their chances of getting in looked bleak. With the grumpy PA Tor away on her hols, and after chatting to us on the way in about our slim chances of getting spare tickets, Geri signalled over two junior production staff.

'Can you get these two in, please?'

It was finally happening!

'Ahhh, thank you so much for doing this.'

'You're welcome. You two have been at every bloody thing I've done this campaign and you're the only ones here today. This is my special thank you. Besides, I'm off on a long holiday tomorrow and I'm *really* bloody excited!' Geri beamed.

'Ha! Screw you, Tor!' Gemma muttered in my ear, as we walked hand in hand into the studios behind our pint-sized pop icon. It was a bizarre afternoon: sitting in the cafeteria next to Geri's handsome troupe of pink-haired Italian dancers, gobbling down Carbonara and cans of Coke. We couldn't understand a word they said, apart from when one asked, 'Why are you inside today and not on the street?' to which we didn't really have an answer. Every time we walked past Geri's dressing room to go to the loos and she had her door open she asked us if we were having fun. It was a surreal but utterly perfect day! Inside the intimate show's audience, Geri literally got us to sit *on* the stage she was performing on, awkwardly craning our necks to watch her sing (mime).

Geri jetted off on her well-deserved holiday as 'Bag It Up' landed straight in at Number 1, securing her third solo chart-topper. Despite an equally gruelling promotional campaign for the past five weeks, B*Witched's 'Jump Down' single hobbled in at Number 16. I was gutted for them. It was bouncy and boisterous, what went wrong? But Geri was unstoppable, it seemed, while the B*Witched girls' pop careers were falling apart around them – this industry was brutal.

♦ ♦ ♦

That week at the airport I was standing there alone in Terminal 1 Arrivals, looking out for the B*Witched girls, while trying not to look at Tasha, Steph and Charlotte, waiting opposite me. To my surprise they walked over and struck up a conversation. I was guarded at first, not knowing how to take this dubious olive branch being handed to me after ten months of bitter rivalry. But we got chatting, to my surprise (not to mention the B*Witched girls, who were dumbfounded at us being pals again!) and, now all slightly older, the rifts slowly started to heal.

♦ ♦ ♦

One Tuesday evening that April, Gemma enlisted me to see her pop queen Britney at Heathrow again, back on these shores to promote her new single and album, *Oops!... I Did It Again*, a song presumably about her trying to make a run for it into Tie Rack. After a brief 'hi', her team led her into Starbucks, where she ordered a coffee. Gemma and I stood slightly back, not wanting to get in their way, but made sure we were keeping an eye on her at the counter. Upon ordering, a woman from Britney's team kept rudely shouting 'DECAF!' over her and instructing what milk Britney supposedly needed. One of the biggest pop stars on the planet and she was being so controlled by her label and managers that she couldn't even order a triple, venti, fat-free caramel macchiato for herself!

Our paths crossed again at *Top of the Pops* and the Capital FM Awards over the coming days. En route to Borehamwood I went shopping for general tat in Camden Market and found a cheap strappy top with the word 'OOPS' in big lettering sprawled across it (and the word Jeanwear in tiny text underneath). In the days long before you could order T-shirts emblazoned with slogans and song lyrics, this was too good to resist. I bought it for Gemma to put on in the *Top of the Pops* loos. Britney fawned over it on stage, chatting to us in the dead time before and after her performances.

The same week, a group of us headed down to the Royal Lancaster Hotel for the Capital FM Awards. Our repeated BRIT Awards success had given us more confidence, so we headed there to see what we could get up to. We watched the usual stars arrive on the red carpet, but that wasn't the thrill it once was. How could we make this more interesting? After scoping out the building and taking a chance on a side door, a group of us ran in, navigating our way through gaudy-carpeted halls before finally finding the awards room as the tipsy stars were filing out from their boozy lunch. We accosted anyone who was anyone, from Gabrielle to Texas, and The Corrs to Daphne & Celeste, then swiped table plans, programmes and ticket stubs (all still neatly stored in my parents' attic). This included Britney's awards speech memo card on the floor by the podium and Craig David's 'Best Newcomer' award! The cheap lump of glass had already broken off from its base but who cared? I could easily glue that back together. *That'll do nicely*, I thought as it disappeared into my zipped-up Adidas anorak. We were like the cast of *Oliver!*, pilfering from the adult world around us with shameless ease, giving a whole new meaning to the phrase Craig David and the Artful Dodger.

While loitering in the foyer, chatting to Billie Piper, I spotted a familiar face across the room: Louise! She was back, after two years in the pop wilderness, with her trusty manager, Wendy. I made my apologies to Billie and ran over for a friendly reunion with Mrs Redknapp. I asked what she was up to. Wendy said it was all top secret, but insisted Louise had big plans for a return.

I went home that evening, but Gemma and Paul stayed out, going on to meet Britney at her swanky hotel in St Martins Lane after the awards. I'd spent half an hour earlier that day composing an 'Oops!... I Did It Again' ringtone on Gemma's Nokia phone for her to play to Britney. Personalised ringtones were a new creation in early 2000 – if you wanted pop songs to play out in monophonic bleeps, you had to compose them yourself back in the day. When Gemma and Paul met Britney in the hotel foyer they treated her to my reinterpretation of her new single in high-pitched bleeps. She apparently patiently listened with an amazed look in her teenage eyes and a huge grin across her face, declaring she loved it!

If I was jealous about missing out on that iconic moment, then the phone call I received from them a few minutes' later made me green with envy. Some of the stars had carried on the party post-awards at Britney's hotel and while Gemma and Paul were waiting in the foyer, a boozed-up Geri and bezza mate George Michael staggered out from the bar into the foyer. Paul decided to give me a treat, handing Geri his phone and telling her Malcolm was on the other end, and I had a brief and painfully slurred chat with her. My teenage life was just too bizarre and unbelievable to explain to people a lot of the time.

♦ ♦ ♦

That Saturday afternoon I was sat at my till at Waitrose, back in the real world but constantly daydreaming about my escapades up in London, when a meek little voice called my name from the end of my till: 'Hi Malcolm!'

It was Keavy, one of the twins from B*Witched, and she was right there – standing at the end of *my* checkout! This time the tables had turned and the stalker had become the stalked! People at college had recognised her strolling around Weybridge recently and figured she must have moved to the area (*to be near me?*). We chatted for ages while I did an extremely bad job of scanning items for the old lady I was supposed to be serving, as a huge queue developed at my till.

That night I got pissed with all my groupie mates at Charlotte's eighteenth birthday party, in a pub in Richmond, and recounted the story to them all. Too old for these squabbles, we'd all buried the hatchet. Life was good.

13

Time to Burn

Spring was in the air. Record labels were gearing up for summer by pushing the cheesy hits we'd all be dancing to in Spanish resorts. There were just a few weeks left of the first year of my Media Studies course. It had flown by! Probably because I was hardly there. I couldn't *wait* for another summer of 24/7 pop stalking. Who wouldn't want to spend nine weeks of freedom sitting on a kerbside outside a recording studio? There was still another year of studying to go before college was over, but that all felt a very long way off.

◆ ◆ ◆

To prepare us for the world of work, every student on our course was instructed to find a couple of weeks of work experience. Somehow, they thought a fortnight of making tea and photocopying would prepare us for a high-powered career in the world of media. Thanks to my extracurricular exploits, I had contacts in the TV industry. I phoned up Suzanna, a runner at Molinare – a Soho TV studio where a pop programme called *Videotech* was recorded.

Videotech was a turn-of-the-Millennium vision of the future. All CGI (computer-generated imagery) green screens and inflatable furniture, which pop stars and celebs would attempt to balance on during interviews. The CGI backgrounds looked more like dodgy screensavers, rather than special effects from *The Matrix*, and the programme's USP was terrestrial TV exclusives of music videos, weeks after MTV first showed them. In case you were wondering, the future didn't turn out as they had expected.

Suzanna was more than happy to have me tag along behind her at work, declaring this was my opportunity to grow up and transition from desperate fanboy to industry professional. She was perky, trendy and could see straight past all the bullshit egos of the self-important bigwigs that dominated the industry. I diligently spent a week following her round like a bad smell, handing out bottles of water to the likes of Richard Blackwood and standing silently for hours on end while we filmed a Moby interview. But I was bored – being a fan was way more fun than this.

Never one to waste an opportunity, I spent every lunch break pounding the streets of Soho and Covent Garden, looking for pop stars to harass. I even managed to slack off early one afternoon and headed over to the Dance Attic studios in Fulham, where we'd found out B*Witched were rehearsing in preparation for their US tour. Alas, for the girls, the luck of the Irish seemed to be drying up and, as they prepared for the tour, I really feared they wouldn't be jigging around the charts for much longer. Fortunately, Keavy could still afford to shop in Waitrose, though, so I was also getting to say hello while I scanned her Special K and crumpets.

After my week working at the studios I immediately went back to making brief appearances at college for a few hours a week, while jet-setting around London on a child travelcard to see Louise and various Spice Girls the rest of the time.

◆ ◆ ◆

By early June 2000, Louise was in full comeback mode with her single '2 Faced'. Maybe bored of being a housewife, and eager to snatch back her crown from the younger new divas, she threw herself back into the music world with a relentless schedule of TV appearances and record shop signings. She wasn't about to sit back and let Samantha Mumba take all the glory.

Ever since my brief encounter with Louise at the Capital FM Awards, a couple of months back, my obsession for my first love Eternal had been reignited. So I set my Argos alarm clock at the crack of dawn one morning to make it over to the mean streets of Hackney Wick for Louise's first appearance of the campaign, at *The Big Breakfast*. It was just my luck that, on the morning of my special reunion with my teen idol, it was pissing down with rain. The sky was an endless landscape of heavy grey. My heart sank.

On our TV screens, *The Big Breakfast* house looked like an idyllic, picket-fenced canal-side cottage. In reality, it was sandwiched between an industrial wasteland and a stagnant stretch of canal that looked like the scene of a thousand *EastEnders* cliff-hanger moments. Us fans had to walk along the dodgy towpath and crawl through a shoddily patched-up hole in the sharp wire fence to gain entry, or risk running the gauntlet past the (admittedly lax) security guards protecting the industrial estate. I usually preferred the second option, as there was a much lower chance of getting mugged.

The unyielding rain was putting a big dampener on my morning. Once within *The Big Breakfast* compound I surveyed my surroundings for any sort of shelter, like the Virgin Mary on arrival in Bethlehem. Knowing that I wouldn't be granted access to Lockkeepers' Cottage itself, I spotted an HGV in one corner and realised that crawling beneath it was my only hope. I spent a dry couple of hours under there, wedged between the tyres and the fag butt-covered tarmac, waiting for Louise to emerge.

When I finally saw her honey-blonde locks dashing across the car park, it was my time to emerge. I leapt out from the lorry, and managed to give Wendy, Louise's manager, a minor heart attack.

'Oh my God! Where did you just come from?' Louise cried, laughing from under a multi-coloured golf umbrella. She was, of course, flattered by my dedication, but no doubt also questioned my sanity.

'It's a bit wet out here to stop today,' said Wendy.

'Don't worry – it's really dry under here!' I said, pointing to my waterless refuge.

'I am *not* crouching under a bloody *lorry*!' Wendy shrieked, horrified at the suggestion. Louise was in fits of giggles so I used the opportunity to huddle under their brolly.

They seemed so pleased that I'd come down and that anyone was still showing support to her after her career break. Wendy recited a list of every upcoming public appearance that Louise was making over the coming weeks, like a middle-aged Rainman in a Debenhams mac and pearls.

Louise's next appearance was on the Jim Davidson variety show. We actually sat through the whole dire performance just to see her sing for five minutes – it was worth it though. Mainly because, before going into the theatre, we mingled with The Netherlands' third-biggest cheese export – the Vengaboys – in a local 'Buffalo' shoe shop as they bought up the entire stock of platform trainers, before jumping back onto the Vengabus and partying their way to Ibiza via The Hague. We then turned the corner and bumped into Five, who were swaggering down the street, gleaming with sweat and testosterone, having just finished dance rehearsals at Pineapple Studios. I felt like a proverbial shit, and pop stars were my flies.

♦ ♦ ♦

'Surely it's on at the Odeon in Leicester Square? Check again!' Gemma commanded, as I scanned through the cinema listings in the back of the *Evening Standard*.

'It isn't, Gemma. They must have only shown it for a week.'

We were confused. All Saints, one of our favourite bands, had just released their debut film. But unlike *Spice World* or *A Hard Day's Night*, it didn't look like Barry Norman would be fondly remembering *Honest* in years to come. The acting from the three Saints in the film (Shaznay opting to dodge the bullet) was hammier than a pound of gammon, but it didn't deserve to be dropped by every cinema showing it within a couple of days. The girls took it on the chin though, and Gemma and I gave them many supportive words to lift their spirits when we saw them a few days later at the recording studio, laying down vocals for their new album, *Saints & Sinners*.

♦ ♦ ♦

As the college year drew to an end, the guys in my class became remarkably more interested in pop. The Queen of Australia, Kylie Minogue, had reinvented herself with a new single, 'Spinning Around'. After a couple of years of trying, and largely failing, to be a 'credible' indie artist, she had returned to her pop roots with a sexed-up look. Her hot-pant-clad bum had been wiggling its way across MTV for a few weeks, and it seemed to be getting the attention she was looking for. To seal the deal, she announced an appearance at G-A-Y, a rite of passage for any self-respecting diva with a single to flog.

The G-A-Y comeback concert on Saturday, 17 June 2000 was incredible. It was packed to the rafters, and the atmosphere (and temperature) in the Astoria that summer's night was sizzling. Truthfully, the gold lamé-wrapped buttocks didn't do much for me, but I was still transfixed. As Kylie belted out some of her legendary early hits I was transported to being seven years old, dancing round Anja's bedroom to a cassette of her first album. For us teenage fans, it was a moment of revelation... turned out this retro icon still had sass!

By the middle of summer, the Spice Girls were still trying to cobble together their third album, a whole year since we saw them at Abbey Road making the first recordings. They were all too busy trying to peddle solo careers to care about the band by this point. The labels, meanwhile, were still trying to find the *new* Spice Girls. The final, and most desperate attempt, was Simon Cowell's tawdry ensemble, Girl Thing. They looked like a tribute act. When we bumped into Mel C at *The Big Breakfast* one July morning, Arash, my Iranian pop pal, and I were desperate to have her take on Girl Thing.

Mel instantly stopped signing our CDs and gawped at us as soon as we mentioned their name. 'Oh. My. God.'

We broke into mass laughter as she held her breath, smiling and waiting to say her piece.

'There's so much to say... Have you *seen* the fucking video?!! One of them does a bloody *backflip*! It's *mad*, innit?!' She let out a wicked cackle, her gold tooth gleaming in the sun. 'They do say imitation is the sincerest form of flattery, don't they?' she concluded.

Posh was the final Spice to attempt a solo career, so we were all incredibly curious when we found out she would be doing a pre-recorded performance of her single at *Top of the Pops* one week that July. I'd heard she was duetting with Dane Bowers, and there was a rumour it would be Garage, but beyond that it was all a mystery. After a classic line-up of Five, Queen, Artful Dodger, Robbie Williams, Destiny's Child, Mel C (*yes*, double Spice action that night) and various other acts, it was VB's turn.

She emerged, a few feet away from us, performing 'Out of Your Mind'. The single was an attempt to be futuristic, but the reality, a couple of decades on, is that it is painfully of its era: costumes inspired by *The Matrix*, a UK Garage beat, excessive use of autotune and a bloke from Another Level. The backing dancers did martial arts in trouser suits while Victoria and Dane mimed in white pleather. It was never going to age like a fine wine but we were blown away. Surely something this 'out there' was bound to bag her a Number 1 when it was released a few weeks later?

◆ ◆ ◆

The highlight of my summer was not to be a chance encounter on the streets of London, though, but a transatlantic adventure, thanks to Tasha. One evening she was listening to Capital FM's show in her bedroom, in the posh bit of Romford, when the DJ announced a competition to win an all-expenses trip to Washington, D.C. to meet the boy band *NSYNC on their monumental stadium tour.

'Call us up with the craziest thing you will do for this trip of a lifetime to meet *NSYNC in the US!'

Tasha picked up her weighty mobile, scrolling through her contacts to find 'CAPITAL FM'. To her surprise she got through to an operator quite easily and landed herself on the air, where she made the bold bid to the DJ, James Cannon, that she'd shave all her hair off. Everything; the lot – a *bald* bid, if you ask me.

After a fair bit of deliberation, and all of Groupie London listening in at home, Tasha was crowned the winner – provided she came in live on air the next evening to shave off her barnet.

'You're a lesbian, you were probably going to shave it off anyway!' I told her, as we sat waiting in the studio.

Cannon then fired up the clippers and, with a graceful sweep across Tasha's head, her brunette locks gave way to a stubbly scalp. She was overjoyed at the prospect of going to the US, and Steph was the lucky bitch chosen to go with her. Unfortunately for her, and luckily for me, Steph couldn't go, so I selflessly stepped up to the mark and took her place, with just a week to go! I told Waitrose where to go after they refused to give me the time off. Who cared? I could find another job.

Before heading stateside, there was just one big weekend of divas to enjoy in London. Christina Aguilera was in town, to perform at Party in the Park the next day. In previous years, we would have all been on the front barrier for the annual pop extravaganza but, by 2000, we thought we were above that. Twelve months into her career, nineteen-year-old Christina already had a reputation for being a somewhat challenging chanteuse, though she was nothing but sweetness and smiles to me when I accosted her in her hotel lobby – I must have rubbed her the right way. Following that, Arash and I headed to the sticky Astoria dance floor for the launch night of the G-A-Y compilation CD, with performances by Louise, Billie Piper, Bananarama, Shola Ama, Honeyz, Dina Carroll and All Saints – the latter clocking me at the front and giving me high fives.

The next day, the most biblical of storms descended upon London as the vast crowds gathered at Party in the Park. I was so glad we weren't there. Instead, a bunch of us congregated at Heathrow Terminal 1 to meet Geri on her way back from a gig in Ibiza. I can only imagine the disappointment among the pilled-up clubbers when they were expecting Judge Jules-style Eurotrance at one of the island's superclubs and instead got Geri miming to 'Mi Chico Latino' in a gypsy skirt.

Upon landing, Geri orchestrated a mass group photo of the eight or so of us fans in the middle of the teeming, stuffy arrivals hall. Looking at the monsoon rain outside, I was quite happy with staying safe and dry inside with her.

There's a reason why you won't find footage on YouTube of Kylie Minogue's medley of hits at the sopping Hyde Park gig. One of the few performers actually singing live, comeback queen Kylie had no working in-ear monitors, thanks to the sound desk tent drowning under the deluge, so she performed her numbers as best she could – some half a second behind the track blaring out the speakers to the sodden and disheartened crowd. Ever the professional, Kylie carried on regardless, despite skidding around perilously on the stage that she likened more to an ice rink.

But we weren't there to witness it (thankfully) as, after seeing Geri, we were actually getting on a plane ourselves for once! Tasha and I were euphoric to be jetting off to the States, skipping through Duty-free in giddy glee, only pausing to drench ourselves in a dozen perfumes and face cream testers. Due to the horrific weather that was spoiling everyone's fun in London, our flight was delayed, but it meant we had time to buy *NSYNC's new album *No Strings Attached* in the Virgin Megastore. We'd at least have something to get signed and importantly, we would look like proper fans. In the UK the group were still seen as less-successful Backstreet Boys clones, fronted by that guy with the curly hair – whatshisname? – Britney's boyfriend.

Tasha and I knew a lot about pop. Like, A LOT. But even we weren't prepared for how big a deal the band was in the States. They were the biggest pop stars in the country, having just broken the record for first-week album sales, with *2.4 million* CDs purchased there in the *first seven days* (Backstreet Boys and Eminem only managed half that figure).

Upon our late arrival at Washington Airport, we were greeted by the charming driver of our private limousine. Finally, we were being treated like the stars we spent our lives chasing! Using our driver's phone, we made a call to Tammy, our contact from Jive Records, who'd been frantically calling our hotel. We headed straight for the stadium, unfortunately hitting the gridlocked freeways. We were so late arriving that Tammy and her colleague flagged us down and literally ran with us, up a maze of ramps, deep into the bowels of the stadium till we reached the small room where the meet and greet was about to commence.

'I'm so happy we got y'all here in time!' Tammy, our all-American chaperone, beamed in her Southern drawl.

We took seats at the back for the serious Q&A session. All the questions were from blubbing girls, hysterically asking 'Will you marry me?' to various grinning, bored-looking band members. The fans then slowly filed past with various pieces of merch to get signed. When we finally reached the desk the guys took one look at Tasha's fuzzy head and realised who we were.

'Oh my God, you're the British kids!' Lance, the blond one, boomed excitedly in his deep-toned voice.

'HEY! It's the girl who shaved her hair off!' Joey, the big Italian-American one chimed in. 'Welcome to the US!'

'We've heard *all* about you – you're so crazy that you shaved your hair off *for us*!' Chris, the squat, goateed one added.

'Yep,' Tasha replied, with a wincing grin. 'That's us!'

'You're mad! I hope ya'll love the concert,' Justin said, in his dulcet Tennessee twang.

Back home, during the last couple of years, Justin had been my only real attraction to *NSYNC. I'd thought he was pretty good-looking from their videos, and that time we briefly bumped into the band passing through Heathrow, eighteen months earlier. But sitting there right in front of me, with his mesmerising blue eyes framed by perfectly thick eyebrows, nestling below a woodland camouflage bandana, I was *transfixed* by the nineteen-year-old enchanter.

Stop looking at him... stop looking at him... I repeated in my head, before being drawn back to his flawless face and sweet lips. Justin was truly the most beautiful guy I'd *ever* seen. He was the quietest of the band by far. Mysterious. The others couldn't *stop* talking.

'We're so happy you're here! We love London and Capital Radio!' JC, the preppy, muscled one said.

After a couple more minutes of chatting to the *NSYNC boys and trying not to stare at Britney's boyfriend, Justin, it was time to wrap it up – all the other fans had been ushered out and the guys needed to prepare for the concert. We each grabbed a group photo with them and said our goodbyes.

Tammy treated us to some quality American food: hotdogs, fries and the biggest buckets of Pepsi I'd ever seen. 'Welcome to America!' she said, flashing us her perfect smile. We gorged on 17,000 calories of processed food, wowed by the immensity not only of the Pepsi, but also the concert. This was a no-holds-barred technical extravaganza. Lance spotted us a few rows back, in the crowd of tens of thousands of besotted schoolgirls, and waved at me and the bald girl at my side. *NSYNC managed to sing live *and* do acrobatic dance routines – this was miles better than watching Dane Bowers mime in Borehamwood.

Back at the hotel, Tasha and I stayed up talking it over, fumbling through our tour programmes and signed albums, occasionally going on missions around the hotel to find working vending machines for snacks. I stared at Justin's page in the CD booklet. I wasn't a fan of boy bands back home, but I had a new appreciation of them after witnessing *NSYNC's live show. Those guys were something else, mainly thanks to Justin.

Why wasn't he famous back home?

After a big shopping day, mainly spent trying on everything in the Abercrombie & Fitch store (the hottest brand that all the US pop stars were seen in), and a final day spent by the poolside, it was time to fly home. We were such moronic kids we didn't do *any* sightseeing. Unfortunately, I'd ignored all of Baz Luhrmann's warnings about wearing sunscreen and by the evening, I was glowing pink and shivering. As we jetted home across the Atlantic, I slowly turned redder than the upholstery on our Virgin plane, while Tasha laughed at my delirious state.

I spent the rest of the week at home in terrible pain, Mum nursing blisters on my neck and shoulders. Ever a hypochondriac, for *two* nights running I was ferried to and from hospital, where I had to be put on an intravenous drip to stop the allergic reaction my body had to the burn.

♦ ♦ ♦

I finally emerged from my sick bed a week later to see Louise at her swanky album launch, at St Martin's Lane Hotel. She said she couldn't let me in because I was underage, but kept coming over to speak to me from the roped-off terrace where the stars (my old mate Kelle, All Saints, Honeyz, Martine McCutcheon, Precious and Steps) were downing champers.

'Oh my God! What happened to you?' Louise asked when she spotted my beetroot face (she could hardly miss it). It was great to see Kelle too, after so long, and she seemed genuinely concerned about my gross, peeling skin.

After months of promo, Louise's comeback track '2 Faced' became the highest-charting single of her career, going straight in at Number 3. Amazing, considering most radio stations had shunned it. Tasha, Steph and I awarded her with a giant cookie at Heathrow with the words 'HOORAY NUMBER THREE' imaginatively written across it in piped icing. Louise was so overjoyed by this celebratory biscuit that she got her PA to take a snap of us all on her Polaroid, the cookie obviously taking centre stage.

◆ ◆ ◆

Louise was *over the moon* with her Number 3 placing. But that was failure in the eyes of another songstress. Victoria Beckham's single 'Out of Your Mind' was getting stacks of airplay that summer, supported by a full-on promotional campaign. With its release date set for 14 August 2000, we were all confident that Britain's favourite WAG would bag the top slot.

But a storm was brewing in Wagland. A Balearic club track was on the horizon, fronted by a porcelain-faced, privately educated vixen named Sophie Ellis-Bextor. She made Posh, in her head-to-toe Burberry clobber, look like Kat Slater in comparison. Sophie's spot as guest vocalist on Italian dance producer Spiller's track 'Groovejet (If This Ain't Love)' was making waves across Europe, from the dance floors of Pacha in Ibiza to the bars of London.

Victoria was evidently aware of her competition, but eager to avoid the perceived desperation of her old mate Geri Halliwell when she'd battled Emma Bunton the previous year. She began her single campaign pretty casually with the usual TV and radio appearances. After a heavy, sweaty night out clubbing, a group of us walked to Channel 4's headquarters, where Victoria and Dane, or 'Posh and Decks' as they were being hailed, were appearing on teen TV show *T4*. After one too many Smirnoff Ices the night before, I remember being woken up on the steps outside by a concerned Dane Bowers, asking Arash if I was alright.

A few days later, we went up to Posh's family home to drop in on Victoria and our BFF Jackie Adams. Seeing that Gemma had a rare promo CD of the single that Jackie desperately wanted, we took twenty quid off her to track down another copy for Mother Posh.

Realising that 'Groovejet' was getting a lot of attention in clubs around the Med, Victoria and Dane headed out to Ibiza to drum up some interest in their track. Sadly, Garage didn't seem to be quite as popular as they had reckoned. We met them at Heathrow when they flew back, and chatted to Victoria as they made their way out of the terminal, at one point all piling into a lift together. Also in the lift with us was Dane's girlfriend Jordan (aka Katie Price), sulking in the corner with a scowl on her face, evidently not keen on playing second fiddle to Mrs Beckham. It was surreal. Especially when the lift doors opened at the top and David and Brooklyn were waiting to collect Mummy!

In a bid to secure chart victory, Victoria announced a series of signings around the country, and that David would be joining her. Maybe she was taking a leaf out of Geri's book after all? During the week of release we met her at Heathrow, returning from Manchester. A couple of Westlife fans spotted Victoria chatting to us, and shoved some scraps of paper in her face for an autograph.

'Have you bought the single, girls?' Victoria asked them with an air of superiority as Gemma and I watched on.

'Not yet, but we're *definitely* going to. We love it!' came the sheepish reply.

'Okay, well, there's a Virgin Megastore over there. Go and buy it, I can wait,' Victoria said, with a cheeky grin.

The two girls looked dumbfounded as Victoria shooed them away in the direction of the record shop on the other side of the terminal.

They duly waddled off to buy her single, as Victoria turned to us two, also stunned. '*What*?! It's two more sales, isn't it?' she said, grinning.

The race had been tight all week, but Gemma was adamant that by going the extra mile, Victoria would push herself and Dane into the top spot. Miss Ellis-Bextor, meanwhile, had taken the laid-back approach. By the weekend, the over-eighteens crept out of the woodwork though and plumped for 'Groovejet' by a sizeable margin, shifting 20,000 more copies than its rival. I listened in horror, that fateful humid Sunday evening, at the announcement that Posh was Number 2.

To add insult to injury, the posh girl who had stolen Posh's crown was splashed across Monday's newspapers in a T-shirt emblazoned with the word 'Peckham' and a cheeky finger in the air, declaring she was *numero uno*. Sophie even accused Victoria of underhand tactics and desperate measures. Such behaviour was clearly beyond the pale for the double-barrelled daughter of a *Blue Peter* presenter.

♦ ♦ ♦

With the battle over, summer was drawing to a close. I was facing the prospect of one final year at college, painfully aware that I had not been *particularly* studious in the current one, and was none the wiser about how I could get some sort of interesting career. To make matters worse, having burnt my bridges with Waitrose, how was I ever going to chat to Keavy again?

14

Same Old Brand New You

September came, and with it, my final year at college. Arash, Charlotte and I were spending loads of time together, while Gemma and I were going through one of our 'rocky patches'. The Luton Girls had placed their autograph books firmly back on the shelf and scarpered to universities in provincial towns across Britain, lured by the prospect of Scream Pubs and Skool Disco club nights. Before the five girls went away, they hosted a farewell party for the finale of *Big Brother*. We'd all been gripped by the thrilling antics of an Irish nun and a marketing manager from Hemel Hempstead. For the first time in history, but certainly not the last, a captivated nation welcomed a dozen new 'celebrities' into the world and asked themselves, 'Why have we wasted a whole summer watching people sleeping and squabbling over tea?'

I started the second year of my Media Studies course with great intentions. I wasn't fussed in the slightest about getting good grades for university, I just wanted a job in the glitzy record industry as soon as college was over next summer, so that I'd never have to face the realities of life outside the pop bubble.

♦ ♦ ♦

Ever since my trip to America I'd avoided having my hair cut. Not in political protest or to save money, although I *did* need a job pretty pronto. I simply had a desperate urge to look like Justin Timberlake, who I'd been idolising ever since our paths crossed in the green room, back in July. I'd studied him on stage in Washington, with his perfect face and perfect eyes, coveting his cornrow hairdo under a bejewelled bandana, and been captivated by his oversized diamond earrings. His look was totally unlike any of the boring people in Surrey, and in an act of teenage rebellion I decided to mimic his appearance in whatever way I could.

I headed into Camden Town to scour the market for a suitable bandana under which my wavy mop could grow long enough for cornrows. I popped into Argos to pick up some huge cubic zirconia studs. I even bought an American football shirt from JJB Sports to parade around the shopping precinct in Woking. *Screw you, Surreyites!* When I saw my reflection in shop windows, I thought I was embodying Justin. Everyone else just thought I was wearing a dodgy headscarf and my nan's earrings. Every cringeworthy haircut or tragic fashion 'statement' was me trying to project who I thought I really was inside. A miniature act of defiance against my parents, or a way to align myself with a tribe.

♦ ♦ ♦

I saw B*Witched for the first time in months, all bronzed and blissful (them, not me), at their first UK gig after their huge US tour. Not at Wembley or Earl's Court, but a *students' union* in Surrey. They'd done all the school tours and provincial clubs on the way up, and were multimillion-pound pop gods now... Right? Is this what they had been reduced to? A novelty act for pissed-up freshers?

Before the gig we caught up on all the gossip from their tour, but I just kept wondering why they were playing tiny gigs for rowdy students instead of working on a new album. At one point, during the set's pinnacle, 'C'est la Vie', some of the less-impressed students threw tomatoes at them on stage from the balcony. None of them hit the girls – and they laughed it off by aiming the song's cusses ('Get a LOIFE') at the culprits – but we'd never witnessed animosity at any of the gigs we'd been to before, bar the booing that poor old Daphne & Celeste and Billie Piper seemed to attract. Steph and Tasha drove me home late into the night, with Keavy and Edele in the car in front of us the whole way, to Weybridge, making faces at us out the windows. They were clearly in good spirits, but I felt gutted for them, just as I had felt watching Kelle's pop dreams start to fade.

◆ ◆ ◆

There was one girl group enjoying a revival, though: the Spice Girls' third album was *finally* due for release on 1 November 2000. *Forever* was a complete departure from their earlier music, ditching Europop for the US R&B vibes of Destiny's Child and Toni Braxton. But the Spice Girls' rendition of this sound didn't quite hit the mark. The band seemed to be lacking direction and, in a pop landscape transformed since their launch four years previously, *Forever* felt like it took forever to be released. The over-confident girls, each with solo projects to worry about, didn't bother with the usual relentless marketing tour to promote the release. They probably didn't even need to bother with a third album, but they had to prove they still *had it* after Ginger's departure. And I'm sure the record label execs could see a healthy profit in another album.

The entire project was clearly a bit of a fudge. Even Gemma, the most die-hard Spice Girls fan I knew, was critical of the album's dismal artwork. They looked more like four divorcees with questionable hairdos from suburban salons than groundbreaking superstars in their mid-twenties.

The only promotion that they bothered to do was a tiny smattering of TV shows: *Top of the Pops*, *CD:UK*, *The National Lottery Live* and the *MTV Europe Music Awards* in Stockholm. Four appearances to promote the comeback album of the biggest pop band in the world – five if you can count the album launch at a gaudy club in the West End. What made it worse was that it didn't even seem like *they* believed in the whole thing.

Still, I accompanied Gemma to the few appearances anyway. The line-up at *Top of the Pops* included: kings of guyliner, Placebo, Muse, the irresistible Corrs, the barking mad Baha Men, along with the new-look Spice Girls. In order to give them the best chance of securing another all-important chart-topper, they were releasing a double A-side – two songs at once. That night, they changed outfits for *four* different recordings so they wouldn't have to regroup and come back for a while. They'd seen us at the front for a couple of them and so, for the last two, Gemma and I opted to hang out at the back of the audience with Jackie and Tony, Victoria's parents, and eighteen-month-old Brooklyn in giant ear defenders. They were so friendly to us, letting us pull faces at him and prod his chubby cheeks – you'd probably be tasered for merely smiling at a Beckham kid these days! We apologised to Jackie for never finding the CD she had asked us to hunt for her, and still owing her twenty quid. She laughed her head off and told us to keep it. After we left, Gemma turned to me and said, 'I wish we'd taken £50 now!'

♦ ♦ ♦

My friend Lauren from college had an uncle who worked in telly, as executive producer of *The National Lottery Live*. Knowing what a crazed pop fan I was, she offered to get me backstage one week – any week – of my choice. This offer was too good to waste on a third-rate week, so I waited months before setting the date. Gemma had heard from her mole Baby Spice that one of their promotional dates for the new album would be the *National Lottery*.

'Can we come backstage on 7 October, please?' I asked Lauren, shocked I'd finally taken her offer up.

'Erm, yeah. Mel C's on in a couple of weeks. Are you sure you don't wanna come then?'

'No, no – 7 October would be *great*, I've heard that'll be a good week!' I said with a cheeky grin.

Things became clearer to Lauren as the weeks drew on and the guest list filtered down the chain. We met Victoria at the airport a couple of days beforehand and pre-warned her we'd been given special backstage access by a friend who worked there.

'Oh, fabulous!' she said, 'That'll be so nice for you both with the whole band there.'

Yeah, no shit, Vicky!

'You know how much I've always wanted a group photo…?' Gemma asked, 'Well, we really, *really* want one while you're back together again – and backstage at the *Lottery* on Saturday is our *only* chance! Please, please, *please* can you help make it happen?' she whined.

'Sure thing! I'll totally sort that out. When you see us backstage, just remind me then,' Victoria said, reassuringly. 'I promise. *Don't* worry, guys!'

When Saturday finally arrived, we were buzzing. We started the day off at *CD:UK*. The Spice Girls were performing, along with contemporary chart heavyweights: Louise, Atomic Kitten, Honeyz, Stephen Gately, Martine McCutcheon (and The bloody Corrs again!). The Spice Girls were on form that morning, chatting to the die-hards in the front row. They would all be heading over to Television Centre for the *National Lottery* afterwards, but only Gemma and I would have unimpeded backstage access!

Lauren's family were so friendly when we met them outside the studios, although keen to remind us how privileged we were to have this special experience and that we had to be on our best behaviour. After playing it cool at first, Gemma and I desperately flitted about between the canteens, studios and dressing rooms, proudly wearing our BBC guest IDs around our necks, in the hope of finding the girls and getting *that* photo.

We cautiously entered a small cafeteria adjacent to their dressing room and were delighted to discover three Spices in there. And *nobody* else. Just Sporty, Baby and Scary sharing a bottle of bubbly in a sea of deserted tables. Sporty was mid-way through recounting a story, her honey-blonde bob flicking around her face animatedly, when we entered and took a seat at the other end of the room. The three of them sat speechless and open-mouthed in confusion for about five seconds, before Sporty gathered enough composure to say, 'Hi guys!'

Instead of the rapturous friendly welcome we had anticipated, they awkwardly continued nattering in a barely audible tone.

Alas, Posh, the one who held the key to making it happen, was nowhere to be seen. Gemma and I realised we had crossed a line in the girls' eyes, and the tension was unbearable. We awkwardly shared a Twix from the vending machine as the three Spices swiftly polished off their drinks and scooted back to the dressing room with a brisk goodbye.

We returned to the studio, somewhat deflated, where Lauren's auntie asked us firmly where we'd been, before reiterating her previous warning.

'You're here as *guests*. Please do as we say and do *not* bother the celebrities!' She didn't understand that we *knew* them and had been promised a group photo by VB *herself*. Well, that's the way our entitled teenage eyes saw it.

When the Spice Girls finally came on stage to rehearse, Gemma and I watched eagerly, waiting for our moment to leave to catch them in the corridor – exactly what we'd been told *not* to do.

We left to 'go to the toilet' together shortly before the rehearsal was winding up. '*Don't* bother them!' Lauren's auntie uttered in a forceful whisper as we slinked out.

We loitered in the silent hallway, cameras in hand, when the studio doors flew open and a tornado of girl power literally squeezed past us, filling the entire corridor: pop stars, make-up assistants, PAs. Frenzied conversations about outfit changes and microphone packs were being batted all around us. The three Spice Girls up front said 'hi' and carried on their chats, while Posh, trailing behind, greeted us with a bright 'hello'.

'Hi! Victoria – the photo! Can we do it now?!' Gemma asked, her words not hiding our desperation.

'Photo... Oh yes, the photo!' Posh said, remembering our conversation. 'Girls!' The other three and the ensemble were slipping away, pushing through the door to their dressing room. 'GIRLS!' she bellowed. Everyone turned on their heels to see what the commotion was, stopping dead in their tracks as silence fell around.

'What?' Scary hollered.

'I promised these two they could have a group photo. Can we do it now?' Posh asked, receiving the attention of the entire corridor.

'Oh,' Sporty replied, wondering what the huge fuss was. 'Yeah... what, now?'

'Yes, now!' Posh protested.

At this point the girls' PA stepped in. 'We haven't got time now, you need to get changed. I'm sorry,' she said, turning to us, 'they need to get into their next outfits. We'll do one later.'

The girls continued their conversations and began filing out into their dressing room, Victoria being pulled in their direction by impatient members of their team.

'I'm so sorry, I tried my best! We'll do it later, okay?' she shouted, as she was whisked through the doors, taking the tumultuous tornado of pop icons with her.

Gemma sighed and we turned to go back in the studio, hoping we could creep back in, unnoticed. A look of horror passed over our faces when we saw that blocking our path was Lauren and her whole family. Powerful uncle. Angry aunt. Three outraged kids. All with faces like thunder.

'GET. OUT!' the auntie roared, seething with rage. Lauren's uncle was silent, shaking his head in condemnation. 'I told you to leave them alone. Now give me your badges, I'm escorting you off the premises. You've disgraced the *entire* family!' she shrieked.

Gemma burst into tears as the auntie marched us out through a side door, into the glaring daylight of the car park beyond. I put my arm on Gemma's shoulder, reassuring her that it would all be okay now we were outside. We turned the corner on our way to the Tube station only to be greeted by dozens of other rival

Spice fans – a who's who of the groupie world, to whom we'd been bragging all bloody month about our privileged backstage passes. My jaw dropped.

Before blubbing Gemma could become even more hysterical at the prospect of walking past them all in disgrace I swiftly made us do a U-turn. I had no idea where we were going, but doing a complete lap of Shepherd's Bush would be better than our rivals witnessing our hideous comeuppance.

The next day, I called Lauren to try to apologise. She was obviously pissed off at me, and was bearing the brunt of her family's anger. Had we gone too far? The closer we got to the stars, the more I felt like we were overstepping the mark. We always wanted to be one step ahead of the other fans, but I was increasingly aware that we were straying into their personal lives, their downtime with friends and family.

For Gemma though, the *Lottery* experience was too traumatic. Realising her long-awaited photograph would probably never happen, we descended into blaming each other and hurling childish insults. Despite Baby Spice insisting to her a few days later that it was all fine, Gemma never forgave me.

Forever failed to live up to expectations, stalling at Number 2, behind a gleeful Westlife, and the four entered a 'permanent hiatus' a few weeks later.

Gemma and I also entered our own permanent hiatus.

◆ ◆ ◆

That November it was time for me to do my second stint of work experience. Desperate to get a foot in the door in the pop industry, I arranged a fortnight at Arista Records, the R&B wing of BMG. This, I thought, would give me not only a week away from college, but also a week mingling with the stars.

I expected their offices to be something along the lines of Trump Tower: soaring and ostentatious. Alas, all the magic took place in an ugly sixties block in Putney, South West London. The building was divided between various divisions of BMG, with Arista spanning the middle floor and the pop division, RCA, up on the top level. Failing girl band Girl Thing were always lounging around in that office, as was the A&R boss: a flashy, middle-aged guy, with dyed hair and a designer wardrobe called Simon Cowell. He often flounced around the room, bleating about highly important matters to do with Westlife, Five and Girl Thing when I hung out with the lovely ladies who worked in the pop office. Back then he was just a badly dressed wannabe bigwig. Most of that would change when he'd prance onto our small screens as a badly dressed *Pop Idol* judge a year later.

I was mostly downstairs in the glamorous press office of Arista, where the conversations would be dominated by their up-and-coming artists P!nk, Alicia Keys and Dido. Dido was currently riding high at Number 1 across Europe as 'that lass on the Eminem song'. She graced us with her presence one thrilling afternoon while I sat on the floor, stuffing envelopes. Everyone was really excited to have her in the office, but for a hardcore groupie like me this encounter was underwhelming. In fairness, it's hard to get excited by Dido in any situation!

The highlight of my fortnight was one afternoon when an executive came in and threw catty insults at another member of staff. Doors were slammed, expletives hurled and tears shed. It was the first time I'd witnessed proper adults behaving like teenagers. I thought one day that would be me, swearing at a secretary in shoulder pads.

The guy above that person wasn't any better either. I was summoned to the boardroom one day, and found it packed with the label's top dogs. When I timidly entered, a big boss gave me very specific instructions to go to a certain café, a ten-minute brisk walk away, and fetch him a particular coffee. I diligently marched to the coffee shop, reciting the order in my head all the way.

Paper chalice in hand, I returned to the boardroom and presented the special coffee to the big boss. As I was slinking out the room he abruptly called me back over.

'What is *this*?' he snapped, staring inside the cup. 'I didn't ask for foam. *Why* would you have got it *with* foam?'

My heart sank as the room fell silent. 'Um... sorry... I... I didn't realise.'

'Well, I *cannot* drink this! You're going to have to go back and fetch me the drink I asked for.'

I returned to the meeting, rolling my eyes, one *foamless* coffee in hand. The big boss totally ignored me as I placed it next to him.

At least I'm in my dream industry, I kept telling myself, inside questioning whether I was cut out to work with all these self-important people, all bigger prima donnas than the artists themselves.

◆ ◆ ◆

In sympathy, my manager let me leave early to see a much bigger diva than the coffee tosspot. For the second time at Borehamwood's hallowed Elstree Studios I would be witnessing *Her Madgesty*. Unbelievably, Madonna hadn't toured anywhere since 1993, so even seeing her mime a single song at *Top of the Pops* was a huge deal for her devoted followers. Madge's only gig (at the comparatively tiny Brixton Academy) the following week would be mostly filled with journalists and media luvvies. The few fan tickets had been given away in radio competitions and subsequently resold for thousands.

Upon arrival, the scenes were exactly like my first Madonna *Top of the Pops* experience two years earlier: a sea of *ancient* adults – in their thirties and forties – offering eye-watering sums for spare tickets. Tasha and I bagged two spares *for free* again! Although, annoyingly, Tasha sold hers for £500 and *still* blagged another spare to get in with.

I was livid!

Sharing the bill with Madge that night were Wyclef Jean, your mum's fave, Ronan Keating, garage royalty Artful Dodger, Richard Blackwood, Toploader (well, they couldn't *all* be stellar acts) and another famous diva: Kylie.

We muscled our way to the front of Madonna's stage. Warm-up guy Danny hadn't even appeared to give his long-winded introduction when the Queen of Pop confidently strutted on, unannounced, to a confused and hysterical audience. There was their empress, standing just a few feet away in a black Stetson. And it soon became painfully clear that no one was ready. Production staff fluttered around on walkie-talkies as Madonna stood there emotionless, looking indifferent to the rapturous applause being showered on her.

Frenzied wails of 'I LOVE YOU!' echoed around the room. As the crowd began to quieten down, one confident fan – a woman in her late thirties – stuck her neck out and pleaded, 'Can I have tickets to your Brixton show?' to Madge, still standing there motionless in her black leather jacket, her lips pursed.

That was a bit eager, the crowd seemed to think, tittering and scoffing at the lady's nerve. In a scene resembling *The Witches*, everyone then looked to their Grand High Witch for a reaction to this impertinent fan. Madonna, hands on her hips, gazed into thin air. After a long, eerie silence, she lifted her mic to her mouth and scowled sarcastically.

'Yeah, sure, I just happen to have two right here in my *pocket*,' pulling nothing out of the arse of her black flares and rolling her eyes theatrically. The audience roared at the now crimson-faced woman in the front row. 'Jesus, they don't pay me to be a *fucking* comedian!' Madonna seethed when the audience finally died down.

The drummer and keyboardist sheepishly appeared on stage behind her, but still there was something clearly wrong. 'Where the fuck are my backing singers?' Madonna snapped, turning her venom away from the outspoken fan. 'Right, if my backing singers aren't on this stage by the count of ten, they're fucking *fired*!'

'TEN! NINE! EIGHT!...' the audience cheered. 'SEVEN! SIX! FIVE! FOUR! THREE!...' Just then, two flustered women barged through the baying crowd, up the steps, onto the stage. Still fixing their outfits, Madge declared she was ready and the song began. Clearly *no one* was allowed to make the Queen of Pop wait.

The besotted crowd were salivating after seeing Madonna's unrehearsed stand-up routine and cowgirl-inspired performance of 'Don't Tell Me', so when Kylie sashayed on stage next to perform her new single, 'Please Stay', surrounded by Mediterranean beefcakes in plaid shirts, the atmosphere in the sweaty room turned feverish.

What the Flamenco-style single lacked in Kylie sass, she made up for with its outrageously camp routine. Kylie danced atop a pool table in heels. Then her Latino dancers spun her round as she dangled from a pool cue, kicking her legs with glee. Still trying to break out of her box as a faded cult singer from the last decade, the song may not have broken the Top 10 but, by late 2000, Kylie was cementing her place as a modern-day legend, more than capable of keeping up with the younger pop starlets.

Madge came back later on, without the hay and bad attitude, to perform her monster hit 'Music' for the upcoming *Christmas Top of the Pops* show. It went down a storm. I bopped along in my bandana, oversized hoodie and sparkly earrings, like a thug gypsy Esmeralda.

◆ ◆ ◆

Madonna seemed to leave her mark on everyone after being in her presence. If I couldn't afford to buy songs I loved, I used to rip them off the music channels and transfer them to minidisc, but I wanted the HQ version of Madonna's new album, *Music*. Upon returning from *Top of the Pops*, I got straight onto our family PC and (painfully slowly) scoured digital music service Napster for files of her latest songs. Poor Madge hadn't had the best start to her album campaign, as lengthy unfinished clips of the first single, 'Music', had been leaked online months early, via Napster. It threw the campaign into turmoil and spoilt the surprise of a proper launch, a sign of things to come for the whole industry. Poor Madge and her team tried to take on the Internet, demanding that the world delete the MP3s from websites. A cute idea, but as *Rolling Stone* put it at the time, 'Madonna can't stop the music'. The album ended up on Napster, in its entirety, weeks before release: one of the first big cases of an artist's new work leaking.

Unfortunately for me, I hadn't yet got the hang of peer-to-peer file sharing and, after spending the night hunched over our PC in a trance, I ended up with only a few clips, some wrongly titled files and a bunch of viruses. Clearly, I wasn't ready for the future either.

Madonna did try to strike back though, with an MSN webcast of her one-off Brixton gig a few days later, beaming her stingy twenty-minute live set in pixelly, glitchy dial-up hell to nine million fans trying to watch across the world. Say what you want, but I was bloody glad I hadn't paid a ticket tout *a grand* to watch the meagre five-song set with Sharleen Spiteri as warm-up. I did manage to get brief, clear moments of Madge on our PC though, throwing some mum moves in that same fancy dress shop cowboy hat, before technology got the better of me again.

♦ ♦ ♦

With Christmas fast approaching, and an expensive pop habit to fund, Dad was yet again pestering me to get a job. One afternoon I saw a 'Staff Wanted' poster at Weybridge's foremost VHS rental outlet, Blockbuster. I fought off stiff competition from other unemployed acne-ridden adolescents for the £3.50-an-hour job and quickly settled into a routine of gossiping and stealing the popcorn between serving customers. An old friend was a regular visitor: my mate Keavy, who had more time to rent out videos since her pop career was going through a quiet patch. She couldn't keep away from me! I had an agreement with my stunningly pretty work buddy Carolyn. She'd cover the tills for me when I was outside chatting to Keavy; I'd cover the tills for her when she was outside kissing her boyfriend. She later went on to be a singer in the short-lived girl band The 411.

The rest of the family went up to Grantham between Christmas and New Year. I obviously thought I was too cool for that, and made the most of a free house by hosting a two-day long house party for Arash, Charlotte and various other groupie mates. I even managed to clear away the evidence afterwards, with the last stray Bacardi Breezer bottle landing in the bin as Dad's car pulled onto the drive.

♦ ♦ ♦

The year 2001 had arrived, and one Saturday early in the New Year a big group of us went to see Steps at G-A-Y. Steps' gigs there were the stuff of legend, ensuring every groupie in the South of England would turn out and dance till they were dripping with sweat, even in the middle of January.

After chugging back dirt-cheap blue WKDs, and clogging the Ku-Bar jukebox with our favourite hits, a load of us made our rowdy Saturday night journey up Charing Cross Road. On our way up the well-trodden route from Ku-Bar, Charlotte and I lagged behind the others after stopping to get cash out. As we walked past St Martin's College (the one from *that* Pulp song), a ragged-looking man reached out for my hand. In all the commotion on the heaving West End street, I thought it was a friend pulling me towards them. When I realised it was a man asking for spare change, I politely apologised and went to walk on. In a blurry flash he had me in a headlock, taking out a sharp object from his coat and poking it under my T-shirt, ordering me to hand over my wallet. I began to get hysterical, to which he pushed the object much harder onto my skin and demanded I 'stop making a scene'. Crowds of people passed by just inches away, slowing down and looking on with sorrow and concern. But not one tried to help the distressed teen in a headlock. Charlotte stood there, helpless, unsure what to do.

He demanded for a final time that I pretend everything was okay and hand over my cash. I told him I didn't have any, thinking how the twenty quid I'd just taken out was all I had left to fund my evening. He scraped the implement against my abdomen again.

'I'm not messing around. DON'T lie to me! Get your wallet out and hand over your fucking notes!'

So I pulled the £20 from my wallet, handed it over and bolted into the crowded darkness.

I ran to Charlotte and bawled my eyes out as we walked hand-in-hand up the road. When we reached the others, impatiently waiting for us in the queue outside the club, I was a wreck. Tipsy and in shock, I couldn't articulate how I felt. I wanted to go home, but the others wouldn't have it and insisted on paying for me to get in. They were determined not to let it ruin my fun, and plied me with free alcopops and hugs all night long too.

◆ ◆ ◆

A bit later in January I was mugged *again* – this time at a salon in Fulham. After growing my hair for six months, I was finally getting cornrows, just like my beloved Justin from *NSYNC. Although my Rapunzel locks had grown so long under my hideous bandanas it still wasn't quite long enough to braid. For *that*, they said, I'd need to buy a weave. I had to rock down to Electric Avenue in Brixton and pick up some fake hair and return with it the next day so it could be woven into my unwieldy mane.

Now, I thought I was good at withstanding pain but nothing could prepare me for the misery of getting my hair braided in cornrows. I screamed and winced (and quite possibly cried) my way through the two hours of knotting and yanking that ensued, while a salon of late middle-aged black women tittered in hysterics.

When the hairdresser was finished, I was so happy! If you squinted and blocked out quite a lot of my face I looked *exactly* like Justin had done that hazy summer before on tour. An unwanted side effect was that it had pulled my entire face up, leaving me looking like a braided Joan Rivers for the first few days, but I *loved* my new 'do'!

'Well, that's your Christmas money blown,' was Dad's underwhelmed reaction.

Keavy from B*Witched didn't know what to make of it when she stopped by Blockbuster Video to pick up a rom-com, popcorn and ice-cream deal when I was working a shift one afternoon. I *think* she liked it, but she was kind of speechless. One person who definitely was a fan was Louise. I met her at The London Studios one morning after she'd presented *CD:UK* with Ant and Dec. Her music career was suffering, with her recent Wu-Tang Clan-sampled single, 'Beautiful Inside', stalling at Number 13, but she was still as bubbly and chipper as ever. She was with her husband Jamie Redknapp and in-laws and just kept raving about my hair to Jamie.

'Oh my God, J! Don't you think he looks like Madonna?'

'Erm... I can't see it meself, actually,' Jamie replied, bewilderedly.

'Yeah, he does! Madonna! In the *Human Nature* video, where she has the braids,' Louise nagged.

Finally, I had a clue where she was going with this, but Jamie and Harry Redknapp just looked on in utter bemusement while Louise continued heaping me with praise.

Feisty US star P!nk was also on the show that morning to promote her new single, 'You Make Me Sick'. Her dancers were not very good at disguising their laughter at my hairdo outside the studio. And that was the moment when I realised that I looked like a twat. Perhaps it wasn't such a good look for a lanky white boy from Surrey.

15

Pure and Simple

After realising I hadn't quite pulled off the Justin look, and with only a few months until I turned eighteen, it was time to sort out my image – I was a man, not a boy band tribute act. So, I went into Weybridge and found the cheapest salon I could, where the barber completely restyled my mop. Louise would be disappointed the braids were gone, but it was for the best.

To further cement my grown-up status, I got a tattoo – a star, at the base of my spine. Getting one aged eighteen would be fine, but getting one now, aged seventeen, would be *so* rebellious! I was very chuffed with it when I visited Sarah, one of the Luton Girls, at university in Lincoln, a few days later. I proudly displayed this indelible symbol that confirmed I was an adult. It was the first time I'd seen university life first-hand (bar the B*Witched tomato incident) and it looked pretty fun. In two whole days together, Sarah had mentioned every bar and club in the city, without ever discussing lectures, assignments or presentations.

Maybe academia wasn't as tough as I'd thought?

♦ ♦ ♦

I wish I could say that I stayed on this road to adulthood, of delinquent disorder and experimentation, but I got distracted. In January 2001, my friends and I, like most children and teens around the country, became glued to a new ITV show, *Popstars*. This fly-on-the-wall series showed the complete process of putting together a pop group, from the open auditions right through to their debut single release – the first of its kind on British television.

Every Sunday night the nation was treated to rounds of auditions, where hopefuls around the country sang their hearts out, to varying degrees of success. Wannabes would warble their way through 'Livin' la Vida Loca' or 'My Heart Will Go On', and the judges would either shatter their dreams or invite them through to the next round. The audience shared their highs and lows, weeping at a stirring performance of Elton and Kiki Dee or exploding with laughter when a hapless applicant struggled to hit the high note in S Club 7's 'Reach'. Each episode they were whittled down, until only the successful bandmembers would be left.

Other pop acts – like Five, Steps and S Club 7 – seemed to just magically appear in our lives one day with a repertoire of songs and stylised image, whereas, in reality, they had been through the exact same process, only without a camera crew recording every tantrum and ugly cry.

It seems ridiculous today, in an oversupplied world of *X-Factor*-created acts, but at the start of 2001, seeing this felt genuinely different and exciting. It exposed the shallow reality of manufactured pop in which dreams were made or lost in an instant. This was also the first time the public had been acquainted with an opinionated TV judge, ripping apart bright-eyed singing hopefuls with witty putdowns and unashamed honesty, hammed up for the cameras. The public were groomed to get as obsessed with 'Nasty Nige' Lythgoe, entertainment controller at London Weekend Television and frontman of the judging panel, as they were the young fame-seekers.

As the weeks passed, the wannabe stars became more and more talked about in the press, until finally there was a chosen five: a pig-tailed loudmouth from Wigan called Kym, sweet Welshman Noel, who was 'sick of being skint', consummate professional Myleene, timid blonde Suzanne and softly spoken East End geezer Danny. Week after week, they were portrayed as ordinary people who couldn't believe their luck. Thirteen million people, almost a quarter of the nation, tuned in at its peak, guaranteeing the five former nobodies were the biggest band in the country before they had performed a single gig.

Unlike the multitude of talent shows that came in its wake, *Popstars* was neither live nor interactive. By the time the final five were shown being picked by the judges on our screens the band had been secretly living together for the best part of a year in a house in North London. The show continued with episodes covering the band's life together, learning the tricks of the trade, and the climax of the series: having their debut single launched on the, by now, feverish public.

Despite some initial cynicism, I was astonished by the hype surrounding the group: unlike anything I had seen before and, in a world where record labels would overhype every new act, the buzz around this lot was created by the public, off the back of the show. Despite trying to tell myself I was moving on from my days as a pop groupie, I got swept up by all the hysteria and wanted to see how this mania would pan out.

Having been assigned the slightly bizarre (and grammatically incorrect) band name, Hear'Say, the next Beatles' very first performance was to be on Channel 5's show, *The Pepsi Chart* – a knock-off *Top of the Pops*, filmed in a tacky-looking nightclub in Leicester Square.

A load of us groupies arranged to go down after work and college that Tuesday afternoon in mid-February to see what all the fuss was about. I was taken aback by the scenes outside – hordes of fans, paparazzi and journalists. Gridlocked streets. In all our years following bands, we'd never witnessed anything quite like this.

At this point all we'd heard were two demos, both covers, and most of the public had heard *nothing*. In scenes reminiscent of *Big Brother* the previous year, a group of nobodies who had achieved nothing were being treated like national treasures. Being nobodies was their appeal, as it was the first time that superstar status felt within the grasp of you or me. It wasn't the music, but their ordinary personalities that had made the TV show so captivating.

◆ ◆ ◆

I ventured into London a couple of times the following week, along with Charlotte and Tasha, for a few more manic TV and radio appearances, seeing Hear'Say mobbed like living gods by their cult-like followers at each one. But their biggest test was a few days away – at the hallowed BRIT Awards. The newbies would be doing their first live performance of their debut single, 'Pure and Simple', for an audience of thousands at Earl's Court and nine million watching at home. The pop industry though was not happy: how had this untested act managed to wangle this appearance, usually reserved for the year's biggest sellers and a couple of old legends?

As with previous years, a lot of us groupies wanted to be there in person on the night to watch the ceremony, schmooze with celebs and live it up on free booze at after-parties, if we could get away with it. By now, after the last two years, it bizarrely just seemed like a given that we would all be going.

After some squabbles about who would make the shortlist, a group of us met up outside Earl's Court on the Sunday morning to copy the backstage passes. By 2001, the BRITs had upped their security game and the passes were now more complex than ever, most with holograms. I was pretty good at Paint, but I wasn't quite up to emulating those on Windows '95. Realising the 'AAA' passes were just too intricate, we settled on a 'Crew' pass that would be much less scrutinised.

Six of us returned in our glad rags the following evening and busted into the show with relative ease. Steph said they saw Caprice AGAIN on the way in, in her famous bra, pants and beaded fishnet number, and I want to believe that *so* much – our scantily clad lucky mascot! The year 2001 was pretty similar to the previous two years I faked my way in, to be honest. We watched some incredible performances (that year by Destiny's Child, Eminem, Coldplay and Robbie Williams, among others), plus Hear'Say's first performance of 'Pure and Simple'. It was great, albeit slightly bizarre, to witness them sing live to a pretty hostile (even booing) crowd of pissed-up music industry snobs. The BRIT School teenagers in the pit at the front loved it, though, and by this point the band had realised there were millions of fans rooting for them at home.

The evening also offered us our first sighting of Geri since the previous summer – at least, we were told it was her. When Ant and Dec welcomed the former Ginger Spice on stage to present an award, the entire arena was taken aback; not by a bold vision in red, white and blue, but a tottering waif with a peroxide bob. *Eh? What's happened to Geri?*, we all thought, as half the audience seemed to not even realise who she was. Arash suggested we attempt to find her after the show and get the low-down, but Tasha despondently replied that there was no way our 'Crew' passes would get us backstage without being swiftly ejected.

At the end of the show we mingled around the star-studded tables as usual, straight after U2 had closed the show with a snoozesome set. We wandered around, looking for the entrance to the after-party, bumping into an inebriated Sara Cox on the way. We showed her our fake passes and, being so blown away by our ingenuity, she wrote our names down on a napkin to read out on air the next morning!

When we found the after-party, the security guards were having none of it, though. 'Sorry, no crew allowed, guys,' the doorman insisted, triggering a roar of laughter among us. Instead, we opted to clear the unopened bottles of alcohol from the surrounding tables. Cockier than ever before, we found some cardboard boxes and went round filling them up with whole bottles of fancy vodka, rum and bubbly.

A security guy cottoned on to our antics, just as we finished filling our crates, frantically calling his beefy workfellows for backup. He tried in vain to stop the six of us, but the backup was too slow. We legged it out of the venue, chased by a gaggle of guards. As they closed in on us on the red carpet, we all prepared to shed our boxes of booze and sprint. By some miracle – I kid you not – *three* rickshaws were sat at the end of the carpet, waiting to ferry guests off to the Tube station. *For free.* We piled into these makeshift getaway cars, and in scenes reminiscent of a Hollywood action movie, demanded the drivers speed off down the hill into the night. We'd made our escape and in a fit of laughter cracked open our pilfered booze on the back seats. Although most days were surreal, mad adventures for us back then, I do look back and smile in amazement at the crazy, unbelievable situations we got ourselves in at such a young age.

◆ ◆ ◆

The following week, we went to see Hear'Say perform a live show at G-A-Y – where else?! They were poised to prove their worth there on Saturday, 10 March 2001. Compared with anything we'd seen there before, the level of press attention for their billing was off the Richter scale. Newspapers from *The Guardian* to *The Telegraph* had written articles explaining to their readers what G-A-Y was and why so many music stars performed in this dingy gay club on the Charing Cross Road at 1 a.m. every Sunday.

When Saturday arrived, a bigger group of us than normal made the well-trod tipsy pilgrimage from Ku-Bar, up the road to the Astoria. Once inside the club, we were packed in tighter than sardines; more rammed than even a Geri or Kylie show. Hear'Say went down a storm. The *Popstars* TV show was *still* on every Sunday, and we were all filmed in the crowd for the following week's show, adding to the surreal excitement of the evening.

The crowd was more mixed than usual, and contrary to my expectations it wasn't cute Welsh boy Noel who got the biggest screams, but gobby Northerner Kym Marsh. Myleene Klass, the Vanessa Mae of Norfolk, was my favourite though, and I handed her a wilted red rose in plastic wrapping during their set, which I'm sure she treasured. Hear'Say's set was short: two covers and a future single, book-ended by 'Pure and Simple'. Their repertoire may have been limited, but the crowd didn't seem to mind – they were hotter than a microwaved Pop-Tart.

As we were on a high, a group of us forked out on a taxi back to Charlotte's mum's house in Richmond, rather than loitering until the first trains like we usually did. Even the cab driver asked us incessantly about it, and the DJ on the radio took calls from drunken G-A-Y clubgoers travelling home to try and get the gossip. We bellowed 'Pure and Simple' out during the taxi ride home, as well as other new favourites, Missy Elliott's mind-bending masterpiece 'Get Ur Freak On' and S Club 7's 'Don't Stop Movin'.

We spent the rest of Sunday in the recovery position in Charlotte's bedroom, listening to leaked Hear'Say tracks she'd downloaded off Napster and sweating out every Smirnoff Ice that had passed our lips the night before. The four of us lounged around, consuming pizza and SunnyD. Despite thinking we were too old to still be chasing pop stars, we were all caught up in the excitement and agreed that we needed to meet these new icons.

On Monday, 12 March 2001, after months of puff and build-up, the new pop stars finally saw the release of their debut single, 'Pure and Simple'. In scenes reminiscent of *Saving Private Ryan,* up and down the country primary school kids, mums and granddads battled with each other in record shops to grab a copy. That drizzly afternoon, Arash and I waited in line along with many thousands of fans of all ages at HMV's Oxford Street flagship store, where Hear'Say were doing a signing. The queue snaked through the shop and out the door, leaving latecomers like us to feel the full force of the spring downpour outside. We just *had* to speak to those fresh-faced pop titans though and be in on the action!

Charlotte snuck into the queue after finishing work and the three of us finally reached the band's signing table right at the end of the night, several weary hours after they'd begun greeting the thousands of ecstatic faces. We excitedly chatted to them about the scale of their success, but they all looked a bit overwhelmed by the crowds, especially the two boys.

The next day, we traipsed across town to see them at the Nickelodeon Studios in North West London. Yet again the crowds were immense. As we waited among the masses for the band to appear, a familiar face stepped out. Suzanna, the runner I'd known for a couple of years, who had sorted out my first work experience at the TV studios in Soho, clocked me while leaving the studios with a friend.

'Malcolm!' she beamed. 'What are *you* doing here? Are you working for the channel?'

Shit! This was embarrassing. 'Umm, no. I'm actually here to see the band,' I stammered.

'What? The *Popstars* band?'

I nodded.

Suzanna's face dropped. '*Really?* I thought you'd got this out of your system!'

'I just wanted to see the buzz with my friends,' I said, feigning laughter.

'You're a bit *old* for this! You must be nearly finished college now, right?'

I nodded silently again, as if being told off by a teacher.

'Look, give me a call when you finish your course and I'll help you get your foot in the door at the studios.' She gave me a hug and walked away. 'Call me!' she shouted back, from the damp, dark street.

I felt awkward. I knew she was right, but the addictive rush of being surrounded by it all was more exciting than handing out water to Moby, or getting stupid coffees for people in boring office blocks.

The band appeared from the stage doors not long after. They were in great spirits, chatting to us and the hordes of other kids waiting outside. Myleene was definitely my favourite, but, just like at G-A-Y, Kym and Noel were the biggest hits with the fans.

All five looked a bit overwhelmed again and unprepared for the bear pit they'd been thrown into.

A photographer tipped us off that the band were heading on to a *Heat* magazine party on Park Lane. Four of us decided this (comparatively) low-profile appearance would give us the ideal opportunity to meet the band properly.

On the Tube ride there I stayed quiet, thinking about my run-in with Suzanna the runner, and her blunt advice for me. She had a point – I was nearly eighteen, for Christ's sake – but these pop escapades were still such great adventures. There was plenty of time later in life for being an adult.

There was a formal red carpet at the front of the plush Park Lane Hotel and we couldn't see much, apart from reality D-listers Ben Fogle and some Series One *Big Brother* contestants posing for a scrum of flashbulbs. Like most awards we went to, we knew there would be an unguarded side door, where we could creep in – and there was. We made it all the way into a big conference room and tried to get the band's attention, before one of the stylists noticed us and had us thrown out by Security. Undeterred, we sat by the bins and a laundry van, waiting for the band to emerge at the back entrance.

We didn't have to wait long, finally getting to meet them properly, and without a single TV crew or paparazzo getting in our way! Charlotte had a camera with her, with some unused film left, so we took it in turns to have a group photo with the whole band. 'YOU'VE ALL GOT TO PAY ME A POUND TO GET THIS FILM DEVELOPED!' Charlotte demanded, which the band thought was hilarious, not realising quite how serious she was – if we didn't cough up, we wouldn't be getting our pics.

I travelled home to Surrey on the last train of the night, and on my hour-long walk home from Weybridge Station, I recalled all the fun times I'd had over the last few days. I was soon turning eighteen, but it wasn't quite over yet – the glorious groupie days.

◆ ◆ ◆

I got my head down at college over the next week, trying to catch up with group assessments I'd played very little part in, and socialised with my classmates on the college campus and at the local pub. I'd sometimes managed to slip back into my assignment groups at the eleventh hour and take credit in order to pass, but I'd (rightly) failed so many coursework projects over the last eighteen months. I had racked up an enormous number that needed completion – already almost thirty, by that point. But true to form, I buried my head in the sand and got on with my main assignment: to carry on hanging out with the biggest pop band in the country and get reacquainted with Geri.

Over the coming weeks, we saw Hear'Say at various events, including the launch of their official dolls at Hamleys Toy Shop – two weeks into their chart career. The speed of it all was unprecedented. The visual resemblance between the band members and their respective dolls was, at best, poor, and at worst, borderline offensive. Thankfully, we still got in without buying a single one. The band told us we were cheapskates!

We saw them at a photo shoot in front of the London Eye (*so* turn of the Millennium!), a couple of album signings, and, *lastly*, flying overseas from Heathrow. As they mooched around the terminal off-duty, they chatted to us about how crazy the last few weeks had been, plans for their next single and about their upcoming mega (thirty-one-date) arena tour later that year (which was already on sale and, for which, over a *quarter of a million* tickets had already been sold).

The long, hectic month of promotion for their debut single and album was *finally* over. Not only did 'Pure and Simple' break the record for the fastest-selling debut in recorded chart history, but their album *Popstars* broke the same record (a feat they would hold for the next five years, until the Arctic Monkeys ruined everything), *and* they became the first British act to top the single and album charts simultaneously with debut releases. They were simply unstoppable. Long may they reign!

16

Teenage Dirtbag

Geri's appearance at the BRITs in February 2001 was the start of her relaunch on the pop scene. Like Dr Who, she'd been regenerated. From Brazen Ginger Spice to Buxom Ms Halliwell, and, now, her third reincarnation as Geri the Yoga Bunny. After Hear'Say reignited our love of pop stalking, my old groupie mates and I decided we needed to get back in there with our old fave. Would she remember us though? Would she be as warmhearted as she used to be, or would the new, serious-looking Geri be too interested in smoothies and Pilates to hang out with us kids?

She'd been silent for a year, hiding away from the tabloids in America and St Tropez, but now she was back. Her comeback song was a cover of The Weather Girls' eighties campfest 'It's Raining Men', which was also to be the lead single for the much-anticipated *Bridget Jones's Diary* film – she clearly knew her target audience.

Photos of Geri had recently been plastered all over the papers, on romantic breaks and out and about in London, with her reported new boyfriend: the biggest man in pop, Mr Robbie Williams. One grainy photo showed what was supposedly Geri's secret new city pad in Notting Hill, West London, conveniently just around the corner from Robbie's mansion. It was enough evidence for me, Charlotte and Arash to take the afternoon off college and try to track her down. With an *A–Z* in hand, and a crumpled photo of the flat torn out of *The Sun*, we scoured street after street of stuccoed houses, BMWs and kids in straw boaters.

After several fruitless hours we resorted to asking local residents, most of whom looked down their noses at us or didn't seem to know who we were talking about. Two lovely ladies, out walking their pedigree lapdogs and picking up some bits for dinner from the local organic deli, keenly told us, 'Geri? No, don't know where she lives. Sorry, my dears. I don't know where any famous people here live actually... Oh wait – that's Madonna's house there,' pointing to a gated townhouse about ten metres away, 'Oooh! And Robbie Williams – he resides on the next street.'

We thanked the helpful dears and skipped round the corner to Robbie's gaff. I rang the doorbell and a familiar voice answered. It wasn't Mr Williams, it was his D-list friend and housemate, Jonathan Wilkes. Like us, he'd been riding on celebrity coattails for a few years. He even managed to forge a minor career as a TV presenter off the back of his big name bestie.

'Is Geri there?' Charlotte asked him – straight to the point!

'Erm. What?... *Geri?*' Jonathan repeated back to us before bursting into a howling fit of laughter. 'Ohhhhh, that's funny!' he said, still chuckling that some fans had come to his house *not* looking for Robbie Williams, for once. 'She's not here, no. Try her own place...'.

We were *so* close. I could feel it! We bounced around the adjoining streets, our hearts fluttering.

'That's it!' Arash shrieked, holding up the crumpled cutting next to the tiny house at the end of a quiet street, dwarfed by the other Georgian mansions. After just a couple of minutes, a fancy car pulled up and its driver stepped out. It wasn't Geri's old minder Calvin that we used to know, and who would always chat to us. He didn't seem to notice us when he made his way from the car to the little door of the flat. Five minutes later, Geri appeared from the door, as if by magic, behind oversized sunglasses, wearing minuscule gym shorts and a sports crop top, clutching a gym bag.

'Fucking hell, she's thin!' the three of us uttered in unison.

We shouted an affectionate 'hello'. Geri stopped in her tracks, mid-way across the road, turning around in disbelief. She glared at us through her tinted aviators, her pursed lips not returning the greeting, then continued walking to her car.

'Fuck!' said Charlotte.

'What have we done?' Arash asked. 'She's *livid*.'

My heart was in my mouth.

We could see her in the car opposite, ranting and raving to her new driver. What now? We couldn't just walk away. She wasn't even going anywhere. They just sat there discussing it – us. Had we overstepped the line? We wanted to apologise, but didn't want to make the situation worse. Eventually, her minder got out the car and walked towards the three of us perched nervously on the pavement's edge.

'She's not happy, is she?' said Arash.

'We're really sorry – can you tell her we're really sorry?' Charlotte begged.

The man interrupted us with a shake of his head and a little smile, 'It's not you, she loves seeing you lot at airports and shows and all the things you go to.'

I slyly glanced over at the car, behind the man, and could see Geri sitting there with her arms folded, staring over at us, seething.

'She didn't even mind you coming to the last house. She just didn't want to see you *here*. This has been her secret hideaway. She's upset about the picture they printed in the paper. Do you understand?' he asked.

We nodded solemnly and apologised profusely.

'I'm taking her to the gym. She'll see you soon at some TV stuff,' he said, walking back to the car, before zooming off.

Reality dawned. We were older, and suddenly wiser. For perhaps the first time the three of us realised that actually, these heroes of ours were just people. People who had every aspect of their lives dissected by the media, were unable to have any privacy and were expected to permanently be on duty.

We trundled back to Notting Hill Gate Tube station. Despite being penniless teenagers, we agreed the best thing to do to try to make amends was to club together for a bunch of flowers. We left them, and a note, with her housekeeper, who said Geri would really appreciate them, and went home hoping that would be true. It certainly didn't look like we'd be gossiping in her garden with her anymore, like we had been a year before.

♦ ♦ ♦

My eighteenth birthday was just a couple of months away. This transition to adulthood would bring great change to my life: namely, guaranteed entry into nightclubs. I could finally dispose of my crinkled fake birth certificate and be able to buy sugary alcohol freely.

My elated countdown was dampened though, when in March Mum and Dad sat us three kids down for a 'family meeting'.

Oh God, we don't ever do these! Something's coming. Divorce? Another kid? Mum's been arrested for shoplifting?

'I've got a new job.' Dad announced. 'In Worcestershire'.

Sophie started hyperventilating. 'WHAT?'

'Where the hell's that?' I asked.

'In between Birmingham and Wales. A great opportunity's come up. We'll need to sell the house and move up there this summer,' Dad continued.

'As IF! I'm not moving to the middle of nowhere!' I snapped. 'I *need* to be near London!'

After failing to congratulate Dad on his new job, I shut myself in my room, hatching a plan. I'd find some other bored groupies to move into a flat with me. *Definitely not Surrey. Probably somewhere central like Soho or Mayfair*, I thought (on part-time wages at Blockbuster?). I scoured my Nokia address book and decided Charlotte seemed like the best option.

'Yes, Mal! It'll be incredible,' she said, agreeing to moving in with me before I'd even told Mum and Dad of my devious plan to avoid Worcestershire. Or was it Warwickshire? Or maybe Wiltshire? Somewhere beginning with W, way outside the M25.

♦ ♦ ♦

The next weekend, Charlotte, Arash and I jumped on a train to Manchester to visit a groupie friend of ours, Jodie. This loud, lesbian, Lancastrian acted as our local guide to the famous gay village: the same one that millions across the nation had watched every week on the now-cult TV show *Queer as Folk*, two years earlier.

I wasn't disappointed. It was *exactly* like *Queer as Folk* – almost every bar offered ropey drag queens doing innuendo-infused brassy cabaret! Unlucky for some, it was karaoke night at one of the pubs, the New Union, and I drunkenly put my name down to do one of my favourite numbers by my pals from last summer, *NSYNC. Pissed out of my head, I performed (and I use that word in the loosest possible sense) their hit song 'Bye Bye Bye' on the pub's tiny stage – full dance routine, the lot – the shimmering, metallic gold curtain lit up behind me, like a high-camp version of *Phoenix Nights*.

We ended up in another gay bar, New York New York, till the early hours, where we partied the night away with a drag queen called Campari – a lovely bloke in his late forties, with pantomime dame make-up and broad shoulders squeezed into a glittering Shirley Bassey frock. We danced with him on stage to Steps megamixes and his performance of the current Number 1 song, Atomic Kitten's surprise mega hit 'Whole Again', in which he changed the words 'You can make me whole again' to 'You can lick me 'ole again', which, I can tell you, works best when sung in a thick Bolton accent.

We all got a cab (minus Campari) back to our grotty B&B on the outskirts of the city, where Arash and I carried on chatting and eating chips in our twin bedroom. We'd shared a room many times before at friends' houses, but this felt different; we were far away from home and any of the baggage that we carried back there. It had been such a fun night, but alone in our room, I felt myself tense up. I grew silent and Arash eventually asked what was wrong. I paused, taking some slow, deep breaths before uttering some words I thought I would never say aloud.

'Sometimes I feel confused,' I whispered, staring into space with anguish in my eyes. 'Confused about my sexuality.' It was so painful to say that sentence. What was I doing? I had no idea how this was going to go.

'Mal, that's okay,' Arash reassured me, 'I think *everyone* does at some point in their lives.' He paused. 'Do you think you might be... *gay?*'

'I don't *know*, I don't know... I just know I feel conflicted inside.'

'You know you can talk to me anytime. I won't tell a soul, I promise,' Arash continued. 'Take your time and think about who you really are. You know we'll all support you.'

Our talk continued, venturing from how Arash had known he was gay, to how he came out and even what it felt like to get with a guy. I said I wasn't sure how I'd ever know I was gay without trying it, at which point Arash said I could share his single bed with him, if I wanted to. We blearily looked into each other's eyes. I bit my lip, considered taking the plunge and using my friend as a test dummy. There was total silence across the B&B for a couple of minutes, apart from the boiler, hissing away on the landing, before I politely declined.

'Not tonight,' I answered with a strained smile, 'I'm not ready.'

'No worries. Well, if you want to talk about this anytime, I'm here for you,' Arash said, rolling over and turning out the lamp.

He'd been incredible. After an hour spent discussing my inner unrest, Arash had helped me to feel so much more at ease. After just that hushed twilight conversation it genuinely felt like someone had lifted a ton off me. Things seemed as normal in the morning. There were a few darting glances between the two of us on the train back to London, but my secret was safe with him.

♦ ♦ ♦

A few days later, we'd heard Geri would be appearing on some TV shows to promote her new single, so we headed down to The London Studios and hoped she'd forgiven us for turning up, unannounced, at her secret hideaway.

As soon as she saw us she had a big smile on her face, and chatted like nothing had happened. After a bit of deliberation I thought I would try my luck. 'Sorry about the other day,' I said. 'Did you get the flowers we sent you?'

Geri looked at the three of us and smiled. 'Yes, I did. That was *so* sweet, I really appreciate it. That was a lovely gesture.'

As Arash and I were walking back to the station alone he asked me how I was doing and if I was still feeling confused.

'Nope! I'm fine now. I'm actually not confused at all anymore!' I shrugged. 'I don't know what that was, I'm definitely straight. Thanks for the chat though, it really helped!'

With a concerned look, Arash replied, 'Okayyy... well, if you want to talk I'm h—'

'I'm fine. *Thanks*,' I said, shutting him down before he had a chance to probe my feelings any longer.

♦ ♦ ♦

A few days passed and I was sitting in my kitchen, listening to Radio 1's *Newsbeat* one morning when one of the main stories caught my attention. It went something like this:

The home of former Spice Girl, Geri Halliwell, was burgled on Sunday night, police have confirmed. A police source was quoted saying: 'We are investigating a burglary in Notting Hill on 18 March.' Ms Halliwell has reportedly moved into a hotel after her flat in Notting Hill, West London, was broken into and obscene messages scrawled on the walls. Ribena and milk are reported to have been thrown around the flat and personal items stolen.

Oh my God, poor Geri!
That's gonna be so sticky to clean up, I thought.

I sat there stunned, my spoon floating on my soggy cereal. Mum looked over at me and fumed, 'Is that the flat you went to the other day? And pissed her off by turning up? Oh my *God* – you might be a *suspect*!' I told her to stop being ridiculous but, inside, I thought our names *must* have been mentioned in the police inquiry at some point. Crikey!

We didn't see Geri for a couple of weeks after that – she disappeared off-radar. Paparazzi photos of her started to appear in the papers, outside the lavish Lanesborough Hotel, by Hyde Park Corner, where she was apparently living, post Ribena-gate. But would she want to see us there? For once we decided to leave the poor woman be.

◆ ◆ ◆

A few weeks later, after hearing rumours in the groupie world that Geri had been happy and civil to other fans there, we decided to risk it and head down to the Lanesborough. We waited under the grand, stone-pillared entrance, trying (and mostly failing) to extract gossip from the smartly dressed hotel porter, Dominic, about the world-famous faces who frequented the hotel. Eventually, Geri arrived, returning 'home' from a day out somewhere, looking very tanned and teeny. We kept forgetting how much weight she'd lost and how different she looked now.

She was surprisingly appreciative to see us, even posing for photos and chatting about her *It's Raining Men* video shoot.

'Do you mind us coming here occasionally, Geri? We honestly won't come again if you want to be left alone,' Charlotte asked.

She seemed quite jovial. 'No – I don't mind at all. It's nice to see you lot at the moment. Things have been pretty shit,' she said with a smile.

We clearly weren't suspects in the Ribena investigation.

Over the next fortnight we returned to the Lanesborough a couple more times. We went down after college on the day of the *Bridget Jones's Diary* premiere. As the singer of the main single from the film's soundtrack, we knew Geri would have got an invite.

We had only gone down there to see Geri on her way out to the Leicester Square premiere, but while we were waiting patiently, a gleaming Mercedes pulled up. Instead of a tiny Geri tottering out of reception, Hugh Grant, Renée Zellweger *and* Colin Firth, the film's main stars, appeared in their glad rags!

Before they had a chance to disappear into the limo we said 'hello' and Charlotte asked Renée for a photo. A smiling Renée agreed and walked around the car towards us. But by that point Charlotte had already begun walking round the car in the other direction. Charlotte laughed and apologised, but Renée got the hump, snapping, 'Oh, just *forget it*!', jumping in the car and slamming the door. We stood there confused, laughing hysterically at how we'd somehow riled up Bridget Jones within ten seconds of meeting her.

Geri appeared a few minutes later, looking gorgeous in a turquoise sequinned gown, white furry shrug and her sleek blonde bob. She didn't stop for long that day but it was nice to see her looking so happy and excited.

When I saw the papers the next day, she was splashed across the front pages, as usual. Upon arrival in Leicester Square, just after seeing us, Geri had picked a boy out of the crowd outside the cinema and given him her spare ticket as her 'date'.

OMG! As if she didn't pick me?!

♦ ♦ ♦

Despite all the politeness and smiles when we saw her at the Lanesborough, or outside TV studios, Geri seemed more distant with us nowadays. A couple of years previously she'd been so genuinely warm, but now she seemed different. Something had changed. No one could put their fingers on *what* exactly, but we all saw that she wasn't the same woman we'd got to know years before.

After a tiring day of flat-hunting with Charlotte, and realising we couldn't afford to live quite as centrally as we'd naïvely imagined, I went to get a new haircut before going to *Top of the Pops*. We knew Geri would be performing, as 'It's Raining Men' was that week's Number 1, Geri's fourth as a solo artist. I was ready for a new look, so, while visiting Charlotte's hairdresser friend that afternoon, got her to buzz my neat locks off in yet another attempt to demonstrate my rebellious streak.

As well as Geri's performance on the show that week we also got to see the unstoppable Steps, the genuinely lovely Stephen Gately and Dido. During one of Geri's 'Raining Men' performances, there was a moment where she was standing high up, on top of a cheap, school production-esque yellow taxi prop, surrounded by a harem of dancers. As she stood there, towering above the crowd, she scanned the cheering audience around her until her eyes reached me. She gave me a confused look for a few seconds, before she grinned, ran her hands over her own head a few times and offered a big thumbs-up.

I'd had my first feedback on the skinhead!

I guess it was for moments like this that we all still did it – a personal encounter with your idol that no one else could take away. Those moments were becoming rarer with Geri, though, as she seemed increasingly indifferent to fans in real life now, but still acted up as the loud, happy pop star on TV.

◆ ◆ ◆

On the eve of my birthday, a load of my groupie friends organised a surprise dinner for me at an Italian restaurant near Waterloo. I'd said I didn't want a fuss, but Charlotte was adamant and I loved lapping up the attention. My life had changed so much in the last few years. Turning eighteen, I had a host of friends wanting to celebrate with me – a far cry from the birthdays of my school years, usually spent alone or with Conor. It was actually great to hang out with these people while *not* waiting for a pop star for a change.

I'd managed to blag two tickets for Geri's album signing by repeatedly sending competition submissions on her somewhat primitive website. It was taking place on release day: Monday, 14 May 2001. *My eighteenth birthday.* It's like she'd planned it. So, the day my adult life finally began and I was still waiting on a pavement to meet a bloody pop star!

When we got to the table where Geri was stood she scrawled the words 'Happy bday Malcolm' on my album after being prompted by Charlotte and Arash chanting, 'HE'S EIGHTEEN TODAY, GERI!'

'You're a man now!' Geri said warmly, with an arm around me while posing for photos.

So, start acting like one, she probably thought.

17

Can't Get You Out of My Head

In spring 2001, my career prospects were looking bleaker than B*Witched's. Having devoted myself full-time of late to studying the pop phenomenon Hear'Say, I had neglected my actual studies. I'd ignored the warnings of my parents, my teachers, even my groupie mates, and had accumulated a magnificent thirty-three assignments to complete in just three weeks. Crap! *This was going to require more long nights, cheap tricks and desperate measures than a divalicious chart battle*, I thought to myself as my head emerged from the sand it had been buried in for the past year and a half.

I went to a pub in Weybridge with my course mates and we all laughed about my impossible situation and, after a couple of pints of Dutch courage, I headed home to break the news to Dad. 'You're an idiot. You've put chasing pop stars around London above your own future. You won't even have the option to go to university now!' He couldn't work out how things had got quite so bad, as I'd been slightly economical with the truth about where I'd been each day. As far as my parents were aware, I'd just been going into London after college, which wasn't *always* the case.

I relished a challenge though. Realising that university was one of the few options to avoid the pain of a full-time job gave me that extra bit of motivation necessary to try and pass. From the minute the computer rooms and editing suites at college opened I would slave away, editing blurry camera footage, typing out assignments, and desperately flicking through textbooks to learn all the stuff I hadn't bothered to turn up to classes for.

Each time a tutor passed me, they'd shoot me a mocking grin and scoff, 'You'll never do it, Malcolm!'

♦ ♦ ♦

In the few minutes I had between assignments I'd keep up with the latest Hear'Say goings-on. It was hard to avoid them. From the *NME* to *Marie Claire*, *GQ* to *Smash Hits*, *The Face* to the *Radio Times*, every magazine in the land had them on the front cover with bold statements like 'Bigger Than Jesus?' that, with hindsight, look like cruel jokes. Still riding high off the back of their first single, the band continued to add dates to their mammoth UK arena tour. They'd been so hyped-up, though, I felt sure it couldn't last.

My college course also looked destined to fail. After a few very productive days I was in the middle of a lull and starting to give up hope. Charlotte phoned to see if I wanted to go and see Hear'Say that weekend, as she'd heard they were performing at Twickenham during the Rugby League Cup Final. I persuaded myself I'd earned a break.

They were performing in front of 70,000 mainly male, uninspired Rugby League fans as the pre-match warm-up act.

Dressed in jeans and rugby shirts, as they belted out their new single, 'The Way to Your Love', in the middle of the pitch, this costume choice looked less of a good move when the heavens opened and a biblical storm battered them on the tiny stage. They kept going, smiling through the horizontal flash flood, looking like drowned rats by the time the song was over and sliding about like Torvill and Dean as they hurriedly ran to shelter. Charlotte and I were standing with some other fans outside the stadium, trying to stay dry under anything we could find during the brief monsoon, while we could hear them singing on stage from within the grounds.

After the match kicked off, the band headed straight out, ready for their next appearance, photo shoot, recording session, rehearsal... whatever it was they did 24/7. They stopped to chat to us though, at the back entrance to the stadium, all five members looking slightly bedraggled and exhausted by their relentless schedule. I told Myleene about my college predicament. She was not happy, and gave me an ultimatum: I wasn't to go and see them until all my assignments were done. I hadn't listened to my parents or tutors, but Ms Klass's words were like the gospel.

If only this second coming could also perform a little miracle for me.

◆ ◆ ◆

Back at home I ploughed on with my essays. With one second to spare I printed out the final report and deposited a huge pile at the desk of one of my tutors, whose jaw dropped to the floor (she hadn't seen their shoddy content yet).

A few weeks later, my marks arrived. I had, against all odds and the better judgement of my tutors, been given a bare pass in my Media BTEC. I celebrated with my college friends in the local pub, before stumbling home and planning my next project: getting the hell out of Surrey. No more twitching curtains. No more ghosts from school. No more parents telling me what to do.

Charlotte and I had found a swanky new flat in Feltham. No, not at the Young Offenders' Institute, although that was next door. It may only have been a few miles down the road from Weybridge and barely within Zone 6, but it was technically London and that was good enough for me. Mum and Dad were happy for me to go it alone, but made it very clear that the pocket money and occasional 'loans' would be stopping.

After ecstatically picking up the keys and settling into our new pad, that first balmy weekend of June 2001, Charlotte and I got to work on the important things: painting every room a garish colour from the bargain bin of dented emulsion tins by the tills in Hounslow B&Q, and inviting our groupie friends around for a massive party. We made full use of our new freedom by staying up late smoking, drinking 'Ibiza in a Bottle' Vodka Red Square, and watching the live feed of *Big Brother 2* till the early hours. Living my best life!

With no more college to worry about, I was free to spend my days with Charlotte and Arash, following Hear'Say on their second single campaign. The band was saturating every possible media to promote 'The Way to Your Love' so it was a real shock to us when we turned up to TV gigs and roadshows and the overwhelming throngs of fans that had greeted them outside four months previously had almost vanished. Where was everyone? They'd sold out dozens of huge arena dates for their autumn tour and had added a dozen more. Scoops and images of the famous five graced the tabloid front pages day in, day out. Clearly, they were still huge, but to us on the ground, something was going wrong.

Their shrinking fan base wasn't the only thing we noticed during the exhaustive promo tour for the second single. They frequently looked exhausted, sometimes downright miserable. For years we'd met pop stars in every possible scenario, and at times saw them looking tired and fed up – they're human beings with feelings and off days, after all! I'm not saying they were the exception to all pop bands, but of all the groups we had ever met, Hear'Say looked the most weary and worn-down. The older, more hardy members, Kym and Myleene, were always warm and chatty, showing their appreciation of our presence and support, but we often didn't know what was wrong with the other three. They were the envy of most kids in the country! Was it really not all it was cracked up to be?

Newspapers started to print rumours of bust-ups between the band members off stage, relishing in details of possible splits and divisions. At a succession of TV appearances, where we saw them either as an audience member or as a devoted fan by the back door, they were starting to attract negative attention from the crowds too. People would yell homophobic abuse at Noel, call Myleene a slag, or accuse them of being talentless nobodies. We always put it down to jealousy. The fact that they were nobodies was the very reason they had captivated the nation; the idea that 'anyone' could become a huge pop star. One irate Blue fan at *CD:UK* took it upon herself to let the band know her opinion of Noel ('Fucking fat gay c***. You're fucking shit, you poofter!'). I responded by picking up a custard pie from the set of the TV show and landing it square in her crabby face as we shuffled out after the recording.

♦ ♦ ♦

The carefree summer days and nights drew on and I was having the time of my life in our shabby Feltham flat. However, many weeks after college had finished I *still* hadn't started looking for a job. After a kick up the arse from Dad, I registered at an agency and got an interview at a mobile phone rental company in Richmond. It wasn't the media role I'd envisaged, but definitely a step up from the Harvester Salad Cart.

Freedom! Money! London!

My first day, at the end of July, coincided with another big life event: Mum, Dad and Sophie fled Surrey for Worcestershire (I *still* didn't know where that was). Anja was moving away too, to Southampton for university. I was getting on so well with my new office colleagues, but inside was choked up all day as the reality sunk in that I was really on my own now. I couldn't believe that they weren't just up the road anymore.

◆ ◆ ◆

Geri was preparing to launch her next single, 'Scream If You Wanna Go Faster', which we knew meant lots of promotional events we could meet her at. But we were wary: she'd been so distant with fans during the 'It's Raining Men' campaign.

When the song came out in late summer, I was already worried that it wouldn't do well. The public reaction was lukewarm and it wasn't a two-fingered statement like her previous offerings. Geri had incredibly scored four Number 1s in a row, so I knew that, in an era where chart positions meant everything, even reaching Number 2 would be viewed as a flop: it got to Number 8. In the first week it sold roughly one seventh of what 'It's Raining Men' managed – a huge fall from grace. The tabloids knew it, we knew it, and I had no doubt that Geri knew too.

One sweaty afternoon in July 2001, we greeted Geri in the climate-controlled coolness of the Arrivals lounge at Heathrow as she was returning from a trip to Paris. Geri was cradling a Minnie

Mouse stuffed toy as big as her, and wearily entered into hollow conversation with Charlotte, Arash and I. We enthusiastically walked alongside her, to her car, through the scrum of people waiting for beloved relatives and suited business partners.

It was packed and stressful, hard to get a word in with her. She put her sunglasses on, possibly on purpose. Charlotte and Arash were asking her about her plans for touring and the summer.

As she got into her blacked-out Jeep, I said to her cheerily, 'Please don't worry about the single not getting to Number 1, we still love you.'

'*What?*' Geri snapped back ferociously, clearly listening by this point. She stared back at me as she sat in the passenger seat.

'I just... mean... er... that chart positions don't matter. Your fans will be there for you whatever number you get to.'

She said nothing but glared at me with lips pursed like Anne Robinson, as though I was the weakest link. Unable to dig myself out of this hole, and with Arash giving me a despairing look, I just awkwardly said goodbye and her PA slammed the door shut.

'Did you *see* her face? She was absolutely raging, Mal!' Arash said, helpfully.

As we walked through the packed terminal building we all laughed about it a bit more – me, pretty nervously.

Like Notting Hill a few months back, we all questioned what we were doing. When our idols were flattered by our presence, we all got an enormous buzz. When we pissed them off, we all felt terrible. When they were laughing and joking with us, we thought they were friends. But when they were being whisked off in limousines, scowling at us for turning up and wanting to be alone, we realised they were actually strangers who wanted to make a living and have a normal life.

♦ ♦ ♦

Less than a month after Geri's Number 8 fiasco, the UK media became fixated on the next big post-Spice release: Victoria Beckham's 'Not Such an Innocent Girl'. Still the only Spice Girl not to have a Number 1 (Emma Bunton having secured one that spring with 'What Took You So Long?'), Victoria's people had obviously underestimated a re-emerging pop icon. Other than Destiny's Child's 'Bootylicious' and Missy Elliott's divalicious remake of 'Lady Marmalade', the only other CD single we wore out that summer was Kylie's 'Can't Get You Out of My Head'. This was pop from the future, a complete departure from anything Kylie had done before, and we weren't the only ones taking notice. From the gay clubs of Canal Street to All Bar One in Exeter, nobody could get Ms Minogue out of their cranium.

The British press widely touted a new ferocious chart battle. Victoria once again pulled every trick out of the bag, appearing at giant outdoor gigs with fake lip rings and anything else she could grab from the shelves of Claire's Accessories, but to no avail. She retreated, bloody-nosed, her single only managing a paltry Number 6, whereas Kylie's synth banger received mass acclaim, sitting effortlessly at Number 1 till summer was a distant memory. I felt a bit sorry for Posh, and knew that Jackie Adams would be gutted, but was delighted the best song had won.

I hadn't seen any of the Spices, bar Geri, since the previous autumn – mainly because Gemma and I had fallen out, but partly because they just weren't around as much. Like the charts themselves, I'd moved on so much in the past few months that my Spice Girls groupie days seemed like a distant memory. One day that August, Arash, a huge Spice fan, begged me to take a half-day and accompany him to see Emma Bunton, still carving out a saccharine solo career for herself, recording an appearance on Jerry Springer's chat show. I begrudgingly agreed, having no dislike of the disbanded four Spices, but no longer having the urge to meet any of them.

I was in the middle of chatting to an excited Arash in the queue full of nans when Emma arrived. As she was marched through the corridor she stopped, grabbed my arm with a beaming smile, and, with a big 'hello', planted a sloppy kiss on *my* cheek before being whisked off to her dressing room.

'I fucking hate you!' Arash muttered in my ear with a wry smile.

◆ ◆ ◆

After six years of pop obsession, by late 2001 so many acts I had loved were calling it a day or struggling on with increasingly dismal record sales and low-grade TV work to pay the bills. My old mate Louise was bouncing back from the disappointing reception she'd had to her album of the previous year with a greatest hits compilation and new single: a syrupy cover of Stealers Wheel's 'Stuck in the Middle with You'.

Steph and I decided to show our unwavering support by turning up to as many of her public appearances as possible as she promoted it, and to thank us, Louise got us on the guest list to be in the audience for many of them. I was finally getting the VIP experience, without the help of Microsoft Paint. Thirteen-year-old me would have *died* to be in this situation. Eighteen-year-old me was flattered and grateful, but getting on the VIP guest list for TV shows and gigs wasn't quite such a thrill anymore.

It was at about this time when I went to meet B*Witched outside their record label, just before a big meeting to discuss their future releases, their contracts and, ultimately, whether the band had a future. I went shopping in the M&S next door with them, having friendly chats while they perused the packets of sandwiches. But the girls were all really nervous. Having been away from the limelight for a year, and with their last singles struggling to make an impact, their careers hung in the balance. Others from the Lairy Lot arrived after work and we all waited for the band in the plush reception of Sony Records HQ.

Hours later, four smiling Irish lasses appeared. The lengthy meeting seemed to go well.

◆ ◆ ◆

Other than the lovely Louise, with summer drawing to a close, there was only one thing on my mind – Hear'Say's much anticipated arena tour. Despite really being too old for this now, and Hear'Say somewhat lacking in credibility, this was my chance to actually be a proper groupie and follow them around the country, having secured tickets for four dates. As my old college mates were going off to university, I was getting ready to be a hanger-on for a bubblegum pop tour.

Less than a year to the day since their first audition, Hear'Say were preparing for their headline tour of thirty-odd arenas. This band were doing everything back to front. Where is there to go when you start at the very top?

We spent several afternoons in a business park in Kennington waiting for them to appear between rehearsal sessions, prior to the tour kicking off. The first night I'd bought tickets for was Wembley Arena, about a week into the relentless month-long extravaganza. We'd secured front-row tickets for two dates there. Another cavernous hall, another set of wailing thirteen-year-old girls and middle-aged couples. Their support act was forgotten gem 'Supersister' – a generic 2001 girl band who looked like a cross between Canary Wharf workers doing karaoke and a

Smack the Pony sketch. Slightly too old to be teeny pop stars, their trashy pun-filled songs such as 'Coffee' were pop GOLD. Gold blend. The genius lyrics are filled with obscene puns and innuendo, about a steamy brew filling their cups, or bemoaning the speed of instant coffee.

Totally inappropriate for the pre-pubescent pop fans. They were, for us though, the highlight of every night.

Straight after Wembley Hear'Say did more London shows. This time across town at my old haunt – Docklands Arena. On the day of the Docklands date, I was passing the time at work flogging mobile phone contracts when the boss appeared from his office and called everyone in with a look of disbelief and panic on his face.

Someone's fucked up, I thought, *or maybe a bollocking from a customer?*

He had the TV on. A sombre-looking newsreader tried to stumble through developing news that two planes had flown into the World Trade Center in New York. Grainy footage of the emerging scene showed flames and billowing smoke, before the dramatic image of the buildings collapsing. Nobody knew quite how to react to this totally unfathomable situation.

The mood at that night's Hear'Say concert was quite different to the last. At the very start of the evening, the band came on stage for a two-minute silence for the victims. It almost seemed like a bad joke when Supersister then appeared to perform their up-tempo kitsch songs like three middle-aged Essex girls on a works night out.

◆ ◆ ◆

Realising Birmingham wasn't too far from Mum and Dad's new gaff, I called them up and told them I would be paying a surprise visit that weekend. My first visit since they'd abandoned me in Feltham.

I got the train up after work that Friday to the bucolic-sounding Great Malvern. After three boring hours chugging through two-bit halts, I stepped out onto the platform of the ornate Victorian station, greeted with a hug from Sophie, sobbing with delight.

'You're here at last!'

I'd missed her so much. Anja was also home for the weekend, up from university in Southampton, where she was studying English, so it was a proper reunion of the family I'd nearly forgotten I had.

The next evening, Dad drove Sophie and I the hour's trip to the Birmingham NEC. I only managed to get two tickets from a tout for seats right at the back, but eleven-year-old Sophie didn't care: her big brother was taking her to see her favourite band *and* he knew them. Just before their encore, I dragged a reluctant Sophie to the entrance to the stalls. After a brief argument with a steward about whether or not I'd really just taken my little sister to the loo and had accidentally left our front-row stalls tickets under our seats, we ran past him as the start of 'Pure and Simple', the show's closer, rang out.

'We're gonna get thrown out,' Sophie fretted, as we pushed our way to the front. Her fear turned to exhilaration when the band spotted me, and Kym reached out to touch my hand. 'This is my sister!' I shouted. Kym smiled and grabbed Sophie's hand for a few seconds while she belted out the pop classic.

Fuck, I'm a good brother, I thought to myself in the car ride back, as an adrenaline-fuelled Sophie bounced around the car. *Beat that, Anja!*

◆ ◆ ◆

The next time we saw Hear'Say was at their Newcastle date, mid-way through their tour. Charlotte, Arash and I had booked a dreary B&B, but that didn't stop us hanging out in the swanky Malmaison by the arena where we knew they were staying. Five jaws almost hit the floor when the band walked through the foyer with their suitcases and saw us three indulging in a genteel afternoon tea. 'Oh, La-de-fucking-da!' Kym boomed. Myleene and I spent most of our meeting discussing 9/11 (as the world had started calling it by then) and the various rumours and reports we'd both been watching on the news into the early hours every night. The performance that evening was, by this point in the tour, well-polished, but having already seen it four times before, it was getting a bit like Groundhog Day.

We didn't have tickets for any more of their shows, and despite having seen them at four venues, I really wanted one last opportunity to witness the spectacle. Even then, I was pretty sure that a Hear'Say tour of this magnitude would never be seen again. Arash suggested we go up to Manchester, the last tour date before the Irish leg. Once we'd agreed to go, we got a bit carried away and decided to pull out all the stops. Charlotte suggested we stay at the same hotel as the band. *Sod it, it's never going to happen again!* By phoning everywhere within a mile of the city centre, using their manager's name, we tracked the band down to the five-star Lowry. For someone whose hotel experience seldom exceeded Travelodge, and a night in a tent on a pavement was acceptable accommodation, this was going to be like The Ritz!

Despite all my stressing about going up there without tickets for the show, we managed to bag decent seats from a shifty-looking bloke in a fleece outside the venue. There would be 20,000 people in the audience, PLUS a live stream being beamed to the country on pay-per-view Sky TV. Even though we'd seen the same repertoire several times by now, Manchester was particularly epic.

Back at the hotel after the show, the dozen or so fans outside were kept at bay by Security, as the three of us waltzed in and hit the bar. The staff were setting up an event: the end-of-tour party would be held in our own hotel! It was also Suzanne's twentieth birthday (yes, tragically, she was only two years older than me!). The hotel pianist played 'Bridge over Troubled Water' on the ivories as the band came into the bar, to applause from guests and tour crew. Suzanne made a beeline for us and jumped on the back of our sofa, wanting to know how she'd done in her solo section of Madonna's 'Express Yourself'.

'You did a great job! No, we didn't notice you mess your vocals up at all,' Arash said, comfortingly, while we all thought, *I'm pretty sure that was mimed*. We bought her a birthday shot and partied in the bar until the small hours. It was just like the BRITs, except this time Security couldn't throw us out.

In the morning, we staggered downstairs hoping to share our hangovers with the band in the lobby, but, annoyingly, they had already headed back to London on the bus at some ungodly hour. We weren't as disappointed as Bong Klass, Myleene's mum, who was waiting in the lobby with us for her beloved daughter. I had to break it to her that the group had already left, as she stood there with gifts for them.

Her face sank. 'Here, if they can't have these, I want you to have them,' said Bong, handing me five bars of luxury chocolate from the hotel gift shop that were meant for the band.

'Erm, okay. Thanks!' I gushed.

'Give them my love when you see them next!' she said, giving me a consolatory kiss and cuddle. I couldn't believe it – poor

Bong didn't know when she'd get to see her daughter again. The band was constantly on the road and even their own parents didn't know where and when they'd be heading next.

18

Because I Got High

One afternoon in October 2001, I jumped on the train from my office in Richmond to do a familiar journey. I was meeting some college friends for a low-grade banquet at none other than mine and Anja's old haunt: the Ottershaw Harvester. I sauntered nostalgically along my old route from Addlestone Station, passing Rosefield Gardens on the way. Mum and Dad hadn't yet found a buyer for our old home in Ottershaw, so the house had stood empty, awaiting a new family, since they moved up to Worcestershire. I was running late but glanced at my jangling chain and saw the old key: maybe I could just have a quick look inside?

None of our elderly nosy neighbours were out in their gardens. No one to recognise me. *What a lovely, quiet street to grow up on*, I thought as I passed the net curtains and neatly trimmed rosebushes. Our house looked the same from the exterior, as though we'd never left. When I slipped my key in the lock and slowly turned it, I was hit by a wave of emotion. Tears dripped slowly off my cheeks as I wandered the echoing, empty shell; the ghost of conversations between Mum, Dad, Anja and Sophie – all so far away – replaying in my mind. Rose-tinted memories of childhood innocence replaced the hatred I thought I felt towards this place. The boredom, the bullies, the isolation all forgotten.

Had I been wrong about my hometown all this time?

I had to go and meet my friends so I said one last goodbye to my childhood home, to its privet hedges and woodchip wallpaper, knowing I would never return. I consoled myself with an extra helping of croutons from the Harvester salad cart.

◆ ◆ ◆

Hear'Say's epic tour had provided unforgettable moments of bonding with the band, and with my other groupie friends. It was bittersweet, though: where would they go from here? Where would *I* go?

Sending faxes to people about phone rentals hardly felt like an inspiring career. With Mum and Dad far away, Charlotte and Arash were my substitute family. We boozed the nights away on Blue WKDs, either up in Soho or in our Feltham bolthole, which now more closely resembled Gary and Tony's ash-ridden, grimy flat from *Men Behaving Badly* than the plush pad we'd envisaged at the start of the summer. If we didn't have promotional tours to attend, we'd live it up with weekend-long parties, or hang out at G-A-Y.

One bleary night on the Astoria dance floor, Charlotte got chatting to a gobby girl by the name of Natalie. The same age as us, bubbly Natalie was charming – a proper cockney from the East End. We couldn't get rid of her all night and she became a regular fixture at ours. Every Sunday I'd wake up and see an array of different sweaty, glitter-clad club kids snoring on our sofa that Charlotte had befriended.

◆ ◆ ◆

After a month off from any groupie duties, I was like a pig in shit with excitement at Geri's upcoming G-A-Y gig. Prior to a performance in Oman for the troops, she was doing a dress rehearsal at the Astoria. There would be almost as many sweaty blokes as in the Arabian Desert. That giddy, butterflies-in-the-stomach feeling had returned at the thought of being in her presence again. During the long hot summer, Geri had been icy with all of her fans. I longed for a look, a smile or a wink like the old days. Both Charlotte and I seemed to be chasing a high from such personal moments with our pop princess that had become so few and far between. Was the old Geri still there?

Some Spice Girls fans we'd known from back in the day were staying at ours and I was eager to get the proceedings underway. By the time they pulled up at the flat, I'd polished off a fair few bottles of booze while dancing around the living room to beloved pop trash CDs. Bored of my nine to five, stuck in a drab office all week, I was gagging to get into town and dance the day away in Soho. Geri was bound to be pulling out all the stops, and her hoards of gay fans and other diehards were ready to party like there was no tomorrow.

By 11 p.m. the Astoria was already hotter than a midday desert. We took trips to the bar in turns to maintain a steady level of Smirnoff Ice in our bloodstreams. Pressed against the front of the stage in anticipation for the pop show of the year, I struggled to understand what Charlotte and Natalie were saying to me, let alone move my limbs and dance. Kylie's 'Better the Devil You Know' rang out as usual at midnight. How was it *still* one hour till showtime? With the stage cleared and five minutes to go, I'd lost all excitement at seeing Geri and just needed air. I couldn't breathe. *What would happen if I fainted*, I thought, as the blood drained from my head.

From there on, it's all a blur. One of the caring Spice Girls fans staying with us, a big lesbian with a crew cut, picked me up and plonked me over her shoulder in a fireman's lift, wading through the sea of bodies to lug me out. *I hope Geri's watching from the wings*, I thought as I came to. *She might let me backstage if she saw me barely conscious.* The paramedics were sure I was high on drugs, so wanted me out. Big Caring Lesbian had to argue profusely that I just needed some cold water and to watch the show from the upper reaches of the balcony. Eventually, they agreed. So there I watched it: Geri's big live show of a lifetime, viewed from the filthy heavens, where the people around me didn't care because they were too busy getting acquainted in shady corners.

As I slowly sobered up, I saw four familiar-looking figures appear: one in leopard print, one in an LBD, one with blonde pigtails and one in an Adidas tracksuit. What on earth? I squinted at the stage and realised this wasn't the reunion to end all reunions, but a bunch of rough-as-fuck drag queens performing 'Who Do You Think You Are' with Geri. Polished they weren't, but they had more oomph than any of the real girls still did!

♦ ♦ ♦

The final quarter of each year was always the most fiercely fought, with the Christmas market still seeing enormous CD sales. Evidently eager to cash in on their supposed golden goose before it ended up at the abattoir, Hear'Say's label made them churn out another album: their second within nine months.

Nevertheless, Charlotte, Arash and I were out there in the bitter cold for its accompanying publicity operation to support our current favourites. Despite their personal lives being daily tabloid fodder, I read in the same papers that pre-sales of the album were disastrous. The single, 'Everybody', would actually have been great, had the boy band Five not had a Number 1 with practically the same song and video two years earlier. 'Everybody' peaked at a fairly decent Number 4, but in its week of release, the album of the same name looked set to miss out on the Top 10 completely. A sprinkling of genuinely great pop gems drowning in a sea of filler ballads was not the album they needed to come back with. The fact that their label lumped a 'new version' of 'Pure and Simple' onto the end of the CD of fresh material only accentuated their lack of confidence in the hastily produced product. Were they resigned to being a One Hit Wonder?

In Hear'Say's usual fashion of highs and lows, in a week that saw them invited to Downing Street by the Chancellor, Gordon Brown, for his Christmas party (I'm suggesting that was the high point, by the way), the pop stars were clearly soiling themselves about their impending musical train crash when I bumped into them the next day at the *Top of the Pops* studios. It was the Thursday evening of the album's release week and Myleene had been told to film all their 'fun antics' on a handheld camcorder for an ITV Christmas documentary about the band. She filmed me between other bands' performances, with Suzanne acting as interviewer.

'You recording? Okay, Malcolm! Have *you* bought the new Hear'Say album?' Suzanne asked excitedly.

'Yes, I have. I *love* it,' I replied with little stage presence but bags of enthusiasm.

'Oh my God! Did you *hear* that, Suzy? We've found someone who's actually bought it!' Myleene laughed nervously behind the camera.

'You're literally the first person we've found this week,' Suzanne said, solemnly. 'Okay, let's be serious now... Tell me which songs you like on it and why!'

Before I could even get seven words out to describe the complex intricacies of my favourite deep cuts, a BBC cameraman shoved Myleene's hand, throwing the camera off course, and thundered at all three of us, 'YOU CAN'T FILM IN HERE! NO RECORDING OF *ANY* KIND ON BBC PROPERTY! I DON'T CARE *WHO* YOU ARE!'

It seemed even the BBC's staff couldn't be bothered with the pretence anymore. We apologised and laughed about it as he stomped off but it was indicative of a change in the air towards 2001's biggest pop darlings.

By coincidence, Geri was also on that week's show to perform her latest single 'Calling' – a ballad that didn't bother the upper reaches of the Top 10, just like her last. She looked through us, and the other couple of long-serving fans in the front row, just as she had a couple of months back when we'd watched her promote her last single. She seemed enveloped by a melancholy air – unless the cameras were rolling. My highlight of the night, though, was meeting Cher again – there to sing her bizarre dancey tribute single for 9/11 survivors, 'Song for the Lonely'. In her platinum wavy wig she looked younger than Anja. As she tottered off stage, I ploughed through the crowd to grab her hand and declare my love for her. As I stared into the twenty-five-year-old looking face, the illusion was shattered when my hand grasped her leathery ninety-five-year-old palm.

It was like shaking hands with my nan.

◆ ◆ ◆

That Sunday, the Hear'Say locomotive finally veered off the shaky tracks. Nine tumultuous months after their record-breaking debut, their second album entered the charts at Number 24. *Twenty-four*. The fall from grace was unprecedented. The band's Svengali – the man who let the Spice Girls escape before signing a contract – had really earned his 'Manager of the Year' award, at the congratulatory Music Managers' Forum, the previous month. *Slow clap*. Meanwhile, Steps, having just completed a humungous arena tour to accompany their Number 1-selling greatest hits album, announced on Boxing Day that they had split up after five years together, upsetting millions of kids, gays and mums, and making one of the top news stories of Christmas 2001. With the pop world still reeling, Kym Marsh flounced out of Hear'Say, shortly after Christmas. It felt like the end of an era for us, with these two pop titans crashing to unexpected ends within a couple of weeks of each other.

Rumours were also flying around online forums that B*Witched – at last about to promote their new album – had been *dropped* by their label. Although we had no way of even contacting the girls to get their side of the story, the jig seemed to be up.

Despite being miserable about the moribund outlook for Hear'Say, and saddened by Geri's and B*Witched's equally bleak-looking prognosis, it was my own future that was causing me the most grief. The pop world that had saved me from the daily torment of school was crashing down around me. What would I do next?

Arash came round and we talked it over, discussing our options and laughing at our pathetic despair over the sudden loss of our favourite hobby, thanks to Kym bloody Marsh!

'Yes, this is fun, but do you really wanna do this forever?' he asked. 'Who are you gonna follow next – S Club-fucking-Juniors?'

We fell about laughing and I put my head in my hands. No, I wasn't about to start chasing around music mogul Simon Fuller's latest pop project – a bunch of twelve-year-olds. I'd had a good innings, it was probably time to hang up my shoes. Arash encouraged me to apply to university, telling me I could probably get in somewhere with my BTEC pass. It seemed like a great idea. Much better than phone rentals.

Sign me up!

♦ ♦ ♦

On Saturday, 19 January 2002, at the crack of dawn, Arash and I headed the half a mile down the road, to a dreary and dark Heathrow Terminal 1. I'd used my blagging skills to locate Geri's flight to Paris for her performance at the NRJ Awards – the French version of the BRITs. Geri had been so cold recently, but I was determined to chase down one more special moment with her, however unlikely that looked.

We sat on a cold metal bench as her new driver scoped out the terminal meticulously for press or fans, but failed to spot us two sat in the corner. When a tired-looking Geri and her PA entered the revolving doors – the very place we'd had so many laughs and chats with her over the last couple of years – Arash and I began to walk over. After looking anxiously around the terminal, she clocked me plodding towards her. She turned to face the check-in desk in exasperation and mouthed two short words very clearly, not even attempting to mask her anger at us being there.

'Oh my *God*! Did you see that?' I asked Arash, us both still shuffling towards her.

'I sure did! What do you wanna do?!'

'It's too late to turn back! Fuck, this is going to be *excruciating*,' I said, my heart racing.

It went as well as can be expected. Geri shot me a curt 'hello' and an icy glare through her sunglasses, giving monosyllabic answers to my couple of questions, just as she had done all those years earlier when I watched Ginger Spice fade away on stage at her final *Top of the Pops* with her bandmates. It was painful. After I'd feigned a smile and said an emotionless goodbye, I trundled off to the Tube with Arash.

'That is the last time I ever go and see that woman,' I vowed. I didn't want to be a burden, and I also didn't want to be made to feel like shit for trying to be supportive.

She was clearly no longer enjoying being a pop star, possibly going through her own inner battles, and wanted to be left alone. Like so much in the pop world we knew and loved, the Spice era had come to an end. In filmmaker Molly Dineen's widely praised 1999 documentary about Geri, at one point Molly comments to the cameraman, 'She'd be happier living on a farm with a husband and two children. But that isn't going to happen, is it?' As I sit writing this book in 2018, that's a bizarrely accurate description of Geri's life now. And she looks happy. Good for her! Because she wasn't then.

◆ ◆ ◆

I accepted that things were approaching an end. Perhaps I wouldn't see the Hear'Say gang again, but Charlotte was still desperate to see Kym. Ms Marsh, her favourite pop star, was hiding away from the limelight while figuring out her next move. We'd seen a picture in the paper of the house in St Albans where she was living with her fiancé Jack Ryder (baby-faced Jamie Mitchell from *EastEnders*, heartthrob to millions). That February, Arash, Charlotte and I trekked around the sleepy commuter town one Sunday afternoon on the hunt for Kym.

Natalie, who Charlotte had come out as now dating, said it was a bad idea, that it was a bit too stalkerish. I agreed, but then I didn't want to be left out.

I had déjà vu as we traipsed around the cul-de-sacs, remembering our terrible run-in at Geri's in Notting Hill. Shockingly, we got stopped by the breakfast show presenter of Kiss FM, also trying to find the Marsh and Ryder residence to bag an interview with the elusive Kym. *The cheek of it! How dare he bother her on a Sunday afternoon*, we thought, as we tried to lose him in the leafy avenues. Having shaken him off, we buzzed the doorbell of the house matching the press cutting. A middle-aged couple opened the door with caution.

'Oh. Ey up! Sorry, we thought you were that annoying man again,' Kym's dad said. 'Wait, we recognise yous. You're those fans... from the tour! Wait here a sec. Kym! KYM!'

Kym and Jack came to the door. She hugged us with a broad smile. 'Come in, it's freezing! I'll fix you a brew.'

We stayed for a surreal couple of hours, chatting to Kym and Jack – still *OK! Magazine*'s darling couple of the moment, gracing their cover every few weeks with the obligatory staged photos 'happy and in love at home' (photographed in a rented show home that bore no resemblance to their modest suburban abode). We talked over everything about the band: the split, the rows with Noel and Myleene, the gruelling schedule, the total lack of time with her children. Later, Arash and I sat watching TV in the lounge with her little ones, David and Emilie, while Charlotte and Kym chatted some more in the kitchen, swapping numbers before we left.

After that bizarre afternoon, Charlotte kept in touch with Kym via text and occasionally phone, where she'd sometimes pass the handset to me to say 'hello'. It didn't seem real. What felt more surreal was the dark February afternoon I came home from work to find a large package addressed to Charlotte with a St Albans postmark. When she got home and opened it, we were speechless to find it full of outfits: Kym's clothes – tops, hoodies and dresses – that she'd worn on the *Popstars* TV show and at events during her whirlwind months in the band. The note read: 'I have no use for these so I thought you'd enjoy them more. Big kiss, Kym x'.

I'd like to say they were treated as priceless memorabilia but, in reality, we paraded around in them, having drunken fashion shows in the weeks that followed. Kym had even given us the eye-catching dress she wore to meet The Queen, a couple of months earlier (if you don't remember it, Google it), which Charlotte and I performed routines in at house parties, me with balloons down my top, Charlotte with little else on. We texted Kym and she loved it. It was so odd, though, that these expensive garments which, just a few months ago, were meeting the rich, powerful and even royalty now meant so little to anyone.

◆ ◆ ◆

Despite all the fun, living with Charlotte and Natalie and having friends stay over every weekend was losing its appeal. My musical horizons were expanding, and although I was still loving chart pop, I was increasingly bored of the new artists, or sick of hearing the same old tunes at G-A-Y.

Charlotte made some 'Crew' passes that February to go to the 2002 BRIT Awards with some groupie friends. Despite having no involvement, they created an extra one for me. I knew security would be tighter post-9/11 and I just couldn't be arsed. I wanted to go to the pub after work, so I turned it down. They got in to watch the show and I wasn't even jealous. How things had changed!

♦ ♦ ♦

That spring, my old mate Louise Redknapp was traversing the country on a thirty-six-date theatre tour, in support of her greatest hits album. I hadn't seen her in a few months, and not once yet since the start of her tour in January, but my long-time Eternal groupie friend Lisa had been to one or two dates. A month or so into the tour, Lisa phoned me up.

'Louise wants to know which dates you're going to. What do you think?' she asked.

'Umm, I don't know... I've got lots on. I'm *so* busy and broke,' I said, feeling flustered. 'I'm definitely going to the London date though!'

Lisa continued, 'Look – you know it's a long, lonely tour out on her own. She'd *really* like you at a couple more if you can, for support. She said she'd put us on her list, so you only have to pay your train fare.'

'I'm sorry, I just can't commit right now!' I snapped, 'Even the Hemel and Crawley ones are gonna cost money I don't have. And I'm really busy,' I said, putting my foot down.

'Okay, fine, I'll let her know. I was only relaying what she said. Call me if you change your mind, mate.'

I felt like shit after that call but just didn't have it in me anymore. I couldn't face traipsing around the Home Counties, even to see my beloved Louise. My enthusiasm for meeting pop stars was waning by the day: I wanted to grow up and find *my* identity.

By the time Saturday, 9 March came around, Louise was a few dates from completing the entire nationwide slog. That evening, I made my way to Shepherd's Bush Empire with Arash. Lisa was there – on the VIP balcony – whereas I was standing near the back of the stalls.

Towards the end of the show, the house lights came up and Louise glanced around the crowd. Without even trying I caught her eye as she was belting out one of her hits. It was glorious to see her face light up upon seeing me. She pointed at me with disbelief and gave me a look of frustrated joy. After a few seconds she tottered to the other side of the stage and I receded into the crowd.

Despite the night reaffirming my love for Louise and the band that started it all off for me, Eternal, I didn't try and get into the after-show party at the venue, or meet her by the stage door. We called it a night.

'I think I'm about done,' I said to Arash.

♦ ♦ ♦

Having lost Kym, Hear'Say churned out *another* ITV show to search for her replacement. The nation were nonplussed though, having moved on to 'Will and Gareth' from *Pop Idol*. Johnny was the new Kym, but nobody seemed to care. Except maybe Lisa Scott-Lee, who ended up marrying him.

Hear'Say's record label, desperate to revive their fortunes, brought in forward-thinking Scandinavian pop producers for their third album in less than two years. Their plan was resolutely thwarted, though, when the five *Popstars* runners-up formed their own band, Liberty X. The moment I heard 'Just a Little', I knew the battle was all but over. Its raunchy lyrics and edgy R&B sound was everything Hear'Say wasn't – it was an *instant* classic. Despite loving the song, I felt sad for Myleene, Danny and co. every time I heard 'Just a Little' (approximately every nine minutes, all summer long).

Summer 2002 was a blur of shit R&B clubs and lazy days with Charlotte, Natalie and Arash or college friends. Sugababes,

Nelly and Kelly and No Doubt were the soundtrack (sneaking in the odd listen on my headphones to XFM when the girls had gone to bed). By now, Natalie had moved into the flat full-time and the dynamic was better than ever. We had endless fun nights in and out. She became the Mother Hen and served up fajitas and pasta bakes most nights. You'd never think she'd go on to win *MasterChef* a decade later, God love her! She and Charlotte were properly shacked up.

Everyone was getting some, except me.

◆ ◆ ◆

Napster had, by now, been shut down, but a number of copycat file-sharing services were appearing every month. Global sales of CDs were down 5 per cent from the start of the hopeful New Millennium, just two years earlier, while UK CD single sales were down 30 per cent from the previous year. The seemingly unshakeable music world was imploding. The dominating record labels struggled to find answers, as new technology threatened to make them obsolete.

Baby, Scary and Posh Spice all 'parted ways' with Virgin Records in spring 2002, while Geri clung to her deal by the skin of her teeth, focusing on her second autobiography, *Just for the Record*. The nineties were well and truly dead.

Would the last one out please turn off the lights?

◆ ◆ ◆

One day that summer I received an unexpected call. An old college stoner friend, now working at WHSmith for his sins, phoned to ask if I'd bought Geri's new book.

'No. It's not even out yet, is it? Anyway, I don't care anymore.'

'Well, you're in it... page 219. She's written half a bloody page about you and your mate.'

I thought he was winding me up, but as he read it aloud I realised this was real. She'd mangled together two different occasions, but had recalled, very clearly, the time I had spoken out about her ailing chart positions. However, Geri had misremembered my 'we still love you' comment into 'we don't think you're washed up'. I belly laughed down the phone, chuffed that I had made that big an impact, but utterly bemused by it all.

Us half a dozen or so superfans had clearly been of comfort to Geri during some lonely times after leaving the group, but she no longer needed or wanted us. She wrote how supportive and dedicated we were, but that, early in the morning, she found it hard to muster up enthusiasm sometimes. I felt like, through the book, she was being honest about the things she felt she couldn't say to us in person.

◆ ◆ ◆

Later that summer, I went to see Hear'Say make their last-ditch attempt to resurrect their career. I wished they would turn a corner, but held out little hope. Even Charlotte wouldn't accompany me to appearances, with Kym no longer in the group. I wasn't sure why I was going – I no longer needed the gratification of getting close to the stars. The high of seeing Eternal as a fourteen-year-old had given way to complacency and boredom. I wanted to be at the pub with ordinary people. But I felt like I needed to go and show my support to the band. Pure and simple, gonna be there.

I had read in the papers about them getting booed and abuse hurled at them at roadshows that summer. They had become a joke. No longer the much-loved rags-to-riches kids, people seemed to view them as ungrateful and undeserving of the success the public had 'given' them. The UK doesn't like a winner. Myleene was punched in the street. Noel said he wanted to come out as gay (after being told to hide it for so long) but, by the time he felt he could, he thought no one even cared, which is so sad. A number of the band went through mental health struggles in the years that followed, after being chewed up and spat out ferociously by the public who adored them so intensely, feeling like their careers were over by the time they'd barely turned twenty-one. When I went to meet them at the Nickelodeon TV channel, during the promotional campaign for their comeback single, the look of defeat on their faces was painful.

Liberty X's two Number 1s had been inescapable all summer, but radio stations wouldn't even play Hear'Say's new song. When 'Lovin' is Easy' was released and I looked at the B-sides, I couldn't believe my eyes. It wasn't full of the fruits of their labours from the past six months in the studio; there it was – 'Pure and Simple (2002 mix)'. Like Marge Simpson desperately revamping her one Chanel suit to fit in at the country club, somebody, somewhere had decided that what Hear'Say needed to put out with their comeback single was *another* new version of Pure and fucking Simple! I sighed and laughed. The dead horse was being well and truly flogged, ensuring they would be forever damned with One Hit Wonder status.

After a mentally and physically exhausting campaign for the band, 'Lovin' is Easy' went in at Number 6 that Sunday. Not a complete flop, but for a whole summer spent doing roadshows and radio tours promoting it, it was a further fall from grace.

◆ ◆ ◆

After checking out the chart results that Sunday I carried on painting the flat with coat after coat of cheap white paint, in preparation for my departure to university across the other side of London. My boxes were packed, I was ready to go... Well, nearly.

I wanted one final *Top of the Pops* swansong. By late summer 2002, I'd attended around seventy times. For me, the novelty of watching it being filmed never completely wore off. My excitement may have dimmed a bit after the first couple of years, but I never *fully* got over the rush I felt from blagging my way into that studio and seeing my head bopping alongside the biggest music names on the planet the next day to five million people eating their TV dinners at home.

Sarah, my old *TOTP* friend, accompanied me in the absence of anyone else being up for it. For all the Luton Girls, *Top of the Pops* was a distant memory. Even I had only been once in the last nine months. Danny, the warm-up guy, was still there, and gave us 'old-timers' a big shout-out to the audience. Sarah and I reminisced about the innocent years up in Borehamwood. The Thursday afternoons sitting bored in Burger King while the girls lathered themselves up in glitter. I missed them all. We'd kept in touch while they were living it up at uni and now I was starting my own adventures. My music taste had already changed so much. I found myself listening to more and more R&B, indie and even (vomit!) Nu-metal. My ever-changing hair had been restyled: blonde curtains replaced by a brunette crop, highlighted with frosted tips.

That night at *Top of the Pops* we saw Kelly Osbourne, over here to promote her first attempt at a pop career – a 'rock' cover of Madonna's 'Papa Don't Preach'; the Sugababes, riding high at Number 1 with another radical pop banger, 'Round Round'; surf-rockers Incubus and the new UK queen of hip hop and

R&B, Ms Dynamite(eee-heeee). The main event for me though was Hear'Say, giving me a chance to congratulate them on their relative success.

Unlike the old days, my smiles at Hear'Say on stage were not reflected back at me. I thought they would be happy to have made it back into the Top 10 and on the legendary *Top of the Pops* Main Stage, but they just looked pained. I desperately wanted a chat with Myleene before going off to uni.

After the show, when the audience were led out by production staff, I grabbed Sarah and insisted we wait for the band behind a pillar. She stayed for a bit but ended up having to go home. After a few more minutes, just when I was about to throw in the towel, I saw Myleene walking towards me to her waiting chauffeur.

'Malcolm! What are you doing, you nutjob?' she said affectionately, with a huge smile.

'It's so rare I get to see you nowadays!' I replied. 'I wanted to say hi properly.'

We discussed the single, the shit times they had been having of late and their future. The last of the sunset had made London a stunning blend of blues and reds as we talked and watched the sky.

'This is literally the last thing in our diary. Who knows what we'll do next? I don't know if Number 6 will be good enough for the label,' Myleene said, the smile fading from her sun-kissed face. 'And what about you? Aren't you going to uni?'

'Haha, yeah. You remembered!' I beamed. 'I'm nervous. I'm all packed up and ready to go.'

'That's so exciting! You're gonna have the *best* time,' she said, putting her arm around my shoulder. 'Seriously, you'll forget about us and we won't see you ever again!'

'No way! I'll still pop up every now and then.'

'Mal – you'll be too busy partying every night to care about us!' Myleene replied, flashing me a huge smile. 'This is the best thing that could ever happen to you. I'm jealous!'

I laughed. 'No way! I'll still be your biggest fan. I'm always going to be a groupie, I'll *never* be over it!'

19

What I Go to School For

Yeah, I'm over it.

Epilogue

I may have only ventured to the other side of London when I went to university but, as with so many people, the experience changed me and my outlook on life. My pop obsession didn't totally die, it just got shoved into a box and forgotten about (or hidden for fear of mockery). I eventually realised what everyone else had figured out years ago: I was gay. I was finally accepting who I really was inside. I think I'd directed all my pent-up sexual energy into my pop love, and the fact I'd been hanging out at G-A-Y every week for years made the process a hell of a lot easier.

Years later, after going through R&B, indie and electronica phases, I found myself strangely drawn to that compartment of my brain dedicated to pop music that I'd kept locked up. I came out to my friends again, this time as a pop fan. The landscape had changed, though. On the one hand, the Internet had destroyed the old industry as I had known it. The charts had lost their relevance and the BBC subsequently ditched *Top of the Pops* in its original format in 2006 (vintage re-runs branded as *Top of the Pops 2* live on, catering for the nostalgia market, rather than the original teenage audience). The record labels had stubbornly tried to hold back the tidal wave of change, clinging on through post-Hear'Say reality acts. In so many ways, though, pop feels more alive now than it has done since I was growing up. Through social media, kids these days are exposed to more music and more of their icons' lives than we could have dreamed of growing up.

Pop music made my difficult teenage years bearable. It gave me confidence and friendships that I never would have got from school. It allowed me to meet musical legends, little-known future stars, and flash-in-the-pan nobodies. Through the emerging world of technology, and with a brazen adolescent attitude, I'd managed to gain access to some of the most famous people in the world in a way that seems impossible today. I'd lied to my parents and ditched my education. But it made me realise that, even though all the kids called me a freak, there were plenty of other freaks like me.

And finally...

To reach out for help on the issues of gay bullying (for both children and adults), contact the following support organisations:

Young Stonewall

www.youngstonewall.org.uk Find a support group in your area (www.youngstonewall.org.uk/help-advice/whats-my-area)

Rucomingout.com

www.rucomingout.com

Switchboard LGBT+ helpline

www.switchboard.lgbt

Acknowledgements

Writing this book has been a ridiculous three-year adventure that I never expected to be so challenging, emotional, fun and rewarding. I feel like I have physically and metaphorically gone down Memory Lane, reconnecting with friends and revisiting old haunts to get reacquainted with distant memories and vague recollections.

None of these escapades would have happened without Kelle Bryan. You brightened up a desperately lonely boy's life with that phone call, which led me to my *Top of the Pops* adventures and all the friends, confidence and madness that followed. You transformed my teenage years.

To all the band members whose lives we invaded: Edele, Keavy, Sinead, Lindsay, Louise, Myleene, Suzanne, Noel, Kym, Danny, Geri, Emma, the Melanies, Victoria, the Saints. And to Steps, S Club, Honeyz, Boyzone and every countless other pop act we shared random chats and laughs with.

Sorry for pestering you at the crack of dawn, or when you wanted to go home, or when you were hungover. You worked so hard to create the songs that so many of us still love.

To all the groupies, cravens, eccentric autograph hunters, journalists, airline staff, security guards, runners, hotel staff, drivers, makeup artists, TV presenters, DJs, EastEnders cast members, production crew, dancers, musicians, PAs, record label and management staff – *even* the paparazzi – who we shared laughs with over those five barmy years, in between star-studded pop encounters. YOU made it the most fun adventures of my life.

To Claire and Noel Mellor, for seeing something in my ridiculous drunken stories and starting me off in this project. You are the reason I took on this challenge and I'm eternally grateful to you both for telling me I could do it! Thanks to Aunty Trish (Taggart), for urging your teenage nephew to write down all his adventures because people would want to read them one day.

Thanks to countless friends for putting up with me harping on about this project. To Danny Christie, for your encyclopaedic knowledge and unrivalled passion for 90s pop divas. We may have been teenage rivals, but I'm so glad we have a friendship now.

Anna Burtt, Clare Christian and Heather Boisseau at RedDoor – thank you for seeing the potential in my idea and for all your help and guidance along the way. Thanks to Clare Connie Shepherd for designing the cover of this book, and Jane Donovan for casting her watchful eyes over my manuscript.

Thanks to Anja, for all the long chats in the early stages, and pushing me to go on the best writing course I could have done. To Peter Forbes, for the most inspiring course I've ever taken and for giving me the tools to turn my unlikely idea into a reality. Everyone in Tuesday night writing group, for all your feedback, chats and laughs – you know who you are! To Sam Markham, Nikki Phillips and Sarah Finley for your feedback on my early pieces and countless hours of chats throughout the project. To Daisy Malt, for your incredible help in reviewing my first drafts. You really steered my ramblings and cut out so many exclamation marks!

To Sophie, for being *my* biggest fan throughout those years; the only one to listen to my tedious anecdotes every night with the same passion for it I had. To Mum and Dad, for seeing the burning passion in me and doing everything you could to allow your son to escape his dreary world and experience some of the best times of his life. I love you both so much.

And to Matt, the Richard to my Judy, without whom this book would never have happened. I love you. Thank you for your unwavering support and making it a reality. Now I've written them down you'll never have to listen to another anecdote again!

About the author

Malcolm McLean was born in Surrey in 1983, sandwiched between an older and younger sister. He has had an intense lifelong love of music which, as a teenager, provided him with an escape from reality and led to years of obsessively following some of the biggest names in pop music.

When not writing, he works at Goldsmiths University. Malcolm loves Eurovision, long country walks and reading books about the struggles of modern life. He lives in South East London with his long-suffering architect partner Matt.

Find out more about RedDoor Publishing and sign up to our newsletter to hear about our **latest releases**, **author events**, exciting **competitions** and more at

reddoorpublishing.com

YOU CAN ALSO FOLLOW US:

 @RedDoorBooks

 RedDoorPublishing

 @RedDoorBooks